Wadsworth's Media Guide for Introductory Psychology

Edited By

Russell J. Watson
College of DuPage

THOMSON
WADSWORTH

Australia • Canada • Mexico • Singapore • Spain • United Kingdom • United States

CONTENTS

Videos and Films in this Media Guide
(by topic area)

Topic area	Videos	Films
1. **Evolution of Psychology**		
Applied Psychology	12	1
Principles & History of Psychology	8	4
2. **Research in Psychology**	19	4
3. **Biological Bases of Behavior**		
Brain & Nervous System	52	3
Heredity & Genetics	4	2
4. **Sensation and Perception**		
Extrasensory Perception	4	2
Perception	12	2
Senses	18	1
5. **Variations in Consciousness**		
Altered States of Consciousness & Hypnosis	5	2
Consciousness	8	1
Sleep	15	2
6. **Learning Through Conditioning**		
Behavior Modification	18	4
Conditioning & Learning	18	2
Learning Disabilities	1	1
7. **Human Memory**		
Forgetting & Memory Construction	10	
Memory Disorders & Aging	3	3
Memory Processes	12	4
8. **Language and Thought**		
Language & Language Acquisition	25	2
Thinking & Problem Solving	16	1
9. **Intelligence and Psychological Testing**		
Intelligence Testing	17	4
Personality Testing	1	
10. **Motivation and Emotion**		
Achievement Motivation	13	7
Motivation & Emotion in the Workplace	9	9
Sexual Motivation	4	1
Theories of Emotion	12	1
11. **Human Development Across the Lifespan**		
Developmental (Overall / General)	20	
Prenatal & Newborn	9	
Child Development	39	6
Adolescent Development	17	12
Adult Development	17	6

Topic area	Videos	Films
12. **Personality: Theory, Research & Assessment**		
Humanistic Perspective	7	2
Psychoanalytic Perspective	15	2
Social Cognitive Perspective	3	1
Trait Perspective	6	2
13. **Stress, Coping, & Health**		
Alcoholism	6	3
Drugs & Substance Abuse	12	1
Stress	43	7
14. **Psychological Disorders**		
Abnormal Psychology – General	33	20
Anxiety & Relationships	13	11
Mood Disorders	8	1
Personality Disorders	2	3
Schizophrenia & Related Disorders	8	9
15. **Psychotherapy**		
Biomedical Therapies	14	2
Behavior Therapies	14	4
Insight Therapies	7	1
Therapy Options	13	2
16. **Social Behavior**		
Prejudice & Discrimination	10	2
Social Influence	12	2
Social Relationships	33	8
17. **Gender and Sexuality**		
Gender Roles	17	6
Sex & Gender Research	3	
Totals	**697**	**176**

PREFACE

Introduction

The purpose of this guide is to encourage the use of video and film in the psychology classroom. Videos are generally perceived by students as special learning devices, a perception that may not be shared by all faculty. From an instructor's point of view, videos can be time-consuming to locate, be a bother to schedule, present additional paperwork, and create the concern that the media will not be delivered on time or that the equipment will not work. There are at times more excuses not to show a video than to show one. Many of us may feel that we can "tell them" about the concept much more easily and quickly. However a growing number of classrooms are being equipped with video projection equipment, and as this trend continues, we will most likely see a remarkable increase in a variety of visual media: Video (tape and disc), internet projection, and presentation software.

If we adhere to what we teach and apply current research, we know that learning, depth of processing, and length of retention all increase with multiple exposure to a subject. Therefore, lecture, discussion, films, experiments, videos, reading assignments, audio-tapes, field trips, and simulations can all work together to help students learn about psychology. I am not encouraging you to make the classroom a movie theater, but let media help you amplify and illuminate concepts for students.

During the past several years there have been significant increases in the availability of videos for use in the introductory psychology classroom. Film specials and series, videotape programs, and full series of topical treatments have emerged in the media, greatly increasing the menu of audiovisual choices. The purpose of this guide is to be as complete as possible in current media offerings, and to provide specific media that related directly to the topics of the introductory psychology course.

This media guide is special in several ways.

1. We have provided detailed descriptions of each of the videos to give you insight into the best use of media within the classroom setting.
2. We have commented on the strengths of many of the entries.
3. Where two or more videos are available on the same topic, we have illuminated significant differences to help you choose the one most appropriate to your needs in the classroom.
4. We have not arbitrarily set copyright date "limits" on my search. That is, there are a few "classics" in psychology films, a few of them older and in black and white, but significant in that the pioneers of our field are featured. We feel that these classics (so indicated in the commentary) should be listed here and shared with classes when appropriate.

In this media guide we have attempted to increase the bandwidth of variety of media by including both shorter (45 minutes or less) and longer (50 minutes or more) types of media. New media is produced weekly, and I have attempted to provide those media productions that have emerged as popular, leaders, and award-winners in this list. There are thousands of videos available for psychology instructors, and for a more in-depth exploration of the menu, please review the video and film directory on page 13-18.

Feature Films

A unique advantage to this guide is the addition of feature films. These films are intended to help illustrate many themes within the introductory psychology classroom. Because of content, curriculum, and coverage requirements it would be rare to have the luxury of showing feature-length films in the classroom. However, with the common availability of video and DVD rental facilities (i.e. Blockbuster Video), it is probable that many students have already seen some of these feature films, and others could certainly view them inexpensively if they chose. In addition, some professors are inclined to assign extra-credit options, which may involve viewing feature films.

The feature films are presented in one of three ways:

1. There are some films presented with a complete synopsis, specific scene descriptions, and content-oriented questions.
2. Other films are listed, with a few discussion-questions provided.
3. Some films are provided with a synopsis. There was a specific purpose to this method.

In surveying a variety of psychology professors prior to this publication, we learned that some prefer a complete list of scenes and associated questions, others simply prefer a few questions, and many prefer a synopsis only – preferring to craft their own questions.

Psychology instructors tend to be busy people. They also tend to be creative. With that in mind our busy colleagues are able to skim through the lists of media and feature films, quickly selecting the films they prefer, and using their creativity to structure and craft questions for discussion and involvement. Others who may prefer examples of structured questions are given many samples of questions from which to use and modify. We attempted to provide something for everyone, and in a user-friendly format.

SOME GENERAL GUIDELINES FOR USE OF VIDEO AND FEATURE FILMS

IN THE CLASSROOM

Audiovisual materials can be excellent resources to supplement, extend, and amplify classroom lectures and reading materials. Here are some considerations in using and choosing appropriate media:

- **Check with your publisher's representative** to learn which videos may be available upon adoption of their textbook. Wadsworth Publishing offers a variety of videos based on the enrollment of your course.
- **Check the library or learning center** for availability of films and videos at your institution. Then check the availability of film catalogs from other institutions, as well as your institution's rental budget and policy.
- **Review your teaching and learning objectives** for each unit, and determine which media resources could make the learning more effective.
- **Review this guide** to explore the numerous video and film options for the topic areas you are most interested. See the summary table on pages 4-5 to get started.
- **Preview the media you choose**. While doing so, make an outline of the topics covered. I suggest distributing this outline to students before they view the film. Setting the stage helps students become active agents in the viewing process and helps stimulate discussion and evaluation after viewing. A sample outline of this type is provided at the end of this introduction.
- **Select the most relevant portion.** Most students are accustomed to information in sound-bites, you may consider showing a portion of a video media rather than the entire presentation. Stop the media at a specific point to generate discussion, then perhaps continue with the media, or engage a wider topic.
- **Be prepared to follow the film with class or small-group discussion and analysis**. Exploring students' thoughts and reactions to the media helps enrich the experience.

Benjamin Bloom's cognitive taxonomy may be helpful in considering the ways by which video media may amplify each objective. In addition, I believe that students should be active agents in the learning process. Some instructors view media presentation as a passive process. I believe that students can and should be active agents while using media. Therefore, each of the cognitive categories is listed below with suggestions for student-directed activity:

- *Knowledge:* Videos provide students with additional information, define terms, illustrate processes, and illuminate theories, principles, and techniques used in the field of psychology. Student activity:

7

Review sheets of media concepts, with vocabulary, definitions, and so on.

- *Comprehension:* The transformation of knowledge into meaningful applications, relationships, and implications may be significantly enhanced through the use of media in the classroom, especially when coupled with discussion. This process assists students' basic level of understanding. Student activity: Review observation sheets or conduct a postmedia discussion to confirm understanding.

- *Application:* An important objective of any introductory psychology class is to teach students how to apply, generalize, and restructure the basic knowledge into principles, laws, theories, and generalizations. Videos have an especially strong impact in this area, because they illustrate direct application of the principles of psychology in a variety of settings. Student activity: Develop hypotheses in class to apply concepts in new areas, or use case studies or small-group discussions about using the concepts in new ways.

- *Analysis:* Media can help students identify, categorize, or discriminate among various concepts, especially when studying hypotheses, experiments, or assumptions of psychologists. Student activity: Large- and small-group discussions are an appropriate way to develop and refine analysis skills.

- *Synthesis:* Frequently media may be used to stimulate creative thinking about a concept, to design and develop new ideas. Media can also be used to explore theories and test hypotheses. Student activity: Reaction papers, creative papers, or summaries allow students to test new ways of thinking or applying concepts.

- *Evaluation:* Making informed judgments about the world is at the highest level of Bloom's taxonomy. Media may be used to assess, validate, and compare a variety of concepts at a deeper level of understanding. Student activity: Two types of evaluation might be appropriate, depending on the topic. First, self-evaluation through introspection may be a growth-oriented way to explore a topic. Second, external evaluation based on objective criteria may be used to amplify various concepts.

To conclude, remember the excitement that media brought to the classroom when you were a student, and carry that excitement into your own classroom. Use the media and these suggestions in any of the above ways to help enrich the understanding of your students in this wonderful science of psychology. Encourage them to approach learning through reading, discussion, experiment, field experience, and media with that same sense of wonder.

SAMPLE FILM OUTLINE

Film Outline: *Learning* (1971) McGraw-Hill, CRM Productions (28 minutes)

This outline will substitute for film notes that you might otherwise take. After the film, be prepared to discuss some of the topics presented or to write a brief reaction paper to a portion of the film that you choose to respond to or amplify.

1. **Species-specific behavior** in the ring-billed gull (Jack Hailman)
2. **Imprinting** in ducklings (Eckhard Hess)
3. **Conjugate reinforcement** with babies and the sucking response (Richard Sequeland, Lewis Lipsitt)
4. **Classical conditioning** ("How Francis Learns")
   a. Loud noise causes fear.
   b. Rabbit is associated with loud noise.
   c. Rabbit now causes fear.
   d. Operant behavior reduces fear by escape from feared object.
   e. Generalization causes fear of similar objects.
   f. Extinguishing procedure is developed.
   g. Fear of rabbits is successfully extinguished.

5. **Shaping and operant conditioning** (Richard Malott)
   a. Rat learns to press bar.
   b. SHAPING cartoon: "Where do I stand on the issue of war?"
   c. Reinforcers are encountered in college.
   d. Reinforcers work with retarded children.
   e. Pigeons learn to discriminate between pictures of people and pictures of objects.
   f. Reinforcers are generally effective.
6. **Aversive control of behavior**: control of behavior through punishment or pain (Nathan Azrin)
   a. Rats in conditioning box.
      1. Shock delivered.
      2. Rats attempt to escape.
      3. Frustration occurs.
      4. Aggression results.
   b. Prisons.
7. **Positive reinforcement**: Utopian design, Walden Two (B. F. Skinner)
8. **Achievement motivation group** (David McClelland)

Critical Thinking Issues for Media in the Classroom

College-level reading has become a topic and issue related to assessment and general education skills over the past decade. Through much of the research in college-level reading, we have learned that in many ways reading and critical thinking skills are fused together. Offered here is an overview to Critical Thinking skills and how to develop those skills within your students as they view and discuss media in your classroom. Critical thinking is an intellectually disciplined activity. It can be taught. It can be learned. It involves a set of skills to process information, and the ability to use those skills to guide one's subsequent activity and behavior.

Critical thinking frequently involves critical questioning. Developing questions as we view media can assist in this critical viewing endeavor. As some of the feature films listed herein contain a variety of questions, the reader is encouraged to craft their own questions to deepen the understanding and critical thinking ability of our psychology students. In discussing feature films in class, a variety of questions and question stems are provided as seeds for further investigation into the field of psychology.

Critical thinking raises the quality of thought. Increased quality of thought means increased quality of communication, both written and verbal. Increased quality of communication yields increased quality of academic and classroom life. These combine to provide an open, thoughtful, dynamic learning environment for your introductory psychology students.

A "Critical-Thinker's Dozen:" 20 Questions for Critical Thinking

The list below is prepared in the spirit of critical thinking. It is also prepared in the spirit of a user-friendly way to consider any feature film listed herein, and apply any one or more of these questions to the premises of the feature film.
1. From what point of view are we experiencing this media? Is there an alternative point of view that should be considered?
2. Can you explain the main idea and concept in psychology demonstrated in this film?
3. What questions about psychology or psychological principles are being raised by this film?
4. Related to psychological issues, what is the film trying to accomplish?
5. How is information given to the audience? What additional information might be needed that is not supplied in the film?

6. How did you reach your conclusions? Is there an alternative way to evaluate the ideas?
7. Does the film show an awareness of the implications and consequences of their position?
8. Is the film sensitive to alternative points of view and reasoning?
9. Is the information presented accurately? On what basis do you make this judgement?
10. Does the film handle objections from other relevant points of view?
11. Does the film address the complexities of this psychological issue?
12. Is there a clear line of reasoning developed that helps us to arrive at the main conclusions?
13. Are the psychological purposes of the film clear and justifiable?
14. Does the film provide experiences relevant to the psychological issue?
15. Does the film present questionable assumptions without clarifying problems that may arise from accepting those assumptions?
16. What are some key factors in the film that make this a complex and difficult problem or issue?
17. If people take (or fail to take) the line of reasoning seriously, what are the implications of this?
18. What are the primary points of view taken in this film?
19. Are we taking into account the thinking of others, and their viewpoints on this film?
20. By what criteria or standards does this film illustrate a psychological principle, and from what perspective?

Essay: History of AV Media in the Classroom

Audio-Visual media has changed enormously in the past few decades. Within the memories of senior professors reading this essay, A-V media has evolved from 16mm film, to reel-to-reel video, then video cassette, followed by large-format laser disks, and currently to digital recordings on DVDs. The younger members of our professional colleagues may have grown up viewing videotape media only, and have not experienced the chatter of a 16mm projector when the film slipped out of the framer. In a very short amount of time we have witnessed a video evolution.

This essay is addressed to the nearly five decades of educational professionals who have served as ambassadors of the field of psychology to their students: Those teaching assistants and younger instructors in their twenties, through the more experienced professors in their fifties and sixties. Remember a time when you were in elementary school? Our senior colleagues may recall walking into the classroom one morning to see a movie projector in the back of the room, poised with a full reel on the front of the machine. Remember the excitement you experienced? This was going to be a special day because you were going to see a movie. You may be able to recall parts of that movie or other movies you saw many years ago. Perhaps that eager feeling of anticipation and excitement followed you into fourth grade, maybe into fifth. Younger professors will identify with a similar excitement when the teacher pulled a video cassette from their desk, and approached the large-screen monitor. That feeling followed me into college and through graduate school, although (unfortunately) the use of media became more rare.

For me and my age-peers, who experienced second and third grade in the middle 1950s, the media of film followed us through high school and college. For the younger instructors there was a media-shift at some point in their educational experience. That shift in media embraced a new technology called videotape. As the rapid pace of change progresses, even since the first edition of this book was printed, another media technology has emerged: Digital video discs, demonstrating a significant advance in video technology. The students in our classrooms have been exposed to more video media than any previous generation. Therein we find both a strength and a challenge. In the strength we find a generation of college students who have a wide bandwidth of experiences gained through video. In the challenge we find students who may become easily bored by typical instructional videos.

I imagine there are some students in college classrooms in the 2000s who are much like I was in college during the 1960s: Visual learners who are able to grasp a concept much more fully and deeply by viewing a film or video media about it. Scholarly students who easily take notes during a lecture or from the blackboard but who also become involved with learning through audiovisual media. Students who didn't quite grasp last night's reading assignment but for whom the reading becomes meaningful when supplemented by a film or video. Perhaps there are also students in your class who feel a surge of excitement when they see the video player ready to roll, although they may not want to admit it.

During my 30-plus years as a professional educator, I spent 8 years (weekends) as anchorman for a news and talk program in Chicago for NBC-TV (WMAQ). During that time I also hosted an FM radio music/talk program for that network (WKQX). I learned much about sight and sound and how they can be used to capture an audience's attention. Those radio and television experiences have helped me learn firsthand about effective and ineffective media presentations. I have viewed both. We all have.

Effective classroom media may be used to capture the attention of students, capture their imagination, enhance creativity, and enrich the learning process. I have attempted to chronicle and assemble for your classroom use a list of the best media available for introductory psychology and to provide a brief commentary about their strengths or limitations. I hope that the results of this endeavor will be useful not only to new psychology instructors but to veterans as well.

Video and Film Source Directory

Here is a summary list for the producers and/or distributors of the videos referenced in this guide. Note the following Series producers:

- Discovering Psychology: (See Annenberg)
- The Brain Series Teaching Modules, 2nd edition (See Annenberg)
- The Mind Series Teaching Modules, 2nd edition (See Worth)
- CNN® Today Videos (See Wadsworth Publishing)

ABC (American Broadcasting Corporation)
77 West 66th Street
New York, NY 10023

AIMS Media
9710 De Soto Avenue
Chatsworth, CA 91311-4409

Ambrose Video Publishing
Exclusive Distributors of Time Life Video
381 Park Avenue S. Suite 1601
New York, NY 10016

American Psychological Association
750 First Street, N.E.
Washington, DC 20002

The Annenberg/CPB Collection
Dept. HB01 901 E. Street, NW
Washington, D.C. 20004-2037
www.learner.org

Barr Media Group
100 Wilshire Blvd., Floor 3
Santa Monica, CA 90401-1121

Cambridge Documentary Films
P.O. Box 390385
Cambridge, MA 02139-0007

Campus Film Distributors Corporation
42 Oak Avenue
Tuckahoe, NY 10707

Carousel Films
260 Fifth Avenue Room 705
New York, NY 10001

CBS (Columbia Broadcasting System)
1330 Avenue of the Americas
New York, NY 10019

Cinema Guild
1697 Broadway
New York, NY 10019

Churchill Media
P.O. Box 3121
Paso Robles, CA 93447-3121

Coast Community College Telecourses
Coastline Community College
Distance Learning Dept.
11460 Warner Avenue
Fountain Valley, CA 92708-2597
714-241-6216

CNN® Today Videos
Available exclusively from Wadsworth/Thomson
Contact your local Wadsworth Publishing Sales Representative
www.wadsworth.com
800-876-2350

Comap
57 Bedford Street, Suite 210
Lexington, MA 02420

CRM Films (also McGraw-Hill Films)
2215 Faraday Avenue
Carlsbad, CA 92008

Encyclopedia Britannica Educational Corporation
310 S. Michigan Avenue
Chicago, IL 60604-9839

Fanlight Productions
4196 Washington Street Suite 2
Boston, MA 02131

Films Incorporated
5547 Ravenswood Avenue
Chicago IL 60640-1199
800-323-4222

Filmakers Library, Inc.
124 E. 40th Street, No.901
New York, NY 10016
www.filmakers.com
Info@filmakers.com
212-808-4980

Films for the Humanities and Sciences
P.O. Box 2053
Princeton, NJ 08543-2053
www.films.com
custserv@films.com
800-257-5126

Focus International, Inc.
1160 E. Jericho Turnpike #15
Huntington, NY 11743

Harcourt Brace & Co.
525 B. Street, Suite 1900
San Diego, CA 9210 1-4495

Indiana University
Instructional Support Services
Franklin Hall
Bloomington, IN 47405-5901
800-552-8620

Insight Media
2162 Broadway
New York, NY 10024-0621
www.insight-media.com
cs@insight-media.com
800-233-9910

International Film Bureau
332 S. Michigan Ave
Chicago, IL 60604

In The Classroom Media
1502 Powell Avenue
Erie, PA 16505
1-888-242-0563 or 814-464-9071
Fax: 814-464-9069
info@intheclassroom.org

Karol Media
350 N. Pennsylvania Ave.
Wilkes Barre, PA 18773-7600

LCA {c/o New World Video)
1440 S. Sepulveda Blvd.
Los Angeles, CA 90025

Macmillan Films, Inc.
200 Old Tappan Road
Old Tappan, NJ 07675

McGraw-Hill Films (See CRM Films)

Media Education Foundation
26 Center Ct.
Northampton, MA 01060

Motivational Media
12001 Ventura Place #202
Studio City, CA 91604

MTI Teleprograms (Coronet Films)
108 Wilmot Road
Deerfield, IL 60015

NBC (National Broadcasting Corporation)
30 Rockefeller Plaza
New York, NY 10020

New York University Film Library
26 Washington Place
New York, NY 10003

NET (National Educational Television)
Indiana University
Bloomington, IN 47402

New Day Films
22D Hollywood Avenue
Ho-Ho-Kus, NJ 07423

NOVA Videos (WGBH Boston Video)
P.O. Box 2284
South Burlington, VT 05407-2284
www.pbs.org/wgbh/nova

PBS {Public Broadcasting Service) Video
1320 Braddock Place or P.O. Box 791
Alexandria, VA 22314-1698
800-343-4727

Pennsylvania State University
Audio- Visual Services
Special Services Building
1127 Fox Hill Road
University Park, PA 16803-1824

Psychological and Educational Film
3334 East Coast Hwy., Suite 252
Corona Del Mar, CA 92625

Pyramid Film and Video
P.O. Box 1048
Santa Monica, CA 90406

Research Press
Dept. 20W
P.O. Box 9177
Champaign, IL 61826

Time-Life Education
P.O. Box 85026
Richmond, VA 23285-5026

United Artists
10202 Washington Boulevard
Culver City, CA 90230

United Broadcast Group, Inc.
9800 D Topanga Canyon Blvd.
Box 104
Chatsworth, CA 91311

University of California, Berkeley
Extension Media Center
2000 Center Street, Fourth Floor
Berkeley, CA 94720-1223

University of Illinois
Film and Video Center
1325 S. Oak St.
Champaign, IL 61820

University of Minnesota
University Film and Video
1313 Fifth St. SE Suite 108
Minneapolis, MN 55414

Veritas Programming
343 Seventh Avenue
New York, NY 10001

Video Nursing, Inc.
2834 Central Street
Evanston, IL 60201

Virginia Tech Film Library
Room 15, Patton Hall
Virginia Polytechnical Institute and State University
Blacksburg, VA 24061

Wadsworth Publishing Company
A division of Thomson
10 Davis Drive
Belmont, CA 94002
www.wadsworth.com
800-876-2350 For your sales representative

John Wiley and Sons, Inc.
605 Third Avenue
New York, NY 10158-0012

WGBH Educational Foundation
125 Western Avenue
Boston, MA 02134

Worth Publishers
41 Madison Avenue
New York, NY 10010
www.worthpublishers.com

1. **Evolution of Psychology**	Videos	Films
Applied Psychology	12	1
Principles & History of Psychology	8	4

* Applied Psych

B.F. Skinner: A Fresh Appraisal. (1999) Davidson Films, (41 minutes)

Other than Freud, no psychologist has been so discussed, critiqued, and at times maligned as B.F. Skinner. Using both archival and new footage, this video takes a new look at who the man was and what he really said in his twenty books. Like other thinkers who broke new ground, Skinner had to invent his own vocabulary to describe the phenomena he was studying. In this video, his terms are introduced in context so the student understands how they were intended to be used and the research that produced them. The video lays to rest some myths and credits Skinner with contributions not often attributed to him. Understanding the complex man behind his work enables students to better evaluate the importance and relevance of the work he inspired.

B. F. Skinner and Behavior Change: Research, Practice, and Promise. (1975) Research Press, (45 minutes)

This video traces the development of modern behaviorism from John Watson to B. F. Skinner. Several professionals from other disciplines discuss the impact of Skinner's theory on their lives. In addition, medical specialists and counselors display different applications of behavior modification techniques. This is a particularly good video for its historical treatment of behaviorism and its applied aspects. Color.

The Bronswick Affair. (1980) CRM, (24 minutes)

Just how much do the media and advertising affect consumer purchasing? This film explores the concept of the self-fulfilling prophecy and shows how a manager's expectation alone can influence a worker's performance. The Pygmalian Effect is presented through a combination of live action and animation to illustrate both the theory and practical application of the phenomenon.

Building More Effective Teams. (1978) Indiana University, (26 minutes)

This film discusses the use of behavioral science findings in dealing with the problems of different organizations. Highlights include group sessions in which managers deal with particular problems.

Career Encounters: Psychology. (1991) Insight Media, (28 minutes)

Produced by the American Psychological Association, this video provides a more detailed examination of the field of psychology than the shorter version, Careers in Psychology. It examines various career opportunities in the field including private practice, science, public interest, and education.

Career Paths in Psychology. Arizona State University, (29 minutes)

The video describes nine major areas of career possibilities in psychology, including clinical, health, behavioral, neuroscience, developmental, social, quantitative, industrial/organizational, environmental, and law and psychology.

Careers for the 21st Century, Psychology: Scientific Problem Solvers. American Psychological Association (14 minutes)

This APA video provides an introduction to careers in psychology and to the important subfields of the discipline.

The City and the Self. Time-Life Films, (52 minutes)

This is an examination of urban settings based on the theories and research of Stanley Milgram. The film illustrates the ways in which city dwellers perceive their environments.

A Conversation with B. F. Skinner. (1971) Filmmakers Library, (23 minutes)

This interview with B. F. Skinner centers on the meanings and implications of Beyond Freedom and Dignity. Skinner discusses the concept of behavior modification and the problems associated with implementing the technology in open and closed societies. The film specifically addresses the use and misuse of rewards and punishment to modify behavior on a cultural level. It is a thought-provoking introduction to applied psychology.

Jobs: How the Brother Feels. (1975) CRM/McGraw-Hill, (27 minutes)

This film, in the setting of an encounter group, discusses the problems and attitudes of the hard-core unemployed.

Lifelines: A Career Profile Study. (1981) Document Associates, (26 minutes)

In order to be fully satisfied and productive at work, a person must understand the forces that shape his or her career and make it grow. Using illustrations from three actual case histories, the film explores Schein's concept of "career anchors," patterns by which individuals discover what they are good at and what they would like to do for the rest of their lives.

The Social Life of Small Urban Spaces. (1979) Insight Media, (60 minutes)

Critic and author William H. Whyte uses time-lapse photography to chart the interaction between city-dwellers and their environment. Looking at favorite benches and ledges and how people rearrange movable chairs, the video generates new urban design recommendations.

Feature Films

Specific Scene Analysis:
Norma Rae (1979) **(Sally Field)** Drama

- Central Concept: industrial organization
- Approximate Scene Location: 91 minutes, 45 seconds into the 114 minute film
- Approximate Scene Length: 7 minutes
- Opening Line: Ruben: "You black employees are being told that by going into the union in mass you can dominate it and control it in this plant as you may see fit."
- Closing Scene: No dialogue. Norma Rae is holding up the sign "union" and the workers have shut off the last machine.

Key Concept: industrial psychologist
Characters/Actors: Norma Rae (Sally Field), Ruben (Ron Leibman), Mr. Mason (Noble Willingham)

Scene Description: Norma Rae is a worker in the O.P. Henley Textile Mill in a small town in the South. The mill is the only major industry, and the 800 workers have unsafe working conditions. The wages are low, and some of the employees are suffering physical ailments that are work-related. Norma Rae's mother often suffers from periods of deafness from working near machines that are constantly emitting a loud noise. Her father dies from a heart attack while working. Ruben has come to town to organize a union at the plant. He is from New York, a Harvard Law School graduate, and the son of a union organizer. He is a representative of the Textile Workers Union of America. The first meeting of the workers who want to organize is held in a local black church. In his comments to the interested workers, Ruben emphasizes unity; they must be together in their push for workers' rights to a decent wage and safe working conditions. Catholics and Jews, blacks and whites, women and men, all must stick together for a union to work. For the difficult task of organizing the workers, he solicits Norma Rae's help because she appears interested. She becomes a very active promoter of the union, although she is under the constant threat of being fired. The plant management has put a very provocative notice on the employees' bulletin board. Norma is to copy the letter and bring it to Ruben; it will be the first piece of evidence that the company is using illegal practices to keep the union out. The scene opens with Ruben reading what Norma has copied.

Questions/Discussion

1. The oldest issue confronted by industrial organizational psychologists is worker safety. Is this a viable issue today?
    Discuss how safety in the workplace is currently a viable issue. Encourage students to talk of incidences of workplace violence they have read or heard about in the news.

2. One of the functions of industrial and engineering psychologists is to design machines so as to improve safety. Ask students to reflect on the placement of knobs on their stoves. Of the various examples offered, discuss which arrangement is best for safety reasons and why.

3. Ask students whether any have had experiences in job training programs. Solicit different views of the effectiveness of their training.

* Principles and History of Psych

Issues in Psychology. (1990) Coast Community College District Telecourses, (30 minutes)
    Part of the *Psychology - The Study of Human Behavior Series*, this video presents a discussion with leading psychologists and teachers of important topics in psychology.

Landmarks in Psychology. (1990) Insight Media (50 minutes)
    (Recommended & acclaimed by several organizations.) This still-image video highlights the principal contributions of Freud, Jung, Adler, Pavlov, Sullivan, Horney, Maslow, Watson, and Skinner. Through historical narrative and case-study dramatizations, the inter-personal, behavioral, humanistic, and existential approaches to psychology are explored.

New Directions. (1990) Annenberg/CPB, (30 minutes)
    The last of the *Discovering Psychology* films, this video presents interviews with several prominent psychologists about their opinions of the future of psychology in the 21st century. The development of new theories is discussed, along with new directions for research and new applications of the discipline. Interviewed individuals include Howard Gardner, Jean Gleason, and B. F. Skinner. This is a well-produced film about the possible direction that psychology can take to improve the overall quality of life.

Past, Present and Promise. (1990) Annenberg/CPB, (30 minutes)

First in the *Discovering Psychology* series, hosted by Phillip Zimbardo of Stanford University, this program looks at all levels of psychologists' work. From studying the roles of various hormones, to overt behavioral studies such as simple stimulus reaction times, to therapeutic work, the program concludes with psychology's emergence as a science and some of the key early figures in that transformation. This is a good overview and wrap-up to the first lecture on the history of psychology, as well as a preview of psychology's methods. It also introduces students to one of the modern giants of psychology, Phillip Zimbardo.

The Search for the Mind: The Mind Series. (1988) PBS, (60 minutes)

Part of *The Mind* series, this film provides a historical overview of the study of the human mind, ranging from ancient times through the mid-1900s. Aristotle, Darwin, and Sigmund Freud are but a few of the individuals that the film mentions. In addition, the film presents some interesting information on memory, especially the difference between episodic and procedural memory, and some information on split-brain findings.

Sigmund Freud. (1995) Insight Media, (50 minutes)

This video examines the life and work of Sigmund Freud, from his boyhood to his medical training to the development of his theories. It discusses his studies of hypnosis with Jean Charcot and his collaboration with Joseph Breuer on the case of Anna O. The program examines Freud's development of the concept of transference, and explains how through self-analysis he discovered the value of dream analysis and free association. It also explores his collaboration and conflict with C.G. Jung and his theories of drives and the Oedipus complex.

Sigmund Freud: His Offices and Home, Vienna, 1938. (1974) Filmmakers Library, (17 minutes)

This film presents a behind-the-scenes look at the private world of Sigmund Freud. Through the use of rare photographs taken by Edmund Engleman in 1938, we are introduced to the man and the therapist. Eli Wallach narrates. By examining his home, office, and antiquities, students of psychology can gain insight into the famous Dr. Freud. This film is well worth the time.

What is Psychology? (1990) Insight Media (30 minutes)

In this video leading psychologists discuss major approaches, subfields, and historical developments in the field of psychology. They describe how in their work they seek to understand the varieties of human behavior. These experts assert that psychology offers explanations that enable us to understand and, at times, to predict and control human behavior.

Feature Films

Analyze This **(Billy Crystal, Robert DeNiro)**
1. Which theory of psychology would you use in working with DeNiro's character if you were his therapist? Why?
2. At the beginning of his therapy sessions, DeNiro's character believes that his problems are "fixed" as soon as he feels a difference in himself, although Crystal's character tries to convince him that there is more to his problems than that. How would you try to make him realize that his problems were more deeply rooted and that he needed to continue exploring deeper into his problems?
3. Do you believe a person such as DeNiro's character would be a good candidate for therapy, and would you, as a therapist, be able to work with him? Why or why not?

Freud (**Montgomery Clift, Susannah York, Larry Parks**) Drama
Various crises in Freud's (Clift) private and professional life are related to his theoretical conclusions by means of dream sequences. Other scenes are of Freud and his patients, one of which is with a young man suffering from an Oedipus complex. A good historical drama about Freud.

Session 9 (**David Caruso**) Drama
Filmed on location at an abandoned mental hospital in Danvers, MA. An asbestos removal crew takes on a difficult task of removal against a one-week deadline. The natural light filming in the creepy deserted building slowly reveals a variety of cruel and primitive means of treatment of unstable patients several decades ago. The film also uncovers some of the additional baggage of each of the laborers. While not a documentary, one sees some of the deserted rooms and equipment of the abandoned mental hospital.

2. **Research in Psychology**	Videos	Films
	19	4

Do Scientists Cheat. (1988) NOVA, (58 minutes)

This is an interesting and provocative Nova program exploring the possible motivations for dishonest research, professional reactions, and the methods of those who have exposed the issues. There is a brief simulation of a hoax early in the 20th century, followed by more recent cases of dishonest research, and the program concludes with a discussion of safeguards to reduce cheating. The "publish or perish" syndrome present in some academic environments also receives some attention.

Ethics in America: The Human Experiment. (1988) Columbia University, Annenberg/CPB, (58 minutes)

(Program 9 in series). Although this film does not deal directly with psychological experimentation, it does present the ethical considerations one needs to consider. It is primarily a medically oriented film, presenting the views of four doctors: Vincent DeVita (National Cancer Institute), Arnold Relman (New England Journal of Medicine), Alexander Capron (professor of law and medicine, University of Southern California), and Frank Young (U.S. Food and Drug Administration). These professionals discuss the ethics of experimental testing, including the need for information versus the rights of the patients.

How to Use PsychLIT on CD-ROM. (1988) APA, (18 minutes)

This video provides an effective introduction to the use of PsychLIT CD-ROM technology as a literature review tool. The straight forward format utilizes student "actors" engaged in an actual search. Through the student you are introduced to the basic keystroke commands and logic needed to complete any literature review.

How to Use Psychological Abstracts. (1988) APA, (12 minutes)

This video is designed to introduce students to the logic behind a literature search in psychology utilizing the *Thesaurus of Psychological Index Terms*, the *Psychological Abstracts Indexes* and the *Psychological Abstracts*. The video follows a student as they attempt to find information on how children are affected by the threat of nuclear war. Mechanical, but effective.

Inferential Statistics: Hypothesis Testing - Rats, Robots, and Skates. (1975) Wiley, (27 minutes)

Three humorous examples illustrate the basic premises for testing hypotheses. First, a scientist tests the hypothesis that a new food will make his rats smarter. Next, an argument is settled by two street toughs. Finally, college professors debate the premise that a teaching robot may be as effective as a live professor. This video/film was designed to illuminate central concepts for either beginners or those reviewing inferential statistics, rather than to teach specific formulas and procedures. It demonstrates the concept of statistical significance and Type I and Type II errors. The program is presented in a newscast format, which is both entertaining and an excellent learning vehicle in an area perceived by some students as dry.

Inferential Statistics: Sampling and Estimation Saves $122,000,000! (1975) Wiley, (20 Minutes)

This amusing film demonstrates the primary concepts of sampling and other statistical topics. A company president prepares to spend $122 million to develop and market a five-blade razor. A statistician suggests using a random sampling method to determine the market population for the razor. After finding that most of the sampled population doesn't like the razor, the president concludes that inferential statistics has saved the company millions of dollars. The program explains the concepts of defining a population, random sampling, using random numbers tables, conducting a survey, and doing interval estimates. Because it presents the concepts involved in the statistical procedures, rather than the formulas, it is an excellent film to use independently or with the companion film on hypothesis testing. It is especially good if students in your class show signs of math or statistics anxiety. Color.

Methodology: The Psychologist and the Experiment. (1975) McGraw Hill/CRM, (31 minutes)
This film provides an informative visual account of the standard methods which all research experiments employ. Independent and dependent variables, control groups, random assignment to groups, and other basic statistical concepts are explored. Schachter's experiment in "fear and affiliation" is documented as well as Riesen's physiological psychology experiment on the development of visual-motor coordination.

Mysteries of the Mind. (1988) Films for the Humanities and Sciences, (58 minutes)
This video examines the neurochemical and genetic components of various psychological disorders and some of the latest research into the mysteries of the brain. It may serve as a good advance organizer for other topics to come in the introductory psychology class.

The Nature of Science. (1972) Coronet Films, (11 minutes)
A look at some of the shortcomings of sensory experience as a primary source of information about the environment. Illusions are used to demonstrate situations where sensory experience is inadequate and to give examples of the ways in which scientific methods produce more reliable explanations.

Order from Chaos. (1985) Insight Media (28 minutes)
This video builds on intuitive understanding of basic concepts and leads the viewer to an understanding of how statistical principles are applied to solve practical problems.

Prisoners of Silence. (1995) PBS (60 minutes)
Excellent for showing how testimonials can be proven erroneous with good experimental design. Fascinating footage of how a technique called *facilitated communication* (supposedly used to allow autistic children to speak by having an attendant guide the hands of an autistic onto a keyboard) was shown to be false. Very good design elements and the logic behind them are demonstrated.

Research Methods. (1990) Coast Community College District Telecourses, (30 minutes)
Part of the *Psychology - The Study of Human Behavior Series*, this video shows footage of lobotomy, autism, and police investigators employing cognitive interview techniques.

Research Methods for the Social Sciences. (1995) Insight Media, (33 minutes)
Examines types of experimental design, describing when they would be most appropriate. It considers the use of control and experimental groups and dependent and independent variables, and discusses clinical, correlational, and field methods. It details the seven steps of the scientific method and explains how to gather and interpret data. It also considers ethical issues in experimentation.

Scientific Method. (2000) Films for the Humanities & Sciences, (25 minutes)
(Recommended by *School Library Journal.*) This program examines the basic elements of the scientific method: defining and researching the problem, forming a hypothesis, gathering information through experimentation and observation, analyzing the data, forming a conclusion, and communicating the results. Practical applications of the scientific method, such as testing new medicines and analyzing the performance of sporting goods, are included as well. A Cambridge Educational Production.

Statistics and Psychology. (2000) Films for the Humanities & Sciences, (25 minutes)

A look at how to statistically test the relationship between experimental data and reported historical findings. This program uses data from the Applied Psychology Unit at Cambridge University, which studies the negative effects of certain patterns that can cause eyestrain, headaches, and epileptic fits. Clear illustrations are given of the use of the Pearson correlation coefficient; positive and negative correlations and what they mean; the difference between linear and nonlinear associations; the rationale behind the Spearman approach; and contingency table analysis.

Statistics at a Glance. (1977) Insight Media, (27 minutes)

An animated presentation of basic descriptive statistics.

Understanding Research. (1990) Annenberg/CPB, (30 minutes)

Host Philip Zimbardo of Stanford University presents an overview of psychological research, the scientific method, and empirical thinking. The video explores various methodologies, data collection, and statistical analysis. Interpretation of findings is discussed as it relates to critical thinking skills. The program moves quickly without getting bogged down.

What Is Statistics? (1988) Annenberg/CPB, (30 minutes)

Program 1 examines the impact of statistics in our daily lives. The programs are designed for science and statistics students, not specifically for psychology classes. However, with math and statistics anxiety infiltrating the ranks of psychology students and faculty alike, this may be an appropriate way to explore some important ground. Program 2 demonstrates the use of patterns and distributions for statistical analysis in the meteorology, television programming, traffic control, and health care fields.

Why Use Statistics? (2000) Films for the Humanities & Sciences, (20-25 minutes each)

This four-part series includes *Handling Variability, Describing Data, Using Samples,* and *Bivariate Data: When y Depends on x.* May be purchased separately or as a set.

Feature Films

Dead Man Walking (**Susan Sarandon, Sean Penn**) Drama

Based on a true story, which explores the issue of capital punishment through extensive work and research by Sister Helen Prejean (Sarandon), a nun, teacher, and activist living in Louisiana, who has often worked with prisoners sentenced to death. This can be used to discuss several aspects of psychology, and the research activities.

In Cold Blood (**Anthony Edwards, Sam Neill, Eric Roberts**) Drama
The viewer is taken inside the mind of a pair of killers during a murder of a farm family in Kansas during the 1950's. A famous case, subsequent novel, and film that can be referenced as a research example.

Instinct (**Anthony Hopkins, Cuba Gooding, Jr.**) Thriller

Ethan Powell, (Hopkins) a famous anthropologist who studies the behavior of mountain gorillas in Rwanda, decides to live among them as primitive man once did. After two years of living with the gorillas, poachers kill several of the gorillas and Powell retaliates by killing two of the poachers. Powell is sent to prison, and receives a psychiatric evaluation by Theo Caulder (Gooding), who realizes that he has much to learn from this complex man. This film provides rich content for discussion of research, environment, and ethics.

Julien Donkey-Boy (**Ewen Bremner, Chloe Sevigny**) Avant-garde/Experimental

An avant-garde film that is a series of vignettes about bizarre characters, centered on Julien (Bremner), a schizophrenic who works in a school for the blind. Julien lives at home with his pregnant sister (Sevigny), a brother who is a wrestler, and a violent father. Julien leaves the home environment and interacts with people on the street. Some connections here with the characters, bizarre behaviors, and research background. An R rating with some adult situations.

The Truman Show (**Jim Carrey, Ed Harris**) Comedy
1. If we were conducting an experiment and were only studying Truman, what kind of study would that be? Why?
2. Would it be possible to conduct a naturalistic observation on Truman, considering his whole world is controlled by the television producers, much like the control over factors that could be found in a laboratory? Why or why not?
3. If given the opportunity, would you participate in an event where all of your actions could be viewed by millions of people, much like in the television series "Big Brother?" Why or why not?

3. **Biological Bases of Behavior**	Videos	Films
Brain & Nervous System	52	3
Heredity & Genetics	4	2

* The Brain & Nervous System

CNN® Today Video Vol. I: *Section 2: The Brain*

Addicted Brain (2:50)

Shrinking Brains (3:30)

Memory Drugs (1:59)

Warrior Mentality (2:54)

Dyslexia Study (2:45)

Brain Conference (2:41)

CNN® Today Video Vol. II: *Section 1:The Brain*

Hyperactive Brains (2:11)

Brain Mapping (2:29)

Smell Memory (2:21)

The Brain and ADD (1:51)

CNN® Today Video Vol. III: *Section 1: The Biological Bases of Behavior*

Mood Chemicals (1:10)

Stroke Brain Repair (1:54

Human Gene Repair (1:46)

Alzheimer's Disease, from *The Mind Teaching Modules*, 2nd Edition, # 19 (2000) Worth (7:06)
This is a case study of Eleanor who has Alzheimer's disease.

Anatomy of the Human Brain. (2000) Films for the Humanities & Sciences, (35 minutes)
Neuropathologist Dr. Marco Rossi dissects and examines a normal human brain. Using three methods of dissection-coronal plane, CT-MRI plane, and sagittal plane – Dr. Rossi separates the hindbrain from the midbrain, and removes a portion of the brain containing the substantia nigra. The anterior and posterior of the forebrain are dissected, and each section is examined, along with the left occipital lobe. After separating the brain stem from the cerebellum, both are sectioned and examined.

The Behaving Brain. Discovering Psychology Series (1990) Annenberg/CPB, (30 minutes)
The Behaving Brain is part of the *Discovering Psychology* series hosted by Dr. Phillip Zimbardo. This video provides an excellent review of basic brain structure including: the functioning of the neurons, subcortical structures, and neurotransmitters. Application highlights include a description of several methods for assessing brain activity, the effects of neurotransmitters on memory and learning, and a discussion of the possible use of brain transplants for curing Parkinson's disease.

The Biology of Behavior, from *Psychology- The Study of Human Behavior Series*, (1990) Coast Community College District, (30 minutes)

Focuses on the human nervous systems and neurotransmission.

Birth of a Brain. (1983) McGraw-Hill/CRM, (33 minutes)

This film illustrates the genetic origins of the brain, the importance of the environment in its development, and the corresponding behavioral manifestations. Dramatic visuals include microphotography, computer graphics, and a live birth sequence.

Brain and Nervous System: Your Information Superhighway. (2000) Films for the Humanities and Sciences, (25 minutes)

This program explores the brain and nervous system, using the analogy of computers and the Internet. Topics discussed include electrical impulses and how nerve messages travel; parts of the brain and their functions; how the brain and spinal cord are protected; the senses; and diseases, drugs, and their effect on the brain and nervous system.

Brain Anomaly and Plasticity: Hydrocephalus, from *The Brain Teaching Modules*, 2nd Edition #7 (1998) Annenberg/CPB (7:02)

The emphasis here is on plasticity. This video emphasizes two points. First, brain injury that occurs early in life is different from brain injury experienced after maturity. Second, hydrocephalus' individuals, although their brains are distorted, have a cortex which is essential to normal human brain function.

Brain Mechanisms of Pleasure and Addiction, from *The Mind Teaching Modules*, 2nd Edition #6 (2000) Worth, (6:51)

This video focuses on biological motivation and addictive behavior. These studies provide an excellent backdrop for class discussion about the application of animal research to the human situation and the ethical implication of human brain stimulation.

The Brain-Mind Connection. (1990) Insight Media, (30 minutes)

This video examines how the brain influences and is influenced by thought and the environment. It explores hemispheric lateralization and the effects of enriched environments.

The Brain Series, General Psychology Teaching Module 1. (1988) Annenberg/CPB, (various times)

General Psychology Teaching Modules: The Brain Series contains brief excerpts from *The Brain Series* originally co-produced by WNET/New York and Antenne 2 TV/France. The first module in the series contains sixteen, four to ten minute segments covering key topics like: overview of brain organization, language & speech, Broca's & Wernicke's areas, split brain, brain transplants in Parkinson's patients, and hormones & sexual development. This abbreviated video format lends itself well to use in an introductory course where you may not want to spend an entire class session showing a video on only one topic.

Brain Transplants in Parkinson's Patients, from *The Mind Teaching Modules*, 2nd Edition, #31 (2000) Worth (11:09)

This video describes the surgical procedure of implanting human fetal brain tissues into the basal ganglia of Parkinson's patients. The results of the operation are dramatic.

The Divided Brain, from *The Brain Teaching Modules*, 2nd Edition #5 Annenberg/CPB, (6:46)

This module will demonstrate to students the effects of having a split brain on behavior and mental processes. It should help clear up any confusion about the role of the corpus callosum in brain functioning.

Dopamine Seduction: The Limbic System. (2000) Films for the Humanities and Sciences, (25 minutes)

This program illustrates the function of the limbic system in a subject named Greg, following the activity of his brain as he staves off danger and hunger. Extraordinary 3-D computer animation such as the release of hormones into the bloodstream and brain cells transmitting nerve impulses.

Effect of Mental and Physical Activity on Brain/Mind, from *The Mind Teaching Modules*, 2nd Edition #18 (2000) Worth (9:27)

This video shows the effect of aging on both mental and physical decline.

Endorphins: The Brain's Natural Morphine, from *The Mind Series Teaching Modules*, 2nd Edition #5, Annenberg/CPB (3:57)

Describes and illustrates the way in which endorphins prevent pain in the body through animation. The purpose is to help visual learners in particular grasp the "lock and key" concept for neurotransmitters.

Eric's Brain. **(1994)** NBC News, (20 minutes)

A news magazine style report showing brain surgery on a man having a tumor removed. Fascinating footage of the effects of surgery on behavior and thought.

The Enlightened Machine. (1984) Annenberg/CPB, (58 minutes)

This film from *The Brain, Mind, and Behavior* series uses microphotography and interviews with neuroscience experts to explain the functions of the brain. The research of Gaul, Florence, Broca, and Wernicke is discussed, and the viewer is introduced to modern recording techniques: CAT, PET, and EEG. This film also discusses several degenerative brain disorders that reveal information about the brain's function (stroke, Parkinson's disease, epilepsy, Huntington's disease, multiple sclerosis, hydrocephalus, and others). It is an excellent film concerning the relationship between CNS illness and behavior.

The Frontal Lobes and Behavior; The Story of Phineas Gage, from *The Brain Teaching Modules*, 2nd Edition #25, (1998) Annenberg/CPB (12:03)

This program is a reenactment of the tragic accident that destroyed Phineas Gage's capacity to function normally.

The Hidden Universe: The Brain. CRM, (Part I, 23 minutes, Part II, 25 minutes)

With David Janssen as host, this film provides an overview of the functions of the brain, including motor control, memory, and sensory perceptions. Featured is a live scene in an operating room where doctors perform a craniotomy, probing different parts of the patient's brain as he indicates the sensation this causes. Following this, a discussion of the separate function of the right and left hemispheres is highlighted with scenes of a young man who has a "split brain." The film also features a woman who has an electric stimulator implanted in her back, and a doctor who is using computers in an effort to cure blindness.

The Human Brain. (1997) Insight Media (25 minutes)
The Human Brain takes a look at how brain function and development is influenced by environment.

Inside Information: The Brain and How it Works. (1992) Films for the Humanities and Sciences, (58 minutes)
Award winning video focusing on the latest brain topics. Includes a discussion of pattern recognition, individual part functioning and possible computer analogies. It is visually memorable and packed with information.

Language and Speech: Broca's and Wernicke's Areas, from *The Brain Teaching Modules*, 2nd Edition #6 (1998) Annenberg/CPB, (7:44)
Both Broca's area and Wernicke's area are presented in terms of their importance in language comprehension.

Language Processing in the Brain, from *The Mind Teaching Modules*, 2nd Edition #8 (2000) Worth (6:19)
This video shows the versatility of the PET scan as a research tool.

Left Brain, Right Brain. (1980) Filmmakers Library, (56 minutes)
Dr. Norman Geschwind introduces this film on recent breakthroughs in brain research. As the film indicates, in most people the left hemisphere processes information with an analytic time-dependent sequential strategy, while the right hemisphere processes information with a holistic strategy that is independent of time and order. Researchers demonstrate a variety of tests which pinpoint the exact geography of brain functions. Highlight includes a fascinating demonstration of split-brain research techniques.

Marvels of the Mind. (1980) National Geographic Society, (23 minutes)
This film explores the complex structures and function of the human brain. It features Olds's stimulation research with rats and includes split-brain research on a woman who has had her corpus callosum severed. The film also includes information about the effects of stimulation on dreams and several computer simulations of synaptic communication processes. This overview of the human brain should help clarify the important functions of the CNS.

Mysteries of the Mind. (1980) National Geographic Society, (59 minutes)
This film examines the structure and function of the human brain to unravel some of its mysteries. It uses sculpture and animation to display the chemical and electrical processes of neuronal communication in some parts of the brain. It also uses computer graphics to show the relationship between CNS blood flow and behavior. In addition, the film documents several feats of mind control over human behavior.

Nerves. (1992) Insight Media, (24 minutes)
This BBC presentation uses animation to demonstrate the formation and propagation of action potentials and the transmission of an impulse across a synapse. It investigates the roles of transmitters, agonists, antagonists, and second messengers, and shows techniques used in studying brain slices and

single neurons. It also considers such disorders of the nervous system as Alzheimer's disease, Parkinson's disease, depression, and anxiety.

The Nervous System. (1981) Encyclopedia Britannica Educational Corporation, (17 minutes)
One of the few quality films designed to introduce students to the workings of the peripheral nervous system.

The Nervous System: Decision. (1985) Films for the Humanities and Sciences, (26 minutes)
This film discusses how our brain handles sensory inputs and decides on behavioral outputs. The information-processing theory of cognition is stressed in examples that highlight the role of the cortex in analyzing, storing, and creating behavior. Individual nerve cells and circuits of nerves are discussed in relation to making decisions.

Neurorehabilitation, from *The Brain Teaching Modules*, 2nd Edition #32 (1998) Annenberg/CPB (11:54)
The important message of this program is that people can recover significantly from brain damage. For rehabilitation to be most effective, remediation should be combined with teaching compensatory strategies.

Organization and Evaluation of Brain Function, from *The Brain Series Teaching Modules*, 2nd Edition #1 Annenberg/CPB, (7:08)
This video highlights the brainstem, midbrain, limbic system, the visual projection area, and the frontal lobes.

Patterns of Pain (1980) Filmmakers Library, (28 minutes)
In this film a professor of psychology, a zoologist, and a doctor speak about the perception of pain in the nervous system. Illustrated and discussed are phenomena such as the absence of pain perception by the wounded during battle; pain control through hypnosis, acupuncture, and yoga; thresholds of pain; the body's ability to release its own analgesic; and finally, new surgical techniques for implanting electrodes in the brain to block pain.

The Physiology of Behavior. (1993) Films for the Humanities and Sciences, (60 minutes)
This video includes segments covering recent work on addiction, development of the human brain, dreams, genetic testing, memory, the nervous system, and other topics. A videodisc version allows the instructor to play only those segments wanted, in an easy, user-friendly way.

The Responsive Brain. Discovering Psychology Series (1990) Annenberg/CPB, (30 minutes)
Another in the series hosted by Dr. Phillip Zimbardo. This video shows how the brain responds to internal and external stimulation (i.e. hormones and experience). It shows how the brain changes as well as how it responds to these stimulations in relation to directing behavior. Together, *The Behaving Brain* and *The Responsive Brain* can be used to show students the balance between nature and nurture in determining behavior and mental processes.

The Split-Brain and Conscious Experience. Harper and Row, (22 minutes)
Examines the implications of rare footage showing split-brain patients after surgery. Actual surgery is shown. Patients laugh when a nude is flashed to right hemisphere but cannot explain their reactions.

Triune Brain. (1985) National Film Board of Canada, (30 minutes)

Presents a detailed portrait of the human brain using models from antiquity through the more recently developed triune model, narrated by Paul McLean.

Two Brains. (1984) Annenberg/CPB, (55 minutes)

This segment of ***The Brain, Mind, and Behavior*** series discusses the hemispheric specialization of the human brain in respect to language, thought, and sex differences. The film introduces us to Vicki, an epileptic who has undergone a split-brain operation, and analyzes the results of the procedure. Interestingly, it points out that the Japanese language contains two forms of writing, a phonetic form (left hemisphere) and an ideographic form (right hemisphere), and that a stroke can lead to different symptoms in a Japanese person, depending on the location of the hemisphere problem.

Unraveling the Mysteries of the Mind, from *The Mind Series Teaching Modules*, 2nd Edition Worth, (10:45)

A look at cognitive psychology and its methods. Shows how neuroscience is opening up areas of the brain to help us understand the mind.

Feature Films

Awakenings (**Robin Williams**)

This movie is about a neurologist who works in a ward at a hospital who is very distraught at the sight of his patients. All of the patients had encephalitis enthartica as children, and were left with no ability to speak, comprehend, or even live. The doctor sees a seminar on L-Dopa and chooses one patient to administer the drug to in an experimental run to see if it would help. After a few doses, the patient wakes up and becomes "normal." They start giving everyone on the ward the medication after seeing his progress and they all have the same results. But after a while, the initial patient's progress starts to deteriorate until he is eventually back into his previous state, along with the rest of the patients.

1. When the people regressed into "statues" again, did they feel all the pain was worth the short-lived improvement? What about the doctors?
2. How does encephalitis affect the brain?
3. If you were in the same situation as the patients, would you want to undergo a treatment like that if you knew the improvements would only be short-term? Why or why not?

Midnight in the Garden of Good and Evil (1997) (**Kevin Spacey, John Cusack**) Drama
Specific Scene Analysis:
- Central Concept: the functioning of the autonomic nervous system
- Approximate Scene Location: 145 minutes, 30 seconds into the 155 minute film
- Approximate Scene Length: 4 minutes, 30 seconds
- Opening Line: John: "Oh Jim, one more question for the book."
- Closing Line: Minerva: "Don't commune so long with the dead that you forget to commune with the living."

Key Concepts: autonomic nervous system, sympathetic division, parasympathetic division
Characters/Actors: Jim Williams (Kevin Spacey), John Kelso (John Cusack), Minerva (Irma P. Hall)
Scene Description: Mr. Kelso writes for *Town and Country* magazine, and he has flown to Savannah, Georgia, to do a short article for publication. He is to write an article featuring Jim Williams's famous Christmas party. Mr. Kelso is staying at Mr. Williams's carriage house while in Savannah. Jim Williams introduces him to Minerva, who is a voodoo priestess. Voodoo is a system of beliefs that is a

combination of beliefs brought from Africa by slaves, beliefs of peoples indigenous to the land, and beliefs of the Catholic Church. It has numerous followers in the United States and the Caribbean and is recognized as a religion in the country of Brazil. Jim Williams professes not to believe in some of the rituals; however, he does believe in the spiritual forces behind the movement. Communicating with the dead, bestowing curses on others, spirits taking revenge on the living, all are part of an elaborate system of beliefs and rituals in voodoo. Minerva is skilled in these and others aspects of voodoo. The Christmas party takes place and is a grand event. Later that night, Jim Williams shoots one of the hired help for his mansion, Billy Hansen. Jim Williams is charged with first-degree murder, and John Kelso decides to stay and write a book about the trial and other interesting events in savannah. During the trial, it is revealed that Jim Williams and Billy Hansen had an intimate relationship. Meanwhile, John Kelso is becoming acquainted with voodoo through Minerva, who says that Billy is still "working" Jim Williams. In other words, Billy's spirit will not rest in his grave until he gets revenge on Jim for shooting him. Although Minerva tries to calm the spirit of Billy, he is still bent on revenge. Because of mishandling of evidence by the police and skilled performance by his lawyer, Jim is found not guilty of the murder of Billy Hansen. However, Jim has confessed to John that he did kill Billy, partially in self-defense and also in anger at his demanding and destructive behaviors. Minerva says that Billy's spirit is still working John because justice has not been done. The scene opens with John preparing to leave Savannah.

Questions/Discussion:

    1.   In the last scene, what do you think happened to Jim?

Have students offer their opinions of what killed Jim.

    2.   Do you think it is possible that Jim's belief in voodoo had something to do with his death?

Have students give their views.

    3.   For the sake of argument, let's say that it did. How would you explain voodoo's possible effect using information on how the autonomic system functions?

Jim believed in the spiritual forces behind voodoo and therefore was vulnerable to the belief that a person can put a curse on you if you did that person a wrong deed. Although he was found not guilty of the charge of murdering Billy, Jim knows that he did shoot him. He is thinking about Billy, as he is in the room where the crime took place. His fear of a curse from Billy stimulates the functioning of his sympathetic system. The parasympathetic system functions to restore a balance in the autonomic system or keep the life-sustaining organs functioning after a period of extreme arousal of the sympathetic system. Jim was so afraid that his parasympathetic system failed to slow down his heartbeat, and thus he died. His parasympathetic system did not kick in quickly enough to keep the heart functioning at a proper beat.

Raging Bull **(Robert DeNiro)**
This movie portrays the life of prizefighter LaMotta, a man who needs to find purpose and meaning in life outside of the ring. He has all kinds of problems in his life and it gets really bad when he has to remove the jewels from his World Middleweight Championship belt and sell them. He suffers from an incredibly impaired judgment and has other problems associated with concussions.
    1. What actually happens to the brain of a fighter when he is "knocked-out?"
    2. Is the protective headgear worn by amateur boxers effective in protecting against head injury?
    3. The American Academy of Neurology has supported a ban on professional boxing since 1983. Do you agree with that position? Why or why not?

* Heredity & Genetics

CNN® Today Video Vol. I: *Section 4: Genetic Mapping*

> Schizophrenia Gene (4:09)

> Parkinson's Gene Therapy (2:08)

The Birth of a Brain. (1983) CRM/McGraw-Hill, (33 minutes)

Through the use of microphotography, computer graphics, and an actual birth sequence, this film illustrates the effects of heredity and environment on the development of the brain and the resulting behavior of the individual. Because of the live birth sequence, you may want to screen the film before showing it to your students. Color.

The Responsive Brain. (1990) Annenberg/CPB, (30 minutes)

This segment of the *Discovering Psychology* series, which is hosted by Philip Zimbardo of Stanford University, examines how the brain analyzes environmental information and controls behavior. It explores the relationship between the organ's structure and its function. Several results from human, maternal, and touch studies are provided that support current theories of active physical and psychological growth in infants. Animal-enrichment studies are also used to support the idea that the environment has a powerful influence on development of the brain. There is good use of comparative data to support the contention that environment influences brain development.

Feature Films

Gattaca **(Ethan Hawke, Uma Thurman)**

Genetic engineering is the main topic of the film. The official site of the picture contains cast and picture information, an interactive game and trailers from the movie. *http://www.gattaca.com*

1. Do you believe that sometime in the near future that you will be able to "order" what your child will be like by altering the genetic code of the developing embryo, like the people in Gattaca?
2. What type of problems do you see being alleviated and what type of problems do you see being created by altering the genetic makeup of individuals?
3. If given the opportunity to correct all possible genetic problems before they actually start in a developing embryo and you are able to make the child be exactly what you want him/her to be like, would you do so? Why or why not?

Regarding Henry **(Harrison Ford, Annette Benning)** Drama
1. What area of the brain was most affected by his injury? What is this area responsible for?
2. Do you believe his portrayal of the effects of brain injury were accurate? Why or why not?
3. How do you think you would cope with an event such as this occurring to you?

4. Sensation and Perception	Videos	Films
Extrasensory Perception	4	2
Perception	12	2
Senses	18	1

CNN® Today Video Vol. III: *Section 2: Sensation and Perception*

Elderly Taste (2:02)

Sleep and Hearing (1:34)

* ExtraSensory Perception

ESP- The Human "X" Factor. Indiana University, (30 minutes)
Illustrates extrasensory perception and interviews J. B. Rhine.

Experimental Parapsychology. (1977) CTV Television Network Ltd., (145 minutes)
Looks at the problems and patterns of alleged cases of paranormal events. Program contains a series of five cassettes 29 minutes each.

The Case of ESP. (1984) WGBH for Nova (57 minutes)
If you cover ESP as part of the unit on sensation and perception, this is an excellent video about formal research and business enterprises dedicated to the study of ESP in the areas of archaeology, criminology, and warfare. It presents vivid replications of ESP studies, as well as rare footage of some Russian ESP experiments. Among the many topics for discussion it includes are precognition, psychokinesis, and clairvoyance.

Secrets of the Psychics with James Randi. (1993) NOVA, (60 minutes)
In this video, the Amazing Randi spends time debunking a number of parapsychological phenomena and demonstrating the P.T. Barnum effect. There is also a discussion about why humans want to believe in the supernatural. A thorough and fun presentation.

Feature Films

The Sixth Sense **(Bruce Willis)** Drama
1.   What type of ESP abilities did this little boy have in the movie?
2.   What was the significance of the dropping of the ring?
3.   What was the purpose of the little boy's ESP?

What Lies Beneath **(Michelle Pfeiffer, Harrison Ford)** Drama/Suspense
1.   What was the perception of Michelle Pfeiffer's character's accident before the awareness of her husband's infidelity?
2.   What strong sensations of the spirit of the dead girl were in the house? Name three.
3.   Do you believe that spirits with unfinished business communicate with those who are alive? Why or why not?

* Perception

The Doors of Perception. (1991) Insight Media (58 minutes)

This highly acclaimed video explores the means by which humans construct an internal representation of their external world. Includes discussions of consciousness and culture and uses the works of William Blake to illustrate important concepts.

Infancy Research Methods. (1983) Indiana University, (18 minutes)

If you lean toward teaching research methods as an ongoing part of your course, this film is for you. It brings research, perception, and developmental psychology together, covering the visual and auditory abilities of infants from birth to one year of age. The four research methods covered include preference, eye movements, conditioning, and habituation. The film encourages a multi-method approach for the most accurate interpretative data.

The Man Who Mistook His Wife for a Hat. Films for the Humanities and Sciences, (75 minutes)

This is a collection of case studies of patients suffering neurological damage. The film relates the case of Dr. P., a well-known tenor who has visual agnosia, a condition in which he can see but cannot make sense of what he sees.

The Mind and Perception- Part Two. (1984) from *Using Your Creative Brain Series*, Educational Dimensions Group, (42 minutes)

Discusses the psychology, biology, and sociology related to the perceptiveness of the brain.

Perception. (1970) Prentice-Hall, (15 minutes)

This film provides many principles of perception not normally available for classroom demonstration. It begins with an overview of the field and goes on to present illustrations of figure-ground relationships. Bruner's experiment, phi phenomena, Benham's top, perceptual set, color satiation, color mixture, and the trapezoidal window are included.

Perception. (1979) CRM/McGraw-Hill, (28 minutes)

This film shows how perception is an individual and subjective means of viewing reality influenced by upbringing, culture, and media. Several vignettes in business as well as social settings depict the consequences of individuals perceiving the same situation differently. Although people strive for objectivity, the film points out that diverse opinions can be normal and enriching as well as a means to evaluate one's own judgments and decisions.

Perception: the Theories, from *The Psychology of Learning: Part Seven* (2000) Films for the Humanities and Sciences, (45 minutes)

Can perception be explained in terms of sensation? In this program, the senses, including proprioception, are described; the Structuralist, Gestalt, Constructivist, and Direct Perception theories are critically analyzed, focusing on both their strengths and weaknesses; and perceptual models such as those of Ulric Neisser and David Marr are presented. Many examples of the perceptual theories are provided. In addition, the roles of Wundt, Wertheimer, Gregory, and Gibson are discussed, along with key perceptual concepts such as Weber's Law, the Principle of Pragnaz, and the laws of Proximity, Closure, and Continuity. An excellent overview of perception theory and various interpretations.

Seeing Beyond the Obvious: Understanding Perception in Everyday and Novel Environments. (1990)
NASA/Ames Research Center, (45 minutes)

Interesting and informative video focusing primarily on visual perception. The first half of the video is devoted to depth (both monocular and binocular cues). The second half of the video focuses on visual perception in novel situations (e.g., while flying a jet).

Understanding the Senses. (1998) Films for the Humanities and Sciences, (56 minutes)

In this program, renowned neurologist Dr. Oliver Sacks and other specialists reveal the beauty and complexity of visual, auditory, chemosensory, and tactile perception. Sense-related phenomena such as proprioception and applications like a device designed to sniff out dangerous chemical signatures are examined, along with sensory malfunctions including color blindness, phantom limb syndrome, and the inability to see motion.

Visual Information Processing: Perception, from *The Brain Teaching Modules*, 2nd Edition, Annenberg (8:45)

A good illustration of brain research on visual perception in animals. Especially informative is the confirmation of specialized feature detectors, such as lines moving in one direction but not another.

Feature Films

Specific Scene Analysis:
The English Patient (1996) (**Ralph Fiennes, Kristin Scott Thomas**) Drama

- Central Concept: visual system
- Approximate Scene Location: 24 minutes, 33 second into the 161 minute film
- Approximate Scene Length: 2 minutes
- Opening Line: Nurse Hannah: "I should try and move the bed, I want you to be able to see the view."
- Closing Line: Nurse Hannah: "Because I am a nurse."

Key Concepts: visual system, transduction
Characters/Actors: The English patient/Count Almaay (Ralph Fiennes), Nurse Hannah (Juliet Bonita)
Scene Description: The time period for the film is the closing days of World War II in Italy. Count Almaay has led an expedition for the Royal Geographic Society to map the terrain of the desert located in northern Africa. He was returning to the area of desert controlled by Allied forces in a German plane when he was shot down. He suffered tremendous burns all over his body. A nomadic desert tribe rescued Count Almaay, and using their indigenous medicine, they kept him alive. During the ride in a Red Cross truck convoy, Nurse Hannah realizes that he is dying and that the trip by truck over the rough terrain is too painful for him. Alone she takes him to a deserted villa to die, and she has placed him on freshly washed sheets in a semi-comfortable bed. The scene opens with Nurse Hannah talking about their location.

Questions/Discussion:
1.   Why does Count Almaay remark that he can see his wife?

Count Almaay can see his wife although she is not present because of the way the visual system works. We see with our brain as well as our eyes, and the images he has seen of her earlier are in his brain. Thus he can see her by recalling previous visual images.

2.   How do the visual images of what we see enter the brain?
The visual system has receptor cells, which experience the sensations of light from the environment.
Through the process of transduction, the stimulus is converted into neural impulses, which are sent to
the brain. The images are retained in the brain for later recall.

3.   Why is transduction important to the visual system?

Transduction refers to the process in which energy from stimuli in the environment is transformed into
an entity that can be used by the neural system to assist us in responding and adapting to our
environment. Without the transduction process, the energies from the environment cannot be used by
our physiological system.

Lightning Jack (**Paul Hogan, Cuba Gooding Jr.**) Comedy
        1.   Paul Hogan's character requires glasses to read anything in small print. What is this
        condition called and what causes it?
        2.   What are the possible causes of the mutism that Cuba Gooding Jr.'s character displays?
        3.   Although both of these characters seem to be functioning well, do you believe that people
        who really lived in the "Old West" would be able to function as well? Why or why not?

* The Senses (Vision, Hearing, the Other Senses)

Controlling Pain. (1995) Films for the Humanities and Sciences, (23 minutes)
        In this video, the complex process of pain is described. Additionally, it discusses ongoing
research to find ways to alleviate pain, including chemicals and electrical stimulation techniques.

Hearing Conservation. International Film Bureau, (22 minutes)
        This film discusses the prevention of environmentally caused hearing loss.

An Introduction to Visual Illusions. (1970) Pennsylvania University, (12 minutes)
        In a brief time and with simple explanations, this film describes how the eye works and how the
brain perceives distance, perspective, and movement. It illustrates over 20 visual illusions, including
depth, direction, extent, afterimages, reverse relief, diversion, and perceived movement. It also illustrates
size variance as related to vertical/horizontal positioning and gamma movement caused by variations in
light intensity. The film is designed for introductory psychology and science classes, so no complex
terminology is included. It provides some memorable visual examples.

Inverted Vision, from *The Brain Series Teaching Modules*, 2nd Edition #10, Annenberg (5:04)
        This video clearly illustrates the difference between sensation and perception for the student. It
shows a woman adjusting her normal daily activities to seeing things upside down through special lenses
during the course of a week. At the end of a week, she removes the glasses and finds that she has to
readjust to normal conditions, but this takes place in only a few hours as opposed to a week.

Managing Pain. (1995) Films for the Humanities and Sciences, (18 minutes)
        This video looks at what can be done about pain besides taking aspirin. Some of the latest
research on the nature of pain and its treatment are presented.

Phantom Limb Pain, from *The Mind Teaching Modules*, 2nd Edition # 20 (2000) Worth (4:29)
        This video is short and to the point. It presents a vivid example of phantom limb pain and raises
important questions about the origin of the pain.

Sensation and Perception, from *Psychology- The Study of Human Behavior Series*, (1990) Coast Community College District, (30 minutes)

Demonstrates construction of reality from senses, interpretation and organization into meaningful patterns by the brain.

Sensation and Perception, Discovering Psychology Teaching Module 3. (1990) Annenberg/CPB (various times)

The Discovering Psychology Teaching Modules contain excerpts from the *Discovering Psychology Series*. Module 3 in this series (sensation and perception) contains several interesting sections including: a discussion by Hubel and Weisel of visual processing, the rat versus man illusion, and an example of visual compensation. Students are fascinated by the Ames room, and in this program, the apparent size of host Philip Zimbardo increases and decreases as he walks the length of the room several times. The program emphasizes visual perception, demonstrates current experimental procedures in studying edge perception, and explains why it is important to our experiences of the world.

The Sense: Eyes and Ears. (1985) Films for the Humanities and Sciences, (26 minutes)

This film looks at the "distance senses"—eyes and ears. Viewers are shown a young reckless driver careening down a road—and are then taken into his eye where the image of the potential crash site is shown. Also seen are scenes inside an ear, showing how the linked bones vibrate to a sound, and a computer graphic shows how the eye focuses on an image.

The Senses and Perception: Links to the Outside World. (1975) Indiana University, (18 minutes)

A look at the way in which sense receptors send information to the brain which then interprets it based on the information itself as well as on past experience.

The Senses. (1978) Insight Media, (29 minutes)

A basic treatment of sensation with primary focus on transduction.

The Senses: Skin Deep. (1985) Films for the Humanities and Sciences, (26 minutes)

This film looks at those sense receptors that depend on contact with the immediate world: taste buds, touch sensors, and olfactory cells. These senses lie in the skin—the largest organ of the body—which also senses heat, pain, and pressure. The complex world beneath the skin is seen from the viewpoint of the root of these receptors.

Sensory-Motor Integration, from *The Brain Teaching Modules*, 2nd Edition #11, (2000) Worth (3:27)

This video uses Olympic Gold Medalist Greg Louganis as a good example of sensory-motor learning and how natural talent, combined with expert coaching and untiring practice, work together to achieve perfection.

The Sensory World. (1971) CRM (33 minutes)

This classic film does a nice job of summarizing the major sensory systems. There is, however, an emphasis on visual processing issues (e.g., color blindness, illusions).

Smell. (1995) Films for the Humanities and Sciences, (23 minutes)

This video tells students what is known about the complex sense of smell. The process of making scented products is also described.

Treating Chronic Pain, from *The Mind Teaching Modules*, 2nd Edition #21 (2000) Worth (14:23)
 This video provides an excellent example of how psychologists and medical practitioners work together under a shared set of assumptions about cause and treatment of chronic pain.

Understanding the Senses. (1988) Films for the Humanities and Sciences, (56 minutes)
 In this program, renowned neurologist Dr. Oliver Sacks and other specialists reveal the beauty and complexity of visual, audial, chemosensory, and tactile perception. Sense-related phenomena such as proprioception and applications like a device designed to sniff out dangerous chemical signatures are examined, along with sensory malfunctions including color blindness, phantom limb syndrome, and the inability to see motion.

Visual Information Processing: Elementary Concepts, from *The Brain Teaching Modules*, 2nd Edition #8, Annenberg (9:11)
 This video reviews how the visual stimulus travels from the environment to the visual cortex. It will help both visual and auditory learners improve their understanding of the visual process.

Feature Films

Senseless **(Marlon Wayans, David Spade)** Comedy
 A college student (Wayans) earns some extra money by becoming a test subject for an experimental drug that heightens the senses by five times. He finds that his enhanced hearing helps him receive distant conversations, and his increased coordination boosts his hockey game. Comic situations occur when an overdose allows only four of his five senses to be operative at any given time. While a comedy, it provides some food for thought, reflection and discussion about the senses. In discussing this film, it may be advisable to recall with the students the sensitivity necessary in dealing with those who are impaired in one or more senses. Nevertheless, even those with a sensory disability have provided humorous anecdotes as well.

5. **Variations in Consciousness**	Videos	Film
Altered States of Consciousness & Hypnosis	5	2
Consciousness	8	1
Sleep	15	2

* Altered States of Consciousness and Hypnosis

Captive Minds: Hypnosis and Beyond. (1988) Filmmakers Library, (55 minutes)
   This award-winning film explains how long-term conditioning takes place and shows that the indoctrination methods used by disparate institutions are surprisingly similar. Recruits are isolated and worked to exhaustion; confused and frightened, they readily submit to a leader, be it a guru, cult leader, or sergeant. The film shows how the power of suggestion influences behavior and reminds us that we are all vulnerable to psychological manipulation.

Child Hypnosis with Dr. Perry London. (1990) Psychological and Educational Films, (40 minutes)
   In this discussion, Perry London asserts that hypnosis can be an effective treatment in psychotherapy. He notes that it has been found to help relieve symptoms of several disorders related to stress and that it is especially helpful in children, because of their level of trust and susceptibility. Actual demonstrations of the technique on a 10-year-old are provided to display levels of susceptibility. This is a very current film on the attributes of hypnosis and its use in psychotherapy.

Hypnotic Dissociation and Pain Relief, from *The Mind Series Teaching Modules*, 2nd Edition #2, Annenberg (3:03)
   Demonstrates the effect of hypnotic suggestion on pain tolerance using the "cold pressor" task, among others. Students can judge for themselves the efficacy of hypnosis as an anesthetic.

The Mind Hidden and Divided, Discovering Psychology Series. Annenberg/CPB, (30 minutes)
   This program provides examples of how psychoactive drugs change perceptions, thoughts, and moods; it also describes how cross-cultural research reveals ritualistic use of drugs, fasting, and meditation in altering consciousness. It suggests that hypnosis provides a window into the unconscious. The hypnotists' suggestions can direct behavior, alter memory, alleviate pain, and even influence decisions about smoking and eating. Topics covered also include multiple personality disorder and research on the divided brain.

Milton Erickson, M.D.--Explorer in Hypnosis and Therapy. (1994) Filmmakers Library, (56 minutes)
   This new video offers a fascinating portrait of the life and work of the world's foremost authority on medical hypnosis and therapy, Milton Erickson (1901-1980). It contains rare archival footage of Erickson at work, allowing the viewer to see firsthand his extraordinary ability to heal both body and mind through hypnosis. The video has both historic value and a powerful message for current psychology classes.

Feature Films

Altered States **(William Hurt, Blair Brown)** Science Fiction
   William Hurt plays a dedicated scientist who wants to find mankind's true role in the world, and submits himself to a series of mind-expanding experiments in a think-tank. Some say that he's trying to think back to the first original human thought. The last of the experiments leads Hurt to devolve into a

Neanderthal-like creature. While a science fiction drama, the movie provides material for discussion of the think-tank movement of the 1970s, as well as variations in consciousness such as meditation, hypnosis, and think-tank self-reflection.

Bram Stoker's Dracula
1.   What role does hypnosis play in locating Dracula?
2.   Is the very quick induction of hypnosis on Mina the way that actual hypnosis is done? Is the process done quickly or does it take longer than what is portrayed in the movie? Explain your answer.
3.   Do you believe that hypnosis is a legitimate method for helping to uncover information that you just can't seem to access consciously? Why or why not?

* Consciousness

CNN® Today Video Vol. III: *Section 3: Variations in Consciousness*

Wake-Up Call (1:57)

Sleep (5:27)

Approaches to Consciousness. (1992) Insight Media (30 minutes each segment)
Adapted from the ***Thinking Aloud*** series, this 120-minute video is divided into four 30-minute programs. If you are limited in class time, I suggest you preview programs and fast-forward to specific sections you wish to highlight in class, or choose one or more sections to view in entirety as a class. Here are the four programs: (1) ***The Evolution of Consciousness***—Robert Ornstein suggests that the mind is composed of many subroutines he refers to as a "squadron of simpletons." Self-mastery requires orchestrating these "simpletons" to work as a team. (2) ***The Nervous System and the Soul***—This program examines the dramatic, musical, and mathematical qualities of the soul as they are available even to the mentally retarded and those with neurological defects. Oliver Sachs maintains that our conventional view of awareness keeps us from appreciating the unique talents of those with Tourette's syndrome and other disorders. (3) ***Working with Comas***—This program discusses the unique methods Arnold Mindell has developed for working with individuals in comatose states. Using the techniques of process psychology, he is able to find channels into the minds of comatose individuals that allow him to establish communication. (4) ***The Art of Psychotherapy***—Irvin Yalom discusses his novel *When Nietzsche Wept*, which highlights the existential issues of human consciousness that are the basis of his own therapeutic approach. The soul-searching self-examination of the philosopher Nietzsche is contrasted with the methodological approach of Joseph Breuer, a renowned physician and pioneer psychotherapist. Color.

Seasonal Affective Disorder. (1993) Encyclopedia Britannica Films, (25 minutes)
This video examines biological rhythms and their influence on the behavior of animals and humans. It illustrates the influence of light and the hormone melatonin, using a variety of natural activities including sleep, mating, and emotional experiences.

Sensation and Perception, Discovering Psychology Teaching Module 8. (1990) Annenberg/CPB (various times)
The Discovering Psychology Teaching Modules contain excerpts from the *Discovering Psychology series*. Module 8 in this series (consciousness) contains several interesting sections including: training people to become lucid dreamers, the structure/function of sleep, and a demonstration of hypnosis.

42

* Sleep

Dreams: The Theater of the Night (2000) Films for the Humanities & Sciences, (28 minutes)
       This film examines several theories of dreams, from Sigmund Freud's *Interpretation of Dreams* to modern biological explanations. Modern sleep research facilities are visited, and positron emission tomography scans are used to answer such questions as why dreams occur and what their functions are. The film also depicts an actual therapy session, with a dream analysis segment. It covers some of the more modern techniques used in the study of dreams.

The Mind Awake and Asleep: Discovering Psychology Series. (1990) Annenberg/CPB, (30 minutes)
       In this video from the *Discovering Psychology* series, Dr. Philip Zimbardo discusses the basic process of sleep, dreams, and altered states. A good review of the history of consciousness in psychology, daydreams, and sleep and dreaming. The program gives considerable attention to the possible function of dreams, from Freud's belief that they are the key to unlocking the unconscious to Hobson and McCarley's controversial theory that dreams arise from spontaneous discharges of electrical impulses in the brain. It also shows how researcher Steven LeBerge of Stanford University trains his participants to report their dreams aloud without waking and gives suggestions for directing their dreams, which some claim enhance creativity and control the unconscious.

On Dreams and Dreaming. (1988) Insight Media, (30 minutes)
       An excellent video if you are interested in exploring dreaming in the context of culture. It specifically addresses lucid dreams and how to take control of one's dreams.

REM Sleep and Dreaming, from *The Brain Series Teaching Modules*, 2nd Edition #15, Annenberg, (8:23)
       A good illustration of how research into sleep and dreaming is conducted. PET scans are used to follow the participant's sleep through the 90-minute cycles of a normal night's sleep.

Rhythms and Drives. (1984) PBS Video, (58 minutes)
       This film from *The Brain* series examines human behavior from the standpoint of subcortical activity. The film discusses how seasonal changes affect the human biorhythm and influence behavior, including sleep patterns. The effects of shift work are also discussed, in relation to physical, psychological, and sleep disturbances. Although most of this film deals with the mechanism of our internal clock, there are also segments on aggressive behavior and sexual behavior.

Sleep and Circadian Rhythms, from *The Brain Series Teaching Modules*, 2nd Edition #13, Annenberg, (6:09)
       An excellent demonstration of how knowledge of our circadian rhythms can be sued to improve both working conditions for shift workers and productivity for management.

Sleep and Dreams. (1990) from *Psychology- The Study of Human Behavior Series*, Coast District Telecourses, (30 minutes)
       Demonstrates construction of reality from senses, interpretation, and organization into meaningful patterns by the brain.

Sleep and Its Secret. (1999) Filmmakers Library, (52 minutes)
       This newly released video examines sleep. It nicely makes the point that, contrary to popular belief, the brain is actually very active during episodes of sleep. Through interviews with

internationally known sleep researchers, it explores topics such as stages of sleep, sleep cycles and circadian rhythms, sleep disorders, and changes that occur with age.

Sleep Disorders... Their Effects and Treatments. (1996) Insight Media, (28 minutes)
　　　This video addresses a wide variety of sleep disorders including insomnia, sleep apnea, and narcolepsy. It also provides practical advice for adapting to shift changes and travel as well as advice for helping children sleep through the night.

Sleep: Dream Voyage. (1985) Films for the Humanities and Sciences, (26 minutes)
　　　What happens to the body during sleep? This film explores the mystery of REM sleep, observes a computer display of the waves that sweep across the brain during sleep, and presents an interesting piece of footage of a cat "acting out" its dreams. The analogy of sleep to a ship on automatic pilot illustrates how some functions must and do continue while the conscious brain is asleep.

Sleep: The Fantastic Third of Your Life. University of Illinois, (52 minutes)
　　　A comprehensive presentation of current scientific knowledge about sleep. Describes recent research findings about sleeping and dreaming.

Sleeping Well. (1997) Films for the Humanities and Sciences, (28 minutes)
　　　This program from *The Doctor Is In* provides specific information on how to get a good night's sleep. The topics of breathing disorders such as apnea are discussed, along with the conditions of narcolepsy and restless legs. Dr. Peter Hauri of the Mayo Clinic and Dr. Allan Pack of the University of Pennsylvania Center for Sleep Disorders offer tips on how to fall asleep, and how to manage sleep when working night shifts or traveling across time zones. For parents, Dr. Richard Ferber explains ways to help infants and children fall asleep and stay asleep. A Dartmouth-Hitchcock Medical Center production.

The Sleepwatchers. University of Illinois, (25 minutes)
　　　Shows various procedures used by scientists to learn more about the complexities of sleep.

States of Mind. (1984) PBS Video, (58 minutes)
　　　Part of *The Brain* series, this film explores the various states of consciousness within the human brain. Dreams are discussed in relation to chemical changes in the brain, and the lack of control in one's consciousness is examined in multiple personality disorder. The film also examines changes in consciousness produced by Alzheimer's, stroke, and drug use. Although the opening comments on dreaming are fairly basic, the concluding segment on transplantation work with acetylcholine-producing tissue as a treatment for Alzheimer's disease is very well done.

Wake Up America: A Sleep Alert. Films for the Humanities and Sciences, (24 minutes)
　　　This program covers the functions of sleep and why some people need more sleep than others; circadian rhythm and events that can disrupt our sleep-wake cycles; the different kinds of sleep problems, including sleep apnea, insomnia, and narcolepsy; signs and symptoms of a sleep disorder and how stress, anxiety, and depression affect sleep patterns; the pros and cons of over-the-counter sleep medications; and the workings of a sleep lab.

Feature Films

The Cell **(Jennifer Lopez)**
　　　1.　　What stage of sleep were the two people in when she was able to enter their dreams?

2.   Compare and contrast the states of consciousness experienced by Lopez's character, the little boy, and the killer.
3.   Do you believe that it will be possible one day to enter someone's dreams to see what they are thinking? Why or why not?

Specific Scene Analysis:
The Last of the Dogmen (**Tom Berenger. Barbara Hershey**)

Central Concept: dreams
Approximate Scene Location: 98 minutes into the 118-minute film
Approximate Scene Length: 3 minutes
Opening Scene: Indian hut with dying campfire. Men on horseback with flashlights are coming into the village
Closing Line: Louis Gates: "Lillian, we cannot let anything happen to these people. No one must ever find out, no one."

Key Concepts: dreams, unconscious, consciousness, latent content, manifest content
Characters/Actors: Louis Gates/Tracker (Tom Berenger), Lillian Sloan/Anthropologist (Barbara Hershey), Yellow Wolf/Leader of Dogmen (Steve Reevis), Indian Girl (Dawn Lavand)
Scene Description: The film opens with a scene of state prisoners escaping from a prison bus and fleeing into the wilderness. Louis Gates is hired to track them down and bring them back to prison. He tracks them to a meadow in the Oxbow Quadrangle, located in northwest Montana. When he gets to the site, all he finds is a lot of blood, a piece of clothing worn by a prisoner, an arrow, and tracks of unshod horses. However, no bodies are found; they have mysteriously disappeared. In the area is an anthropologist, Dr. Lillian Sloan, who has a grant to conduct an archaeological dig to study Indian cultures. Gates goes to her for an explanation of the arrow. She gives him the historical account of the Dogmen arrow he has found. Approximately 128 years ago, a Cheyenne chief, Black Arrow, wanted to make peace with the white man. He was promised protection if he brought his tribe to Sand Creek and camped there. After assurance that his people would be safe, he led them to the campsite. A volunteer group of militia from Colorado surrounded the camp and massacred the tribe; two-thirds were women and children. Approximately 20 men, women and children escaped. The fleeing Indians were led by Lone Wolf, the leader of the Dogmen. Within the Cheyenne tribe was a military society of the strongest and bravest warriors who were unyielding in their defense of the tribe. They often acted as decoys when the tribe was under attack so that others could get away. They called themselves dogmen; the U.S. military called them dog soldiers. Lone Wolf and the others escaped into the wilderness of northern Montana. Gates, accompanied by Sloan, who spoke Cheyenne, set out to find the group that had shot the arrow. He and Sloan are captured by the Cheyenne Indians in Oxbow meadow and are carried to their secluded, well-hidden village. The Cheyenne tribe was isolated and had continued its traditional lifestyle. Gates and Sloan were accepted into the tribe and shared the challenges and pleasures of life in the village. Preceding the opening scene of the film clip, showing an Indian hut, was a scene of Sloan, Gates, and members of the tribe around the campfire telling stories.

Questions/Discussion
    1.   What is the content of Gates's dream?
Gates dreams that the modern world, represented by the soldiers with flashlights and high-tech machinery, will destroy the traditional lifestyle of the Cheyenne. Yellow Wolf, as one of the last of the Dogmen, is challenging the intruders to give members of the tribe time to escape.

45

2.   How does his dream support Freud's explanation of the meaning of dreams?
Freud postulates that dreams serve as expressions of the unconscious and thus reflect our innermost desires, wishes, and needs. The content of the unconscious cannot be expressed directly because of the pain, unacceptable feelings, and guilt that will be evoked. Dreams function to code and disguise material in the unconscious in a manner that is acceptable to the conscious. The contents of dreams reflect the individual's desires for fulfillment of wishes and needs and concerns about emotional issues. The wishes and needs in the unconscious are the latent content of the dream that is transformed into manifest content, the characters and events that make up the narrative of the dream. What to do about the discovery of the last remnant of the Cheyenne tribe is what is preoccupying Gates's thoughts.

3.   Does Freud's position have empirical support?
There is evidence to support Freud's idea that dreams have psychological meaning. However, there is no evidence for Freud's idea that dreams reflect wish fulfillment.

The Matrix (**Keanu Reeves, Laurence Fishburne**) Science Fiction
This is a complex, but popular sci-fi film that has a premise that a massive artificial intelligence system has tapped into people's minds and created the illusion of a real world, while using their brains and bodies for energy, then tossing them away when through. Reaves character plays a computer employee who discovers the premise, and is convinced by Fishburne's character that he is 'Neo,' the one who can crack open the Matrix and bring his people both physical and psychological freedom. Very creative visual effects in this film bring many sources of topics for discussions on states of consciousness, psychology, and philosophy. What if virtual reality wasn't just for fun, but was being used to imprison you?

6. **Learning Through Conditioning**	Videos	Films
Behavior Modification	18	4
Conditioning & Learning	18	2
Learning Disabilities	1	1

* Behavior Modification

B. F. Skinner: A Fresh Appraisal. (1999) Davidson Films, (41 minutes)

    Other than Freud, no psychologist has been so discussed, critiqued, and at times maligned as B. F. Skinner. Using both archival and new footage, this video takes a new look at who the man was and what he really said in his twenty books. Like other thinkers who broke new ground, Skinner had to invent his own vocabulary to describe the phenomena he was studying. In this video, his terms are introduced in context so the student understands how they were intended to be used and the research that produced them. The video lays to rest some myths and credits Skinner with contributions not often attributed to him. Understanding the complex man behind his work enables students to better evaluate the importance and relevance of the work he inspired.

Behavioral Treatment of Autistic Children. (1988) Pennsylvania State University, (44 minutes)

    This film presents a detailed explanation and demonstration of Ivar Lovaas's intensive behavioral treatment project for autistic children and illustrates various outcomes from the project, including normal functioning in half the children. It provides follow-up data from autistic children treated in the 1960s, seen 25 years later as adults. This is a new follow-up to the original film, *Teaching Language to Autistic children,* listed below. This is an excellent and powerful work.

B. F. Skinner and Behavior Change: Research, Practice, and Promise. (1979) Research Films, (45 minutes)

    This film features discussions with Skinner and others on the topics of theory, practical methodologies, and the ethical implications of behaviorism. It also explores behaviorism's philosophy, practical applications, and early development. It makes good use of field applications and intervention strategies in mental health, counseling, medicine, and education, which are good topics for discussion about the ethics and social implications of behaviorism.

A Good Night's Sleep. (1990) ABC 20/20, (17 minutes)

    This segment features Dr. Richard Ferber, a children's sleep expert, demonstrating his behavior modification technique for getting children to sleep through the night. This film follows one family's successful effort with Dr. Ferber. This 20/20 segment is really liked by general psychology classes.

Behavior Modifications: Teaching Language to Psychotic Children. (1969) Prentice-Hall, (42 minutes)

    This is a superior film for instructors wanting to demonstrate the clinical and therapeutic uses of behavior modification, although the narration is a bit dry. We see behavior modification techniques pioneered by O. Ivar Lovaas used with several autistic children. Baseline, therapy, and posttherapy charts show dramatic reductions in undesired behaviors and increases in desirable ones. The rare and bizarre behaviors shown in the children include echolalia (echo-speech), self-destructive behaviors (self-inflicted blows to the head and face), and failure to acquire social and intellectual behaviors. This rare and dramatic film may be somewhat difficult to obtain, but it is worth the extra effort.

B.F. Skinner and Behavioral Change. (1979) Research Press, (45 minutes)

  Distinguished professionals from various disciplines join B. F. Skinner in facing the issues and controversies generated by behavioral psychology. The viewer observes on-site interventions with patients, clients, and students as the film visits (1) a home where parents work with their mentally retarded child, (2) a hospital for treatment of an epileptic child, (3) a youth center where children with social problems learn more effective skills, (4) a marital counseling session, and (5) a school of dental medicine where a child is taught to control fear of dental procedures.

Learning. (1971) McGraw-Hill, (30 minutes)

  An award winning film that steps through classical and operant conditioning, motivation, imprinting, and punishment. This classic film does an excellent job presenting the basic principles of most of the major issues in learning theory. This tongue-in-cheek approach shows "Little Albert" as a college applicant with a fear of white furry things.

Learning. (1990) from *Psychology- The Study of Human Behavior Series*, Coast District Telecourses, (30 minutes)

  Focuses on classical conditioning, operant conditioning and real-world applications to behavioral psychology.

Learning as Synaptic Change, from *The Brain Series Teaching Modules*, 2nd Edition #17, Annenberg, (8:19)

  This short segment illustrates the physiological effect of learning, however it is acquired. This short segment shows how new synapses are developed in areas of the brain associated with certain learned behaviors. Its purpose is to remind students of the physiological basis of our mind, and remind students that psychology is a unified discipline.

Learning: Discovering Psychology Series. (1990) Annenberg/CPB, (30 minutes)

  In this video from the *Discovering Psychology* series, Dr. Philip Zimbardo discusses the major players in traditional learning theory (e.g., Pavlov, Watson and Skinner) and the impact of these theories on modern life. For example, it describes how reinforcement is used to train dogs to assist in the care of disabled persons and how clinicians use behavior therapy to treat learned helplessness and agoraphobia. The behavioral perspective is highlighted throughout, but observational learning is not covered.

Mind Over Body. (1974) Time-Life, (49 minutes)

  This documentary looks at a wide spectrum of cases to show a whole new area of research that straddles psychology, physiology, and medicine. The links are demonstrated by the research explained in the film. In the future, many persons may be able to use self-therapy to alleviate psychosomatic illnesses.

Nine Days of Hell--Japan's Toughest School. (1993) Filmmakers Library, (18 minutes)

  During holiday time, Japan's most ambitious parents send their children to a very intensive school to prepare them for the tremendous pressures of the Japanese school system. Up before dawn, drilled before eating, constantly quizzed, prodded, and harassed to learn by rote, the children are on constant alert except for a few hours of sleep at night. Each student must pass an oral examination, grilled by a stern panel of academicians, who goad and mock them and exhort them to present their ideas more fiercely. While many Japanese approve of this privately run program, some question whether it stifles creativity and independent thought. This award-winning video is brief, but powerful.

Observational Learning. (1978) Harper & Row, (23 minutes)

  This film shows the famous Bo-Bo doll experiment, vicarious emotional conditioning, modeling therapy, and children imitating what they have seen on television.

Pavlov Himself. Films for the Humanities and Sciences, (25 minutes)

Presents an historical view of Pavlov and incorporates rare documentary footage of Pavlov at work in his laboratory. Produced by USSR Central Television with English narration.

Pavlov: The Conditioned Reflex. (1975) Films for the Humanities and Sciences, (25 minutes)

Portrays the Pavlovian conditioning of the salivary reflex in dogs.

The Power of Positive Reinforcement. (1978) McGraw-Hill Films, (27 minutes)

Documents the systematic on-site application of behavior management and its emphasis on positive reinforcement. Examines its use in the Valley Fair Amusement Park in Minnesota, on the defensive line of the Minnesota Vikings, and in the streets of Detroit, Michigan, with the Sanitation Department. Portrays behavior modification as a powerful tool for managing human performance.

Reward and Punishment. CRM, (30 minutes)

Dr. James Gardner narrates this film which focuses on operant techniques used in the management of children's behavior. The appropriate uses of reward and punishment are also discussed.

The Skinner Revolution. (1979) Research Press Films, (45 minutes)

This film presents interviews and conversations with B. F. Skinner, attempting to show him as an individual against the background of his contributions to science and philosophy.

Feature Films

1984 (**John Hurt, Richard Burton, Suzanna Hamilton**) Science Fiction
Winston Smith (Hurt) living in the totalitarian state of Oceania, breaks the law when he falls in love with the Ministry of Truth worker Julia (Hamilton). Winston and Julia attempt to escape but are hunted down by the Thought Police. Both have to be re-educated into loving the State and dictator Big Brother.

Specific Scene Analysis:
An Officer and a Gentleman (1982) (**Richard Gere, Louis Gossett, Jr., and Debra Winger**) Drama

- Central Concept: instrumental conditioning
- Approximate Scene Location: 57 minutes, 52 seconds into the 126-minute film
- Approximate Scene Length: 6 minutes
- Opening Line: Sgt. Foley: "Prepare for inspection."
- Closing Line: Sgt. Foley: "All right, Mayo, on your feet."

Key Concepts: negative reinforcement, punishment
Characters/Actors: Zack Mayo (Richard Gere), Sgt. Foley (Louis Gossett, Jr.), Perryman (Harold Sylvester), Sid Worley (David Keith)
Scene Description: Zack Mayo's mother committed suicide when he was approximately 7 or 8 years old. He was sent to live with his father, a sailor stationed in the Philippines. Zack meets his father for the first time when he arrives at the naval base. Zack's father confesses to not wanting to fulfill his role as a father. He states that he is out to sea three weeks out of the month and when he is home, he is not interested in being a daddy. Zack is left alone most of the time and has to take care of himself in a strange culture. He lives in his father's apartment in a low-rent district of the city, where he is exposed to harsh street life. When Zack is older, his father has been stationed in Seattle and he has finished a local college. After graduation, Zack enrolls in the Naval Academy to become a naval aviator. His class of officer candidates has Sgt. Foley as a drill sergeant. Sgt. Foley is tough and demanding. He uses every means

necessary to expose the candidates' weaknesses and determine whether they have the personal attributes and physical qualities to fly naval jets. If a candidate discloses any weaknesses or experiences failures during the 13 weeks of basic training, Sgt. Foley asks the candidate to submit his DOR, Dropped On Request. As part of the training, candidates have to keep their belt buckles and shoes shined so they can pass inspection. Mayo has a scam of getting local people to shine buckles and shoes for which he pays them a small fee. He then sells them to candidates who are not prepared for inspection. Earlier one of his roommates, Perryman, had objected to Mayo's for-profit scam. As the scene opens, Perryman is stressed and has to ask Mayo for a buckle so that he can pass inspection.

Questions/Discussion:
1.   Using operant conditioning as a conceptual framework, categorize the behavior of Sgt. Foley toward Mayo.

Sgt. Foley's behavior can be called negative reinforcement. He is trying to get Mayo to emit the response of DOR. He is trying to increase his comments on his treatment until he gets him to say DOR or other comments that will reflect his character.

2.   The concepts of negative reinforcement and punishment are often confused. What is the distinguishing characteristic between the two?

Negative reinforcement attempts to get the organism to increase its responses, whereas punishment attempts to get the organism to stop or decrease its responses.

3.   Why was punishment not the correct answer? Mayo had committed an act that violated training. Wasn't he being punished for that behavior?

If Sgt. Foley were trying to punish Mayo, he would have him perform some tasks or endure some action that was the result of his behavior. However, Sgt. Foley wants him to volunteer to leave the program by saying DOR or offer some comments about his inner self that enable Mayo to judge his character. If Mayo gave comments that indicated the depth of his character, then Sgt. Foley could make a decision as to whether he should stay. He was trying to increase his responding, not decrease.

Fly Away Home (**Jeff Daniels, Anna Paquin**) Family Adventure
Endearing tale of lost geese and a young girl, played by Anna Paquin, who helps them find a way home.
1.   What is the purpose of imprinting?
2.   Describe the steps that were taken for the ducks to imprint to the little girl.
3.   What are the dangers of having the birds imprint on the young girl?

Liar, Liar (**Jim Carrey**) Comedy
1.   Give an example of positive reinforcement used in the movie.
2.   Give an example of negative reinforcement used in the movie.
3.   Give an example of punishment for Jim Carrey that is depicted in the movie.

Mighty Joe Young (**Charlize Theron**) Comedy
1.   What reaction is Joe conditioned to emit when the flashlight is shined through the woods?
2.   Joe also is conditioned to another stimulus. What is this stimulus and what reaction results from it?
3.   If an animal such as Joe truly existed and you were assigned to train him, what would you condition him to do and how would you go about it?

*Conditioning and Learning

CNN® Today Video Vol. I: *Section 7: Learning*

> Virtual Rat (2:44)

CNN® Today Video Vol. II: *Section 6: Learning*

> Head Games (2:29)

A Demonstration of Behavioral Processes by B. F. Skinner. (1971) Prentice-Hall, (28 minutes)
> In this documentary, B. F. Skinner offers an introduction to operant conditioning. In a classroom setting, Skinner reviews the history of operant conditioning and explains the experimental apparatus. He demonstrates differential reinforcement and "shaping" techniques used on a pigeon while showing how pigeons shape their own behavior. Finally, Skinner applies principles of operant conditioning to human behavior.

Albert Bandura, Volumes 1 and II. (1988) Insight Video, (Vol. 1: 29 minutes, Vol. 2: 28 minutes)
Part of the *Notable Contributors* series. In part 1, Bandura reviews his influences in theoretical and research development and discusses cognitive and social behavior modification, social learning, modeling, and aggression. In part 2, he recalls his classic Bobo doll experiment and discusses the effects of aggression and violence in the media, morality and moral disengagement, self-efficacy, reactions to criticisms, and plans for the future.

Ape Language—From Conditioned Response to Symbol. (1986) Aims Media, Inc., (23 minutes)
> This video illustrates and documents research into the nature of language acquisition through the study of symbolic and syntactical skills in chimpanzees.

Behavior Theory in Practice: Parts I-IV. (1966) Prentice-Hall, (each part is 20 minutes)
> Basic and informative, these films present behavioral principles in considerable detail. Included in Part I is respondent versus operant behavior, selection of a response for basic research, the cumulative record, and operant conditioning and extinction. Part II covers schedules of reinforcement, shaping various operants, and programmed instruction. Part III features generalization, discrimination, motivation, reinforcement, punishment, avoidance, and intracranial reinforcement. Part IV describes sequences of behavior, homogeneous and heterogeneous chains, alternative responses, and multiple stimulus control.

B. F. Skinner on Behaviorism. (1977) Insight Media, (28 minutes)
> This video allows students to learn about the learning theory approach to behavior modification, human shaping and programmed instruction from the person synonymous with the operant conditioning perspective, B. F. Skinner.

Biofeedback: Listening to Your Head. (1979) Document Associates, (19 minutes)
> This film explains how biofeedback is used to control involuntary functions.

Classical and Operant Conditioning. (2000) Films for the Humanities & Sciences, (56 minutes)
> This program explains the nature of behaviorism, so central to the study of human behavior, and its important applications in clinical therapy, education, and child-rearing. It clearly explains, discusses, and illustrates the complex Classical and Operant conditioning theories of Pavlov and Skinner, and features archival footage of laboratory work with dogs and present-day research using rats in Skinner boxes as well as numerous examples of conditioning in everyday life.

Further Approaches to Learning. (1998) Films for the Humanities and Sciences, (57 minutes)

Explores alternative approaches and explanations of learning, including latent learning, learning sets, insight learning, ethology, social learning, and neuroscience. It emphasizes the recent move towards a cognitive theory of learning and examines the current research in this area. The program includes archival film featuring B.F. Skinner and Robert Epstein, who demonstrated apparent insight learning in pigeons using behaviorist techniques. Skinner, speaking just before his death, claims that reinforcement rather than higher mental processes is at work in learning.

Ivan Pavlov. (1981) Insight Media, (30 minutes)

Edward de Bono conducts an interview with "Pavlov". This simulated interview helps the viewer to understand the revolutionary nature of Pavlov's work and the impact he had on the study of behavior.

Learning. (1971) CRM/McGraw-Hill, (30 minutes)

This excellent film should be useful in any classroom when the topic of learning is being discussed. It creatively combines experiments, animation, discussion, and humor to illustrate concepts ranging from classical conditioning through behavior modification. It covers many topics in a brief amount of time and provides plenty of fuel for discussion and reaction. This film has won awards for its creative development. If you have time to show only one film, this one covers more topics in a brief amount of time than any other. (See the sample summary of this film in the introduction to this guide.)

Learning, Discovering Psychology Teaching Module 4. (1990) Annenberg/CPB, (various times)

The Discovering Psychology Teaching Modules contain excerpts from the *Discovering Psychology Series*. The three most important programs in this module involve: Historical footage of classical conditioning, historical footage of Little Albert, an interview with B.F. Skinner.

Observational Learning. (1978) Harper & Row, (23 minutes)

This film presents dramatic and convincing evidence of the strong impact of observational learning in children and adults. Excellent visual sequences and excellent narration make this film memorable. It shows footage of Bandura's well-known "Bobo doll" experiments, provides an excellent description of the Papago Indian project, gives examples of emotional conditioning, and summarizes the potential negative impact of television violence on children.

Pain of Shyness. (1984) ABC 20/20, (17 minutes)

This segment features Philip Zimbardo, author of *The Shy Child*, discussing just how disabling severe shyness can be. He also explains some of the techniques that have been used to overcome their shyness, including a demonstration of systematic desensitization.

Pavlov: The Conditioned Reflex. (1975) Films for the Humanities and Sciences, (23 minutes, B&W)

If you cover classical conditioning in detail, this film will assist by providing documentary footage from USSR Central Television and the Soviet Academy of Sciences of Ivan Pavlov at work in his Leningrad laboratory. The film also provides a review of the methodology exploring the conditioned reflex. This rare glimpse of the famous conditioning experiments with dogs allows students to see one of the pioneers of psychology at work. If you do not go into detail on classical conditioning, the film may still be more effective than any equal-length lecture on the subject.

The Question of Learning. (1974) WGBH, Boston, (50 minutes)

This program is an excellent resource to demonstrate concepts from classical conditioning through operant conditioning. It provides examples of animal learning in the wild, including grizzly bears feeding on salmon. The program also shows replications of experiments by Pavlov (dogs with saliva-collection tubes attached to the cheek), W. von Osten's "Clever Hans," the horse, Thorpe's experiments with the songs of finches, Thorndike's law of effect demonstrated with chicks, and John Watson's study of the nesting habits of terns on the Galapagos Islands. The program is part of the *Animal Behavior* series, narrated by George Paige.

Think Like an Animal: Cognition Studies. (1988) Films for the Humanities and Sciences, (51 minutes)
This intriguing program uses behavioral and communication research to open a window into the animal mind, as psychologists present their findings on innate animal intelligence gathered from the Ohio State University's Primate Cognition Project, the Smithsonian's Orangutan Language Project, and studies involving pigeons, parrots, and even octopuses. This research adds weight to the growing body of evidence that indicates animals do go beyond hardwired reflexes and responses to gather, organize, use, and retain information to solve problems.

* Learning Disabilities

Dyslexia: A Different Kind of Mind. (1997) Films for the Humanities and Sciences, (29 minutes) (Finalist, AMA International Health & Medical Film Competition) Dyslexia, a learning disability that affects oral and written language, often masks the presence of a gifted mind. People with dyslexia learn differently. This program from *The Doctor Is In* explores that cognitive difference by examining how dyslexic students learn, and how new teaching techniques are helping them succeed in school. These teaching approaches are explored at the Washington Lab School – a pioneer in the implementation of innovative teaching methods. Thomas West, author of *In the Mind's Eye*, discusses our society's need for the visual talents possessed by many people with dyslexia. A Dartmouth-Hitchcock Medical Center production.

Feature Films

I Am Sam **(Sean Penn, Michelle Pfeiffer)** Drama
Penn stars as a developmentally disabled adult who has been working in a coffee shop and raising his daughter Lucy for seven years. He receives help in parenting from a circle of disabled friends (including two real-life developmentally challenged actors). While he provides a loving and structured environment for Lucy, she begins to surpass him in mental ability. When Lucy begins to intentionally stunt her own mental growth so as not to hurt her father, a social worker removes her from her home and places her in a foster home. Penn seeks the help of a lawyer (Pfeiffer) to take his case to court. During the case, Pfeiffer's character comes to care for her client and his daughter, and considers the limitations of her own abilities as a parent.

7. **Human Memory**	Videos	Films
Forgetting & Memory Construction	10	
Memory Disorders & Aging	3	3
Memory Processes	12	4

* Forgetting and Memory Construction

Exploring Your Brain: Memory. (2000) Films for the Humanities & Sciences, (56 minutes)
Part of a three-part series, this program investigates issues related to data storage and retrieval, including discussions of Alzheimer's, the effect of aging on memory, and steps to improve memory.

Human Memory. (1978) Guidance Associates, (28 minutes)
Bower guides you through a presentation of the basics of memory theory. Includes a rumor-chain experiment.

Information Processing. (1971) CRM/McGraw-Hill, (28 minutes)
Actor David Steinberg introduces this film which utilizes isolated, stimulus-rich sequences from a complex social environment—a Hollywood cocktail party—to illustrate some of the aspects of human information processing. Donald Norman acts as "anchorman," observing behavior from a booth situated above the party. Norman and Steinberg explain what each scene reveals about the ways in which people receive information, store it in memory, and then retrieve it when necessary.

Life Without Memory: The Case of Clive Wearing, from *The Mind Series Teaching Modules*, 2nd Edition #10 Annenberg, (12:35) and ***Clive Wearing, Part 2: Living Without Memory.*** Annenberg, (32:35)
Describes the case of Clive Wearing, an English singer, conductor and composer who was also an expert on the 17th century composer Lassas. The first video depicts Clive's general amnesia, preventing him from recalling most of his past and from learning new experiences as well. Reviews how Clive's hippocampus was destroyed by a bout of viral encephalitis and the subsequent loss of episodic memory and a good deal of semantic memory. However, Clive's procedural memory remains intact, as revealed by his ability to continue to compose, conduct, and sing. Students will get a clear impression of the difference between explicit and implicit memory. Part 2 expands on how Clive deals with his memory loss from day to day.

Memory. (1980) CRM/McGraw-Hill, (30 minutes)
This fast-paced examination of information-processing theory includes a discussion of sensory, short-term, and long-term memory. The film concentrates mainly on the improvement of long-term memory through the use of mnemonic devices, and viewers are provided with several methods for improving their own memories. The film also discusses what interference is and how to overcome it through conscious effort and practice. The applied aspects of this film make it a practical adjunct to the discussion of memory in the classroom.

Memory. (1998) Films for the Humanities and Sciences, (56 minutes)
Memories provide a sense of personal continuity and, to a large extent, define one's identity. This program investigates issues related to the brain's fundamental processes of data storage and retrieval, such as why people remember some things and forget others; how Alzheimer's disease affects the brain

and what treatments are being developed to treat it; how aging affects memory; and what steps can be taken to preserve and improve retention. Panelists include experts from Harvard Medical School and the Howard Hughes Medical Institute, and the author of the book *Searching for Memory*.

Memory. (1990) Coast Community College District Telecourses, (30 minutes)
   Explains research in the nature and workings of memory; defines amnesia and Alzheimer's disease.

Memory: Fabric of the Mind. (1988) Films for the Humanities and Sciences, (28 minutes)
   This film visits several internationally known memory research labs in an attempt to answer questions concerning memory. Brain chemistry is examined and the location of memory is sought. Ways to improve memory are also discussed, along with various reasons why we forget. This is a very good video on modern research into human memory.

A Super-Memorist Advises on Study Strategies, from *The Brain Teaching Modules*, 2nd Edition #20, (1998) Annenberg/CPB, (9:57)
   This video shows Rajan Mahadevan's memory for numbers is impressive. He can recite from memory the first 100,000 digits of pi. This video demonstrates the awesome potential of the brain.

Understanding the Mysteries of Memory. (2000) Films for the Humanities & Sciences, (53 minutes)
   This program explores the extraordinary nature of memory through the stories of people who yearn to remember or long to forget. Includes information on implicit and explicit memory, savant syndrome, traumatic memory, and more.

*Memory Disorders and Aging

CNN® Today Video Vol. III: Section 4: Human Memory

   Alzheimer's Babies (1:36)

Living With Amnesia: The Hippocampus and Memory, from *The Brain Series Teaching Modules*, 2nd Edition #18, Annenberg, (8:00)
   Depicts the role of the hippocampus in creating new memories and how amnesia develops from injury to this vital organ in the brain.

Memory—The Past Imperfect. (1994) Filmmakers Library, (46 minutes)
   Part of the *Nature of Things* series. This new video explores long- and short-term memory, hypnosis as a method of recalling the past, the phenomenon of amnesia, the memories of very young children, and the variability of eyewitness testimony. Several experts share their findings on these topics. This video was produced by the Canadian Broadcasting Company.

Feature Films

I Am Sam **(Sean Penn, Michelle Pfeiffer)** Drama
   Penn stars as a developmentally disabled adult who has been working in a coffee shop and raising his daughter Lucy for seven years. He receives help in parenting from a circle of disabled friends (including two real-life developmentally challenged actors). While he provides a loving and structured environment for Lucy, she begins to surpass him in mental ability. When Lucy begins to intentionally stunt her own mental growth so as not to hurt her father, a social worker removes her from her home and

places her in a foster home. Penn seeks the help of a lawyer (Pfeiffer) to take his case to court. During the case, Pfeiffer's character comes to care for her client and his daughter, and considers the limitations of her own abilities as a parent.

Memento (**Guy Pearce, Carrie-Anne Moss**) Mystery
   Leonard (Pearce) is a man who struggles to put his life back together after the brutal rape and murder of his wife. Leonard was severely beaten by the same man who killed his wife, and the after-effects include a complete loss of short-term memory. He cannot retain any new information, so resorts to note-taking and Polaroid photos to keep track of each day's events. He retains long-term memory, including the murder of his wife. He becomes obsessed with finding and taking revenge on the man who ruined his life. This mystery brings many concepts of memory to the discussion table, including long term and short term memory, as well as memory devices to improve retention.

Sommersby (**Richard Gere, Jodie Foster**) Drama
   Gere plays Jack Sommersby, a wealthy landowner who returns to his small Tennessee town three years after the Civil War's end. The soldier is ready to resume his life with his wife Laurel (Foster), except that Laurel, thinking her husband was dead, has become engaged to another man. She cancels the engagement. We learn that the War experience has made a dramatic change in Sommerbsy. He is no longer the cruel, callous, feared pre-War Sommersby. He is now sensitive, charming, and very caring for his community and the people in it. Some think he is an imposter pretending to be Sommersby. He is arrested and charged with a murder he committed years before, and the courtroom uncovers even more information about the past. This drama can surface much conversation regarding memory, memory disorders (amnesia, fugue state, post-traumatic stress disorder, etc.), as well as other memory-related topics.

* **Memory Processes**

Learning and Memory. (1984) PBS Video, (55 minutes)
   An introduction to one of the more interesting of the brain's functions, this film highlights some of the brain research on the formation, storage, and retrieval of memory. It presents chemical and physical theories of memory creation and storage and discusses the specialized functions of several brain structures, such as the hippocampus and amygdala. This media presentation is well produced and will greatly enhance the text's discussion of memory.

Locus of Learning and Memory, from *The Brain Series Teaching Modules*, 2nd Edition #16, Annenberg, (6:49)
   This program explores the track of memory formation in the brain, and the role of various structures in creating memories.

Memory Fixing. (1985) The Program Source, (67 minutes)
   This film features an interview with Kenneth Cooper in which he explains the various levels of human memory. He discusses the type of information that is encoded and sorted in our memories and explains how people can "program" their subconscious memory to solve problems and inform their consciousness at a later time. The film is interactive and demonstrates several mnemonic devices for organizing thoughts: placing them in logical order, grouping them according to similarity, and linking them with language. This presentation of our ability to remember is an interesting blend of psychoanalytic and information-processing theory and should be a valuable adjunct to a lecture on memory.

Memory Skills. (1992) Insight Media, (30 minutes)
   This video provides basic instruction on how one can improve his or her memory. It examines how elaborative processing can enhance memory for a wide variety of materials.

Memory -- The Past Imperfect. (1994) Filmmakers Library, (46 minutes)

This video represents an excellent presentation of recent work on memory. It builds on the theme that memory is not a video recorder, but rather a fallible system. Included in the topics discussed are hypnosis and memory, eyewitness memory, children's memory and amnesia.

The Nature of Memory. (1991) Films for the Humanities and Sciences, (26 minutes)

This video examines the definition of memory in relation to its function. How does it work? Is it reality or a creation of our subconscious? And can it be manipulated by dreams or hypnosis? These are but a few of the questions answered by this film. Computer demonstrations provide insight into the processes of memory, and human amnesiac studies are discussed in relation to the encoding, storage, and retrieval of memories. The film also provides some information about how emotions affect memories and how they can be altered.

Persistence of Memory. (1980) PBS Video, (58 minutes)

This is one of the films in the *Cosmos* series, narrated by Carl Sagan. He discusses the evolution, function, and physiology of the human brain, especially as it pertains to the storage of information. Cognition is discussed in relation to genetics and the brain's memory function. The film concludes with a discussion of the development of external information storage as a logical extension of human memory.

Remembering and Forgetting: Discovering Psychology Series. (1990) Annenberg/CPB, (30 minutes)

Program 9 in the series. This film examines the complex processes involved in the creation of memory. Philip Zimbardo, the host, discusses how environmental stimuli are translated into neural codes that our brain can process, understand, and store. Several explanations of why we forget are mentioned, and the film concludes by demonstrating common retrieval aids that we can use to improve our memories. This half-hour film presents a clear overview of the process of memory with excellent graphics and commentary.

Sensation and Perception, Discovering Psychology Teaching Module 5. (1990) Annenberg/CPB, (various times)

The Discovering Psychology Teaching Modules contain excerpts from the *Discovering Psychology Series*. Module 5 in this series (memory) contains several interesting sections including: the anatomy of the brain, and a memory demonstration with Dr. Philip Zimbardo.

Studying the Effects of Subliminal Stimulation on the Mind, from *The Mind Teaching Modules*, 2nd Edition #9 (2000) Worth (4:46)

This video presents an example of how researchers study a construct like the unconscious with the state-of-the-art-technology. This video is a good example of the impact that Freud has had on psychology.

Thinking. (1988) PBS Video, (30 minutes)

This film, part of *The Mind* series, examines the background and history of memory research. It focuses largely on prefrontal and frontal lobe studies and identifies these areas as the place where memory and other cognitions occur. The segments on prefrontal lobotomies are interesting, as are the examinations of stroke victims' memories.

Understanding the Mysteries of Memory. (1998) Films for the Humanities and Sciences, (53 minutes)

This compelling program explores the extraordinary nature of memory through the stories of people who yearn to remember or long to forget. Case studies and interviews with experts, supported by computer graphics, throw light on the mechanics of implicit and explicit memory, savant syndrome, traumatic memory, flash-backs, "Flashbulb memories" such as the space shuttle Challenger explosion, mistaken identification, and memories twisted or even totally invented through suggestion. The effects of short-term memory damage, trauma-induced amnesia, and Alzheimer's disease are investigated as well.

Feature Films

Fire in the Sky (**D.B. Sweeney, Robert Patrick, Craig Sheffer, Peter Berg, James Garner, Henry Thomas**) Sci-Fi/Fantasy
A man claims to be have been kidnapped by aliens, but no one believes him.

Were there any memory disturbances for the abducted character? If so, give examples from the movie.
   1.	What are some reasons for repressed memories? Did any of the characters exhibit repressed memories?
   2.	Having a similar experience as the movie's main characters, how do you think your memory would be affected?

Overboard (**Goldie Hawn**)
   1.	Goldie Hawn's character displays total amnesia after falling overboard. What exactly is the cause of her amnesia and what are some other ways that someone may develop amnesia?
   2.	Hawn's character starts to remember parts of her life at first, and then she remembers everything about her life at one time. What triggers this to happen, and what could possibly explain the instantaneous recovery of her memory?
   3.	Do you believe that someone's personality could change, like Hawn's character, if during a period of amnesia, you were made to believe that you were someone you really weren't? Why or why not?

Specific Scene Analysis:
Total Recall (1990) (**Arnold Schwarzenegger**) Action drama

- Central Concept: memory
- Approximate Scene Location: 16 minutes, 23 seconds into the 113-minute film
- Approximate Scene Length: 4 minutes, 30 seconds
- Opening Line: "Doug, it's Bob McCane. Nice to meet you."
- Closing Line: "Ready for dreamland."

Key Concepts: sensory memory, working memory, long-term memory
Actors/Characters: Doug (Arnold Schwarzenegger), Bob McCane (Ray Baker), Dr. Lui (Rosemary Dunsmore), Lab Assistant (Erik Cord)
Scene Description: The action in this film takes place in a futuristic world. We are traveling in space and have colonized Mars and Saturn. Advanced technology is apparent in all the scenes. Doug wakes up from a dream about Mars in which he is in danger. He wakes up from his nightmare and is comforted by his wife, who tries to get him to forget about Mars. She tells him he did not like it when he was there. While traveling to work on the metro, Doug sees an advertisement by Recall Inc., a firm selling memories of pleasant vacations. In this technologically advanced world, dreams and memories of events can be purchased and implanted in your brain. Doug stops by Recall Inc. on his way home from work. Bob McCane, sales representative for Recall, greets him and tries to sell him a memory of a glorious vacation. He will store the memory in Doug's brain.

Questions/Discussion:

    1.   How do we store events in our memory?
There are three types of memory to be stored: sensory memory, working memory, and long-term memory. Each type operates differently as memory is processed for possible storage in long-term memory. Have the students discuss the distinguishing features of each type of memory.

    2.   Do you think it will be possible in the future to implant memories in people's brains?
The advancements in science that have increased our knowledge of how the brain functions suggest that it will be possible.

    3.   Ask the students whether they would like to have memories of vacations stored in their brains as suggested in the film clip. What are the advantages and disadvantages?

While You Were Sleeping **(Sandra Bullock, Bill Pullman)** Comedy
    1.   How did Sandra Bullock's character come to be engaged to her first fiancé?
    2.   How easily do you think people are influenced to believe false memories? Have you ever been influenced to have false memories?
    3.   How accurate is oral information? Remember to cite examples from the movie that support your view.

8. **Language and Thought**	Videos	Films
Language & Language Acquisition	25	2
Thinking & Problem Solving	16	1

CNN® Today Video Vol. II: *Section 6: Learning*

Head Games (2:29)

CNN® Today Video Vol. III: *Section 5: Language and Thought*

Babies and Birds (3:48)

* Language & Language Acquisition

Animal Language, from *The Mind Series Teaching Modules*, 2nd Edition #27, Annenberg
Discussion of nonhuman communication systems and research with chimpanzees, elephants, and giraffes in language acquisition is reviewed.

Behavior Modification: Teaching Language to Psychotic Children. (1969) Prentice Hall, (42 minutes)
This film, also recommended to supplement Chapter 6 (conditioning and learning), is a superior treatment of language acquisition, learning theory, behavior modification, and experimental psychology (although the narration is somewhat dry). It chronicles the work of O. Ivar Lovaas, who used stimulus-fading techniques to teach speech to psychotic children. Bizarre behaviors are shown, such as echolalia, self-destructiveness, and pervasive failure to acquire social and intellectual skills. The goal with these children is to develop speech for spontaneous conversation. If your audiovisual budget or class time is limited, this excellent film is a good choice because it covers many topics and vividly demonstrates applications of psychological theory. Note: A sequel to this film has been produced examining Lovaas's patients twenty years later.

The Bilingual Brain, from *The Mind Series Teaching Modules*, 2nd Edition #26 Annenberg, (7:29)
This short program reviews research into the functioning of the brains of bilingual people. It explores how they might operate or be organized somewhat differently than the brains of monolingual individuals.

Chimp Talk. (1998) Films for the Humanities and Sciences, (14 minutes)
Paul Hoffman, editor of *Discover* magazine, explores the controversial issue of language use by apes with primatologist Dr. Sue Savage-Rumbaugh. Dr. Sue Savage-Rumbaugh's 20-year study with chimpanzees reveals that they can use language with the astounding accuracy of a two-year-old human, which includes a rudimentary syntactical ability. However, Petitto's research indicates that humans have a cognitive predisposition for language lacking in chimps, which leads to the conclusion that although apes communicate by associating symbols with objects and actions, they do not have language abilities in the way that humans do. If the scientific community should eventually accept language use by apes, will the last scientific distinction between humans and animals be lost?

Dyslexia: Diagnosis and Therapy. (1995) Films for the Humanities and Sciences, (52 minutes)
This program features eight children and adults of different ages who have had their lives severely affected by dyslexia. The video stresses the importance of early recognition and alerts students to the signs of dyslexia and possibilities for therapy.

Exploring Language: Thinking, Writing, Communicating--Apes and Language. (1981) International University Consortium, (29 minutes)

  The series of language videos of which this program is part has two primary purposes: to explore the social, psychological, and political implications of language and to teach the fundamentals of clear, concise writing. This program studies the debate over whether apes are capable of using language. Filmed examples are used, as well as comments from some of the leading ape language researchers, including Herbert Terrace, Roger Fouts, and Duane Rumbaugh.

Exploring Language: Thinking, Writing, Communicating--Men, Women, and Language. (1981) International University Consortium, (29 minutes)

  This video builds on the purposes of the series, which are to help us understand language and learn skills useful in producing clear written communication. In this part of the series, social psychologist Jean Berko Gleason and neurologist Richard Restak discuss some of the differences in how men and women use language. They comment on the biological, sociological, and cultural origins of these sex differences.

Faces of Culture: Language and Communication. (1983) Coast Community College, (30 minutes)

  Program 6 in the series. This video discusses the structure of language and its relationship to thought. It examines the influence of culture on language, explores body language as a form of communication, and studies speech as a reflection of culture. Comments from linguists Keith and Claudia Kernan are included.

The First Signs of Washoe. (1974) Nova Series, (58 minutes)

  This classic film is widely known and used. It provides an interesting and amusing glimpse of field research by the Gardners with the chimp Washoe during a five-year language-acquisition study using American Sign Language. The film also chronicles the work of Rumbaugh and von Glasersfeld at the Yerkes Primate Institute with the chimp Lana, who communicates through a specially constructed language used with a computer. Fouts's research, which is also explored, attempts to teach groups of chimps to sign among themselves.

Human Language: Signed and Spoken, from *The Mind Teaching Modules*, 2nd Edition #25 (2000) Worth, (6:08)

  The module opens with a scene of a young deaf child communicating with her family through sign language. Next the viewer sees Dr. Ursula Bellugi, who studies the basic elements of signing in an effort to sift out the properties of language that are due to the mode in which language is transmitted— either by signing or speaking. This video also provides an opportunity to enrich the discussion of language by including other subjects such as hemispheric specialization, language acquisition, the nature of language formation, and methodology. This video may also be referred back to in the module on good emotion, specifically on the topic of differentiating between facial expression and body language.

The Ideas of Chomsky. (1995) Films for the Humanities and Sciences, (47 minutes)

  Linguist and political activist Noam Chomsky of the Massachusetts Institute of Technology transformed the nature of linguistics before he was 40. In this program with world-renowned author and professor Bryan Magee, the outspoken Chomsky challenges accepted notions of the way in which language is learned, examines the relationship of language to experience, and discusses the philosophical nature of knowledge. A BBC Production.

Infant Speech Sound Discrimination, from *The Mind Teaching Modules*, 2nd Edition #23 (2000) Worth, (4:03)

This video has to do with infant speech development. It demonstrates how young infants are able to discriminate between very subtle sound differences.

Language. (1990) Coast Community College District Telecourses, (30 minutes)

Part of the *Psychology - The Study of Human Behavior Series*, this video describes how language is the product of learning, environmental influences, and human genetic endowments.

Language. (1995) Insight Media, (23 minutes)

This video explores the relationship of language abilities and specific areas of the brain. This program examines, from an evolutionary perspective, both human and nonhuman animal language development.

Language. (1988) PBS Videos, (60 minutes)

Program 7 in *The Mind* series. This is an excellent video on the evolution of language and the phenomenon of speech. Many examples are illustrated during the hour. It identifies an innate drive in humans to communicate and the linguistic ability that exists even without speech and hearing. The program provides much information and fuel for discussion.

Language and Culture, from *The Mind Series Teaching Modules*, 2nd Edition #28, (1988), Annenberg, (4:42)

This short program relates to possible cultural differences in language and cognition in connection with the linguistic-relativity hypothesis of Benjamin Whorf. It looks at specific language differences as a product of culture rather than reflecting cognitive inferiority. The program's value lies in reaffirming the fact that most cultural differences are due to people in different environments adapting to those environments, not to racial or ethnic inherent inferiority.

Language Development. (1976) Harper & Row, (24 minutes)

Jerome Kagan and Howard Gardner present language acquisition across the child's first four years.

Language Development. (1990) Annenberg/CPB, (28 minutes)

This interesting video, hosted by Philip Zimbardo, describes language acquisition from the earliest coos and babbles. Concepts covered include nature/nurture interaction, cerebral maturation, and physiological development. Examples of several languages and cultures are presented, and similarities are demonstrated with an electronic voiceprint. In addition, the complexities of language in social communication are studied.

Language Development. (1973) CRM/McGraw-Hill, (20 minutes)

This research- and experiment-oriented film illuminates language acquisition in young children. It compares various theories of acquisition and demonstrates the cross-cultural nature of verbal development in infants. Featured research includes Premack's experiments in which chimps use plastic word symbols for identification and communication. Animation sequences demonstrate vocal processes during the first few months of life.

Language Predisposition, from *The Mind Teaching Modules*, 2nd Edition #24 (2000) Worth, (3:44)

This video deals with language, development, and research methodology. It is a good demonstration of our remarkable sound recognition abilities.

Out of the Mouths of Babes: The Acquisition of Language. (1984) Filmmakers Library, (28 minutes)
This award-winning film offers an excellent opportunity to see and hear the chronology of language acquisition during the first six years of life. We see the gradual progression that occurs from random babbling, to jargon and one-word sentences, to the use of complicated structures and linguistic concepts. This film provides a clear, informative description of linguistic development. Also interesting are the carefully structured games and tests that researchers have devised. This video was produced by the Canadian Broadcasting Company.

Signs of the Apes, Songs of the Whales. (1983) Nova Series, (57 minutes)
If your students are already familiar with *The First Signs of Washoe*, here is the sequel: Washoe revisited almost ten years later. In this excellent program, language experiments with chimps, gorillas, dolphins, and sea lions are demonstrated. In addition, the complex signals that whales use to communicate among themselves are explored. This film is excellent fuel for class discussions.

Talk to the Animals. (1987) CBS – *60 Minutes* video, (14 minute segment)
This brief journalistic-type video is significant in two ways: First, it illustrates research in communication with chimpanzees through both sign language and an original syntax designed to be used with a computer. Second, it illustrates the potential of teaching language skills to retarded children. Overall, it is a rather good cross-section of current theory, research, and application in the field, especially if you face time constraints.

You Must Have Been a Bilingual Baby. (1992) Filmmakers Library, (46 minutes)
This new and interesting video explores how babies become bilingual, how school children fare in language immersion classes, and how adults cope with learning foreign languages. It shows a bilingual class in Virginia where Spanish- and English-speaking children learn together while developing a sense of pride in their respective cultures. This video also shows a program where adults have the satisfaction of attaining fluency in a second language.

Unlocking Language. (1998) Films for the Humanities and Sciences, (29 minutes)
Approximately 70,000 years ago, humankind began talking, and hasn't stopped since. In this fascinating program, a diverse group of experts – an evolutionary linguist, a neurologist, a geneticist, a neuropsychologist, a developmental cognitive neuroscientist, and an oxford professor of communication—discuss the birth, development, and transmission of the mysterious phenomenon called language. Topics explored include the ability of language to express abstractions; the role of evolution in the development of languages; language as an innately guided behavior in unborn babies, infants, and toddlers; the parts of the brain involved in language; the relationship between genes and language disorders; and the isolation of the Speech 1 gene.

Feature Films

Dr. Dolittle (**Eddie Murphy, Ossie Davis**) Comedy
In a minor car accident, Dr. John Dolittle (Murphy) hits his head and triggers a gift for holding conversations with animals. While others show concern, Dolittle happily takes on animal clients: birds, rats, rabbits, and other creatures who teach him many things about being human. Technically an excellent weaving of real animals, Henson animatronics, and computer graphics. A whimsical comedy, it nevertheless allows for discussions about the other scientists, namely those who have studied ape and whale languages, as well as those who have taught sign language to primates.

Nell (**Jodi Foster, Liam Neesom**) Drama

Jodie Foster plays a backwoods innocent who barely speaks English yet still teaches valuable lessons to snooty scientists.

1. What rule of language did Nell use when she was first found?
2. What was the first morpheme that was used?
3. Was Nell's language barrier due to innate or environmental factors?

*Thinking and Problem Solving

Brain Traps: Problem-Solving Skills. (1997) Insight Media, (15 minutes)

This short video uses a series of interesting problems to illustrate how normal patterns of thinking can lead us into "brain traps". This video is intended to help students become better problem solvers.

Cognitive Processes, Discovering Psychology Series. Annenberg/CPB Project, (30 minutes)

Psychologist Donald Broadbent viewed the mind as a computer, and today's cognitive psychologists use this type of information-processing model to describe the thought process. Discussion of mental groupings called concepts. Complex concepts, or schemas, are ways of looking at the world that organize our past experiences and provide a framework for understanding our future experiences. This program also explores the physiological basis for thinking, showing how psychologist Michael Posner studies the electrical and chemical changes that occur in the brain as a person solves problems.

Creative Problem Solving: How to Get Better Ideas. (1979) CRM/McGraw-Hill, (28 minutes)

The bottom line of this film is expressed in Professor James Adams's words: "The best way to have a good idea is to have a lot of ideas." It encourages us by showing that creative problem solving can be taught and developed in each person, although it is frequently inhibited by criticism or a lack of self-confidence. Some animated scenes develop Freud's ideas on creativity, followed by the split-brain theory of creativity. George Prince explores applications of the theory through a group problem-solving session with professionals solving real business problems.

The Creative Spirit. (1991) Ambrose Video, (59 minutes)

Each of these four programs blends animation, humor, original music, and on-location action to capture the emerging spirit of innovation and creativity. Through observations of creative people and places, we discover that creative solutions to problems begin with basic human qualities: passion, persistence, vision, caring, and trust in oneself and others.

Decision-Making and Problem Solving. (1990) Coast Community College District Telecourses, (30 minutes)

Part of the *Psychology - The Study of Human Behavior Series*, this video explains rational and irrational influence on human thought.

Faces of Culture: Language and Communication. (1993) Coast Community College, (30 minutes)

One of the few videos to explore the relationship between thought and language, this excellent video's main focus is on the cultural influence on language and how speech reflects one's culture.

Human Consciousness and Computers. (2000) Films for the Humanities & Sciences, (28 minutes)

     In this program two major experts, Roger Penrose of Oxford University and Stuart Hammeroff of Arizona University, discuss the nature of human consciousness and whether computers can ever be taught to think. Excellent animation illustrates many of the concepts presented.

Judgment and Decision Making, Discovering Psychology Series. Annenberg/CPB Project, (30 minutes)

     In general, the program seeks to explain the error and irrationality occurring in much of the human decision-making process. Amos Tversky and Daniel Kahneman are interviewed and discuss their research into decision-making heuristics such as availability, representativeness, framing, and anchoring and adjustment. The value of this video is in the different examples and hearing the explanations from the researchers themselves.

Koestler on Creativity. (1972) BBC Video, (40 minutes)

     Based on Arthur Koestler's book *The Act of Creation*, this film explores creativity and investigates the conscious and unconscious processes used by both scientists and artists. Various experiments are demonstrated, with comments by Koestler, and scenes illustrate how random associations of existing theories or ideas have led to major discoveries. This film is a Blue Ribbon winner of the American Film Festival.

Language and Thinking. (1992) Insight Media, (30 minutes)

     This video explores the issue of phonetic and grammatical acquisition during childhood. In addition, it offers a brief discussion of the relationship between language and cognition.

Maturity and Creativity. (1982) Karol Media, (30 minutes)

     In this film Rollo May discusses his views on maturity and his own work on the process of creativity. In this interview, he also evaluates his contributions to psychology, reacts to his critics, and discusses his future plans.

The Mind Machines. (1979) Time/Life, (57 minutes)

     This film discusses artificial intelligence, including chess-playing machines, computerized medical diagnosis, and computer-controlled robots that can "see" and "learn."

Problem Solving. (1981) Department of Psychology, University of Illinois, (29 minutes)

     This video provides nice examples of some classic problem solving tasks described in the text (e.g., "water jug" problem, "old monk" problem). In addition, there is a discussion of the difference between heuristic and algorithmic methods of problem solving.

Problem-Solving Strategies: The Synectics Approach. (1980) CRM/ McGraw-Hill, (27 minutes)

     This film depicts an actual Problem-Solving Laboratory conducted at Synectics, a unique consulting firm in Cambridge, MA, which specializes in teaching the process of creative problem solving. Viewers are given a simple set of innovative strategies that can be used to stimulate organizational creativity and streamline problem solving.

Thinking. (1988) PBS Videos, (60 minutes)

     Program 8 in *The Mind* series. This video combines the topics of brain physiology and thinking and is a good review of both. The initial focus is on the frontal lobes and the prefrontal cortex, where memory, emotion, and intelligence come together to produce conscious activity. The program explores current research attempts to pinpoint where thoughts originate and how they are stored.

The Unbiased Mind: Obstacles to Clear Thinking (1994) Insight Media, (23 minutes)
> This video demonstrates how we are sometimes victims of flawed thinking. It has a particularly good section on the confirmational bias.

Feature Films

The Cell (**Jennifer Lopez, Vince Vaughn**) Science Fiction, Thriller
> A child psychiatrist (Lopez) has developed a technique that allows her to travel through the minds of her patients. She is asked by an FBI agent (Vaughn) to enter into the mind of a brutal serial killer who has lapsed into a coma, in an attempt to find a girl whom he has kidnapped. Once she enters his mind, she finds getting out to be very difficult. This film has graphic violence and adult situations, and has earned its "R" rating, but it explores questions that scientists have speculated about for years. Will it be some day possible to enter into another person's mind? How are thoughts formed and understood, and communicated?

9. **Intelligence and Psychological Testing**	Videos	Films
Intelligence Testing	17	4
Personality Testing	1	

CNN® Today Video Vol. III: *Section 6: Intelligence and Psychological Testing*

Emotional Intelligence (7:01)

* Intelligence Testing

Aspects of Individual Mental Testing. (1960) Pennsylvania State University Audio Visual Service, (33 minutes)

This black and white film presents a review of the items contained on the 1937 version of the Stanford-Binet Intelligence Test. While some material is dated, the film offers an up-close and personal view of the construction and administration of a classic measure of intelligence.

Better Babies--Raising Intellectual "Superstars." (1991) Filmmakers Library, (28 minutes)

Does prenatal and early childhood learning produce geniuses? This video documents several early-learning programs. We see parents talking to their unborn children in the belief that they will accelerate verbal skills, and other parents in courses on how to raise geniuses. We are shown the hectic schedule of a toddler whose mother teaches him art, music, computers, geography, and Japanese. One couple displays pride in having raised four genius daughters, yet the eldest daughter does not plan to repeat her parents' experiments on her own children. This could be a good discussion-starter for your class.

The Elementary Mind. (1992) Pennsylvania State University / PCR, (28 minutes)

(Part 17 of the *Time to Grow* series). This video examines the fundamental changes that occur in intellectual abilities during middle childhood and how cognitive abilities increase during this period, becoming effective tools for further learning and development. Researchers offer views on intelligence and the problems with IQ tests. Color.

The Exceptional Child. Time-Life, (51 minutes)

Research on non-average intelligence and its causes are examined. Both the gifted and slow learners are discussed.

Intelligence. (1990) Insight Media (30 minutes)

This video offers an excellent description of variations in intelligence (from retardation to giftedness). One of the main focuses of this video is the concern over the effectiveness of IQ tests as measures of aptitude (versus achievement).

Intelligence: A Complex Concept. (1978) CRM/McGraw-Hill, (28 minutes)

Beyond the notion that intelligence helps a person score well on tests, there are hundreds of different ideas about the nature of intelligence. When people on the street were asked, their filmed answers revealed much confusion between what intelligence tests measure and intelligence in daily life. The film explores some of the varied definitions of intelligence including those of Piaget and Guilford.

Intelligence and Culture, from *The Brain Series Teaching Modules*, 2nd Edition #4, Annenberg (4:02)

This video tries to explain how culture can influence traditional measures of intelligence. For many cultures, the cognitive skills necessary for scoring highly on the standardized test are not emphasized because they are not adaptive in the particular culture. Students are given examples of cultures in which this is true and should develop a new perspective of the intelligence of people of color.

Intelligence, Creativity, and Thinking Styles. (2000), Films for the Humanities & Sciences, (29 minutes)
This film explores multiple intelligences, traditional IQ scores, the role of the teacher and the family in shaping student intelligence, and presents Sternberg's triarchic theory of intelligence.

Intelligence: A New Definition for the Information Age. (1997) Films for the Humanities and Sciences, (77 minutes)
Success in the Internet era seems to rely more and more on that intangible quality called intelligence. This thought–provoking program critically examines intelligence and technology in today's world, skewering outdated assumptions and arguing for an all-encompassing perspective that incorporates the full range of human capabilities. Encounters that run the gamut from school children to computer hackers and from behaviorists to brain specialists offer a new perspective on humanity's most mysterious capacity and how it is defined.

Intelligence Tests on Trial—Larry P. and P.A.S.E. (1982) San Diego State College, (46 minutes)
This video focuses on the major issues involved in two federal court cases dealing with the cultural bias of individually administered intelligence tests and the use of the tests in placement of black children in EMR/EMH classes.

IQ Myth. (1975) Carousel Films, (51 minutes)
This is an extremely good CBS documentary, narrated by Dan Rather, on the many ways in which IQ scores are misunderstood and misused. Topics include the origin of IQ testing in America, ways in which tests are standardized and administered, and interviews with leading psychologists, like Wechsler and Kamin who take different positions on the utility of IQ testing.

May's Miracle. (1983) Filmmakers Library, (28 minutes)
This is a fascinating presentation of the abilities of a musical idiot savant. The film consists of an interview with his parents who describe the evolution of his remarkable ability, and he is shown through photographs as he slowly developed his talent.

Mental Retardation: The Long Childhood of Timmy. Contemporary/McGraw-Hill, (53 minutes)
This is a compassionate portrayal of a child with Downs Syndrome and his move from the family to a school for the retarded.

No Two Alike. (1963) Indiana University, (30 minutes)
The film explores measurement of abilities and the meaning of intelligence. It also shows methods of developing creative thinking in the classroom.

Secrets of the SAT. (1999) PBS Video, (60 minutes)
This Frontline program, aired on October 4, 1999, examines the many controversies that surround the SAT's merits. Noting the test's critical role in the college admissions process, the video shows how test preparation has become a multimillion-dollar business with students investing hundreds of hours in an effort to obtain higher scores. The history of the SAT's development, the debate over its predictive validity, and its impact on colleges' racial diversity are all explored. Both supporters and critics of the SAT are interviewed.

Testing and Intelligence: Discovering Psychology Series. (1990) Annenberg/CPB, (30 minutes)
　　　In this video from the *Discovering Psychology* series, Dr. Philip Zimbardo explores the nature of psychological assessment and intelligence. This superior production offers an excellent review of the history of intelligence testing (from Galton to modern times) and the methods used to construct an intelligence test. In addition, the use of a single score as a measure of the complex topic of human intelligence is questioned. The program examines the debate over whether intelligence is a general ability or several specific abilities. Howard Gardner's theory of multiple intelligences receives special attention. The program concludes with a look at research efforts linking intelligence with information-processing speed.

Why Man Creates. Pyramid Film and Video, (25 minutes)
　　　This film is always well received by students and provides a cross-disciplinary introduction to the topic of creativity. This video examines our creative nature through eight episodes, all humorous, some surrealistic. The segments present human accomplishments through the ages, portray the dedication of scientists to solving problems and examines the public's view of artists. Why do people create? The film's implied answer is that people feel they must leave a mark that proclaims their existence and their unique identities.

Feature Films

***Finding Forrester* (Sean Connery, Rob Brown, F. Murray Abraham)** Drama
An aging reclusive novelist (Connery) who hasn't written anything since winning a Pulitzer Prize decades earlier, is apprehensive in mentoring a 16-year-old with a desire to write. Each begins to encourage the other's writing, and they become unlikely friends despite their ages and backgrounds. A study in intellect and the intellectual relationship between two writers of very different generations.

Specific Scene Analysis:
Forrest Gump **(1994) (Tom Hanks and Robin Wright)**

- Central Concept: individual differences
- Approximate Scene Location: 100 minutes into the 145-minute film
- Approximate Scene Length: 4 minutes
- Opening Line: Jenny: "Hi Forrest."
- Closing Scene: Forrest and Forrest, Jr., watching television.

Key Concepts: heritability, individual differences
Characters/Actors: Forrest Gump (Tom Hanks), Jenny (Robin Wright), Forrest, Jr. (Haley Joel Osment)
Scene Description: Forrest Gump tells the story of his life to strangers as he is sitting on a park bench at a bus stop. He was born in Alabama and was a person of limited intelligence with an IQ of 75. His mother was very accepting of Forrest and she told him not to let anyone tell him he was different. The film presents his life story intertwined with historical events during the sixties, seventies, and early eighties, e.g., President Kennedy's assassination, the peace movement, the space age, etc. It details his relationships with Jenny, his childhood friend, who is in and out of his life. It tells of his experiences in Vietnam with Bubba, his best friend, and Lieutenant Dan. As the scene opens, he is still at the bus stop waiting for the bus to take him to Jenny's after receiving an invitation from her. Forrest is told that Jenny's street is five blocks away, and he runs to her apartment, where she opens the door.

Questions/Discussion:

     1.   Why is Forrest Gump's question about the child's abilities important?

Forrest Gump wants to know whether his son is smart or like him. The question of whether or not someone inherits intellectual abilities is one that has been extensively researched.

     2.   What term do social scientists use to describe an answer to Forrest's question: How is it measured?

Heritability refers to the percentage of the variance in any trait that is accounted for by genetic differences among individuals in a population. The best way to measure heritability of a trait is with a twin study research design.

     3.   What are the political and social policy controversies that reflect a misunderstanding of heritability of a trait?

Have the students discuss the following issues and the fallacies in the arguments: (1) African Americans and Hispanic Americans are genetically inferior because of their low scores on intelligence tests in comparison with Caucasian Americans; and (2) the government should not waste taxpayers' dollars paying for Head Start programs.

Specific Scene Analysis:
Good Will Hunting **(1997) (Matt Damon and Ben Affleck)** Drama

- Central Concept: intelligence
- Approximate Scene Location: 22 minutes into the 126-minute film
- Approximate Scene Length: 1 minute, 30 seconds
- Opening Scene: Will writing on the blackboard in the main hall.
- Closing Line: Thomas: "Looks right."

Key Concepts: Gardner's theory of multiple intelligences, intelligence, logical-mathematical intelligence
Characters/Actors: Will (Matt Damon), MIT Professor (Chas Lawther), Student Assistant to the Professor (Richard Fitzpatrick)
Scene Description: The location for the film is Massachusetts Institute of Technology (MIT), a prestigious university in the United States. The noted professor of mathematics challenges his class in advanced studies. He places a difficult problem on the blackboard in the main hall and challenges the students to solve it before the end of the semester. The student who solves the problem will get special recognition. The problem was solved overnight, yet no student has claimed the prize. The professor is puzzled. The professor places another problem on the blackboard in the main hall. The next evening, the professor sees someone writing on the blackboard, trying to solve the problem. The person is a janitor named Will who secretly solved the first problem.

Questions/Discussion:

     1.   Is it possible that a janitor at the school would have the ability to solve the mathematical problems?

Yes. A person's job does not necessarily indicate the level of intelligence the person possesses. Have students discuss instances they know of a person appearing to be more intelligent than the level of their job suggests.

2.   Is there a consensus among social scientists as to what characterizes intelligence?
The definition has evolved over the years from Binet's early attempts to identify students who did not do well in school so as to provide special instruction. Currently, intelligence is not viewed as a single ability that is measured on a limited range of behaviors so as to rank persons on a dimension. A contemporary approach is to investigate the cognitive processes involved when attempting various types of demanding activities. The conceptual framework for this view is the information processing approach.

3.   What theory of intelligence best explains Will's abilities?
Gardner's theory of multiple intelligences best explains Will's abilities. According to the theory, there are seven well-defined types of intelligence that are independent of one another. These various types of intelligence are located in specific sections of the brain. The type of intelligence exhibited by Will is classified as logical mathematical, or the ability to engage in abstract thought.

The Last Castle (**Robert Redford, James Gandolfini, Mark Ruffalo**) Drama
General Irwin (Redford) is court martialed and sent to The Castle, a maximum security military prison. Irwin does not get along with Warden Colonel Winter (Gandolfini) and rallies a group of convicts together to lead them on a revolt against Winter. Winter retaliates with a violent confrontation. A film that challenges the intellectual resources of the characters in the midst of this struggle, leaving them with few material resources.

Rain Main (**Dustin Hoffman, Tom Cruise**) Drama
    1.   Do you believe Raymond was intelligent and if so, what type of intelligence?
    2.   In what areas did you see savant tendencies?
    3.   What is the normal intellectual level of those individuals diagnosed with autism?

* Personality Testing

Personality. (1971) CRM/McGraw-Hill, (29 minutes)
      This film focuses on the psychological assessment and personality description of a college student. It examines various assessments of personality from self-description to formal appraisal, and it shows the administration of many common inventories, including the Minnesota Multiphasic Personality Inventory, the Wechsler Adult Intelligence Scale, the Thematic Apperception Test, the Holtzman Inkblot Test, and the Forer Sentence Completion Test. This film provides an excellent overview of several objective and projective tests in the assessment of personality.

10. Motivation and Emotion	Videos	Films
Achievement Motivation	13	7
Motivation & Emotion in the Workplace	9	9
Sexual Motivation	4	1
Theories of Emotion	12	1

* Achievement Motivation

Attitude: Your Most Priceless Possession. (1992) University Film & Video, (25 minutes)

This video documents the power of a positive attitude in the workplace. Interviews are included with a variety of employees and employers who emphasize the importance of staying positive and the influence that attitude has on hiring and promotion decisions. Although the video is somewhat basic, it provides multiple perspectives.

Dying to be Thin. (1995) Films for the Humanities and Sciences, (28 minutes)

This video profiles a young woman obsessed with the desire to be thin. It has taken her four hospitalizations and years of outpatient therapy to overcome her problem. Additionally, the characteristics of anorexia and bulimia are explored.

The Impossible Takes a Little Longer. (1987) Indiana University, (48 minutes)

This remarkable and memorable film should be viewed if time permits. It profiles four highly accomplished, seriously disabled women: one is paraplegic, one is quadriplegic, one is blind, and one is deaf. Although their disabilities vary, their determination to succeed in spite of many obstacles is a unifying theme. The demands on their personal and professional lives are high, but each woman demonstrates self-acceptance and a strong sense of self-worth. Each has developed ways to cope with an insensitive public and to solve new problems creatively. In addition to profiling these four women, the film demonstrates some of the devices used to assist impaired people with mobility and communication.

Konrad Lorenz's Discussion with Richard Evans: Motivation. (1975) Association Sterling films, (30 minutes)

Lorenz discusses his notions of the role of social approval, Harlow's rhesus deprivation research, and instinctual versus learned behavior. The film presents Lorenz's controversial theory that social motives are hereditary rather than learned. Lorenz's accent is occasionally difficult to understand.

Motivation and Self-Actualization. (1969) Psychological Films, (60 minutes)

This film discusses Maslow's hierarchy of needs and variables related to the attainment of self-actualization.

Motivation: It's Not Just the Money. (1981) Document Associates, (26 minutes)

Through interviews with employees, managers, and behavioral scientists, the factors which contribute to satisfaction and productivity on the job are examined. As the film shows, it is becoming increasingly evident that while wages and benefits are important, a range of non-material needs must also be met by modern organizations. The film features a look at the Volvo plant in Sweden, where an innovative approach to manufacturing was established that better met the needs of employees.

Need to Achieve. (1963) Indiana University, (30 minutes)

Documents the research of David McClelland on various aspects of achievement motivation. It shows that people with a high need for achievement are moderate risk-takers.

A New Look at Motivation. (1980) CRM/McGraw-Hill, (32 minutes)

Studies have shown that even when a job itself provides neither intrinsic nor extrinsic rewards, the social environment within an organization may provide an incentive to work. This film examines these needs as they are defined by David McClelland and illustrates the categories and personality types which are usually associated with each.

Pleasure Power. (1998) Films for the Humanities and Sciences, (53 minutes)

The scientific quest to fully understand and harness the mysterious power of pleasure has revealed some exciting possibilities. Enhanced by computer imaging and 3-D animations, this program interviews Mihaly Czikszentmihalyi – author of the best-selling *Flow: The Psychology of Optimal Experience*– and a battery of psychologists, physiologists, and neuroscientists. Together with several recovering addicts, they explore the intriguing nature and effects of pleasure, including biological underpinnings, its role in boosting physical and mental well-being, and if taken too far, it's ability to destroy a person's life.

The Psychology of Eating. (1978) Harcourt, Brace, Jovanovich, (29 minutes)

What motivates animals and humans to seek food? Why do we choose some foods and avoid others? Why do some people eat more than they need and become obese? These questions provide the framework for the consideration of the psychology of eating in this film. Illustrated research includes taste preferences in newborns, conditioned aversions, physiological responses to novel foods, and the capacity of animals to control their body weight by regulating the amount they eat.

Scare Me. (1990) Films for the Humanities and Sciences, (53 minutes)

Under certain conditions, fear can actually trigger a feeling of euphoria, promote group bonding, and stimulate personal growth. In this program, psychologists and other medical professionals – along with a video game designer and a movie director – explore the subject of fear in exacting detail, discussing topics such as the physiological mechanics behind it; factors that enhance and suppress it; the use of extreme sports, horror movies, computer technology, and thrill rides to deliberately induce it; and proven ways to master it. Color.

The Self-Motivated Achiever. (1967) University of Illinois, (25 minutes)

In addition to covering some of the research on achievement motivation, this film shows how to enhance self-motivation.

The Will to Win. (1993) Films for the Humanities and Sciences, (28 minutes)

This video covers the individual's determination to succeed—in early childhood, on the playing field, in business, and in the way the body responds to illness.

Feature Films

Alive **(Ethan Hawke, Vincent Spano, Josh Hamilton, John Haymes Newton, David Kriegel, Bruce Ramsay)** Drama

The true-life adventure of a Uruguayan team of rugby players who survive a plane crash in the desolate Andes Mountains in 1972. For 10 weeks they struggled against impossible odds and freezing temperatures to stay alive.

1. Using Maslow's Hierarchy of Needs, give an example of each level of need that was illustrated in the video.
2. What do you think motivated the survivors to continue to live?
3. How do you think you would react in this situation? Explain your answer.

Billy Elliott (**Julie Walters, Jamie Bell, Jamie Driven, Gary Lewis**) Drama

The young son of a poor English coal miner dreams of being a ballet dancer. The film takes place during a 1984 miners' strike in Durham county where Tony (Driven) and his dad (Lewis) are protestors. Billy (Bell), who's father talks him into taking boxing lessons, meets Mrs. Wilkinson (Walters), a ballet teacher, while working out at the gym. Billy has natural talent and is encouraged by Mrs. Wilkinson to try out for the Royal Ballet School. Billy's father does not approve but slowly comes around to the idea of Billy going into ballet as a way to escape the dangerous life of a miner. An excellent study in motivation, achievement, and relationships.

Good Will Hunting. (**Matt Damon, Robin Williams, Ben Affleck**) Drama

A rebellious 20-year-old MIT janitor Will Hunting (Damon), gifted with a photographic memory, anonymously leaves the correct solution to a problem that professor Lambeau has on the hallway blackboard for his students. Lambeau tracks down Hunting who is having problems with the police and offers an out for him. Hunting must visit a therapist and attend weekly math sessions. Sean McGuire (Williams), the therapist, helps the uncooperative Hunting deal with his past and his future. Can be used as an illustration both in motivation, and psychotherapy.

Mr. Holland's Opus (**Richard Dreyfuss**)

1. What motivated Glenn Holland to accept a teaching position?
2. In time his motivation for teaching changes. What now motivates Mr. Holland to teach? What motivates you to continue to strive for a college degree?

Specific Scene Analysis:
Mr. Holland's Opus (**1995**) (**Richard Dreyfuss**) Drama

- Central Concept: motivation
- Approximate Scene Location: 38 minutes, 2 seconds into the 143-minute film
- Approximate Scene Length: 5 minutes
- Opening Lines: Ms. Lang: "Mr. Holland." Mr. Holland: "You're late and you left your clarinet here."
- Closing Scene: Ms. Lang playing a clarinet solo at the graduation ceremony.

Key Concepts: motivation, emotions, drive theories, incentive theories
Characters/Actors: Mr. Holland/music teacher (Richard Dreyfuss), Ms. Lang/music student (Alicia Witt)
Scene Description: Mr. Holland is a musician with a strong desire to compose a symphony. For economic reasons, however, he has taken a position as a music teacher at Kennedy High School. Mr. Holland pursued a teaching certificate as a fallback occupation rather than from a desire to be a teacher. The students at the high school vary in their interest and desire to learn music appreciation or play an instrument. As the years pass, Mr. Holland's abilities as a teacher develop and the students respond to his love of music of all types, e.g., jazz, classical, rock, etc. He organizes an orchestra and marching band and sometimes gives special tutoring sessions. Ms. Lang is a student who wants to be good at something.

She comes from a very talented family; her brother is going to Notre Dame on a football scholarship, her sister has a ballet scholarship to go to New York, her mother has often won blue ribbons for her watercolors, and her father has a beautiful singing voice. She is trying to learn to play the clarinet so that she can be successful like the other members of her family. She is not a very good clarinet player as the film clip opens. As the scene opens, she is coming to her tutoring session.

Questions/Discussion:
1.   How is motivation defined?
Motivation is a condition that energizes behavior and gives it direction, especially toward pleasant experiences and away from unpleasant experiences.

2.   How does Mr. Holland motivate Ms. Lang to play the clarinet?
Mr. Holland emphasizes the feelings and emotions that go with playing a musical instrument. Playing music is more than being motivated to learn the notes and mechanics of playing. What is also important is to have deep emotional feelings about performing the sounds of music. He asks Ms. Lang what she likes about herself and why. When "a sunset" is part of her response, he tells her to visualize a sunset as she plays.

3.   What are the two major theoretical positions for explaining motivation?
Drive theories postulate a biological explanation for the origins of primary motives that give direction to behavior. The drive is toward satisfying basic physiological needs, e.g., hunger. Other motives, secondary motives, are learned as a result of their proximity to the experiences of satisfying primary motives, e.g., the presence of mother while the baby is feeding leads to the presence of mother when not feeding being pleasurable in and of itself. The other major theoretical position is incentive theory, which stresses and objects of motivational behavior. The emphasis is on the external environment and its role in motivating the individual.

Oh Brother, Where Art Thou? **(George Clooney, John Turturro, Tim Blake)** Comedy
Ulysses McGi (Clooney), Delmar, (Nelson) and Pete (Turturro) are serving time on a prison gang in the South during the depression. Everette knows where $1.2 million is hidden and the three manage to escape to seek their fortune. However, a stranger says that they may find their fortune but not the sort they are looking for. As they take to the road they meet a variety of people and even make a hit record.

Raising Arizona **(Nicolas Cage, Holly Hunter, Trey Wilson)** Comedy
H.I. McDonnough (Cage) is a career criminal who has been arrested so many times that he gets to know the officer who takes his mug shots, Ed (Hunter). Hi and Ed marry after Hi promises to give up his career as a criminal. They move to Arizona and are blissfully happy until they discover that Ed can not have children. The couple decides to kidnap a baby from a couple who just had quintuplets, figuring that they'll have a baby and the other couple will have less of a burden with one less child.

Rudy **(Sean Astin)** Drama
A no-talent kid does the impossible and makes the Notre Dame football team--sort of.

* Motivation and Emotion in the Workplace

Communication: The Nonverbal Agenda. (1988) CRM, (30 minutes)
This film does a nice job in identifying the ways in which nonverbal body language (e.g., facial expression, body movement) can influence communication. Albert Mehraian's work on the relationship between attitudes and nonverbal cues are featured in this color production.

75

Judgment and Decision Making. (1989) Annenberg/CPB, (23 minutes)

Part 11 of the *Discovering Psychology* series. This video explains the hows and whys of making judgments and decisions and discusses the psychology of risk taking and negotiation. It could also be used in Chapter 8 in the section on decision making. Color.

Marjoe. (1972) Cinema 5, (88 minutes)

This is a documentary illustrating how an evangelist induces high states of arousal to motivate his audience.

Motivation. (1990) Insight Media, (30 minutes)

This video offers a great overall review of the major issue involved in human motivation. Using dramatic examples, this video explores why people think, behave, and make the choices the way they do. Motivational factors are explored including curiosity, need for achievement, and intrinsic and extrinsic rewards. The video provides examples of PET scanning used to discover the brain's role in motivation. Maslow's hierarchy of needs is also presented. In another section the topic of risk-taking behavior is addressed.

Motivation and Emotion: Discovering Psychology Series. (1990) Annenberg/CPB (28 minutes)

In this video, which is part of the *Discovering Psychology* Series, Dr. Philip Zimbardo reviews research on several key aspects of motivation including: 1) Freud's approach to motivation; 2) Maslow's hierarchy of needs; 3) Seligman's views of the role of cognitive factors in motivation and emotion and the role of socialization in the motivation process. Also, regarding emotion, the program indicates that the components include physical arousal, thoughts, feelings, and behavior. Robert Plutchik's theory of eight basic emotions is highlighted. His theory proposes that these basic emotions can be combined in different ways to produce a variety of emotional experiences. The video also reviews Paul Ekman's cross-cultural research indicating that facial expressions of certain emotions are identifiable cross-culturally.

Nonverbal Communication. (1976) Pennsylvania State University, (22 minutes)

This film features interviews with leading figures in the field. Stanley Milgram discusses the nonverbal cues involved in body language.

Productivity and the Self-Fulfilling Prophecy: The Pygmalion Effect. (1987) CRM/McGraw-Hill, (30 minutes)

This program, part of the *Behavior in Business* series, may be useful if you are applying the topic of motivation to the business community. It explores ways that managers (and teachers) can affect employee morale and performance, often without conscious knowledge of doing so. It illustrates the research of Robert Rosenthal, Rensis Likert, and Douglas MacGregor. The Pygmalion effect, the power of expectations, occurs whether or not we are aware of it and can influence both negatively and positively. This film explores how it occurs and how we can use it positively to its fullest potential. This film is a Blue Ribbon award winner from the American Film Festival.

Stress and Emotion: The Brain Series. (1984) PBS, (60 minutes)

This video is designed to introduce students to the relationship between stress and emotions. Of particular interest is information concerning some of the major theories of emotional acquisition.

Without Words: An Introduction to Nonverbal Communication. (1977) Prentice-Hall, (23 minutes)

Illustrates the role of nonverbal communication in daily life.

Feature Films

Brian's Song (**Aidan Devine, Dean McDermott**) Drama
Based on the autobiography of Gale Sayers (Phifer) and his friendship with fellow Chicago Bears player Brian Piccolo (Maher). Sayers and Piccolo are in competition for the same position on the team but soon become close friends. When Sayers suffers a knee injury, Piccolo helps him through rehabilitation. It is then Sayers turn to help Piccolo when Piccolo learns that a lingering illness is actually cancer.

Cool Runnings (**Leon, Doug E. Doug, Malik Yoba, Rawle D. Lewis, John Candy, Larry Gilman**) Comedy
The story of a bobsledding team from Jamaica trying to make it to the Olympics begins with Derice Bannock (Leon) realizing that because of an injury he will not be able to compete as a track member in the Olympics. Looking for another sport, Derice and ex-United States gold medal bobsledding winner Irv Blitzer (John Candy) put together a bobsledding team from Jamaica. After setbacks and near disasters the group becomes a team and heads off to the Olympics.

The Green Mile (**Tom Hanks, David Morse, Bonnie Hunt**) Drama
The film, based on a Stephen King novel, takes place in a prison in 1935. Inmates of the Cold Mountain Correctional Facility call Death Row "The Green Mile" because of the dark green linoleum that tiles the floor. John Coffey (Duncan), who was convicted of murdering two young girls, in under the charge of Paul Edgecom (Hanks). Edgecom and his fellow guards soon realize that Coffey is an unusual person who seems to be able to perform miracles of healing. This leads them to wonder if Coffey could have committed the crimes for which he is in prison for.

It's a Wonderful Life (**James Stewart, Frank Albertson, Donna Reed**) Comedy Drama
George Bailey (Stewart) faces the possibility of prison when he comes up $8000 short in his books at the bank. Contemplating suicide George meets Clarence, and angel who has yet to earn his wings. George wishes that he had never been born and Clarence grants him his wish and shows him what life would have been like without him. George comes to realize how many lives he has touched and what a wonderful life he has. A classic film that can be referenced for a variety of ages in your classes, from older to younger.

Lean on Me (**Morgan Freeman, Robert Guillaume, Beverly Todd**) Drama
Joe Clark (Freeman) is a high school principal who in 1987 is given the task of reforming an inner city Eastside High School in Paterson, NJ. The school is considered the worst school in New Jersey and is in danger of being taken over by the state. If Clark is able to turn the school around he may keep his job. His hard line policies and uncompromising campaign helps him achieve his goals and also fame.

OfficeSpace (**Ron Livingston, Jennifer Aniston, Stephen Root**) Comedy
www.officeguy.com
A frustrated office drone does everything he can to get fired but ends up getting promoted instead.

Patch Adams (**Robin Williams, Daniel London, Monica Potter**) Comedy / Drama
Hunter Adams (Williams) is a young man who is enrolled in medical school and believes in healing patients with laughter. He is determined to provide emotional and spiritual relief as well as medicine to his patients. After opening a low-cost rural clinic he his forced to defend himself before a board of jurists who would like to bar him from practicing medicine.

The Patriot (**Mel Gibson, Heath Ledger, Joely Richardson**) Historical Film
Farmer Benjamin Martin (Gibson) fought during the French-Indian wars but after his wife's death he renounces violence and lives quietly on his farm, raising his seven children. In 1776 Gabriel (Ledger), his

oldest son, joins the fight against the British. Gabriel returns from battle wounded and with Lord General Cornwallis seeking his arrest. A skirmish breaks out on Benjamin's plantation and he is forced to give up his vow of pacifism to rescue Gabriel.

***Remember the Titans* (Denzel Washington, Will Patton, Donald Faison)** Drama
In 1971, a court order forces three high schools in Alexandra, Virginia to integrate their student bodies and faculties. Coach Bill Yoast (Patton) is replaced by Herman Boone (Washington) who becomes the school's first black faculty member. Neither students nor staff welcome Boone and the team has no respect or trust for one another. Against long odds, Boone helps his team become a force to be reckoned with and wins their respect and trust.

* Sexual Motivation

AIDS: No Nonsense Answers. (1995) Films for the Humanities and Sciences, (10 minutes)
This brief and extremely informative video demonstrates and motivates prevention behaviors and lifestyles changes while presenting the basic facts about AIDS and HIV. Many questions that your students have will be answered in this film including, "If one in a group of children is positive, are the others at-risk?"

The Differences Between Men and Women. (1995) Films for the Humanities and Sciences, (23 minutes)
The old question "Are the differences between men and women conditioned by biology or by family and social environment?" is answered with recent research, which claims that the male and female brains are far from identical. The video also looks at cultural influences on gender-related behaviors.

Homosexuality: What Science Understands. (1987) Insight Media, (54 minutes)
This video traces research on homosexual behavior from the original Kinsey studies in 1954 through the late 1980s. Highlights of the video include a discussion of the decision to remove homosexuality from the DSR III and the issues of homophobia and AIDS.

Sex Hormones and Sexual Destiny. Insight Media, (26 minutes)
A Reuters laboratory is visited where research has demonstrated that hormones have a measurable effect on masculine and feminine behavior and the structure of male and female brains is different. The influence of the environment on female behavior is also discussed. The film features Dr. June Rainiest, director of the Chinese Institute for Research in Sex, Gender, and Reproduction.

Feature Films

***Boys Don't Cry* (Hilary Swank)** Drama
The true story of Brandon Teena, who seduced young women in a small, rural community in Nebraska and was later discovered to be a woman posing as a man.

* Theories of Emotion

A World of Gestures. University of California, Berkeley, (28 minutes)
This video explores gestures from a variety of cultures, including those for beauty, aggression, suicide, friendship, and love. There is an accompanying Instructor's Guide that provides suggestions for using the video, classroom demonstrations to show the power of gestures, and background reference material on gestures and nonverbal communications.

Constructive Use of the Emotions. (1970) University of California, (22 minutes)
This film reviews the different responses to anxiety and the apparent adaptability of most of them.

Death. (1968) Filmmakers Library, (42 minutes)
Documents the last days of a terminal cancer patient. Discusses psychological defenses used to face death and the reactions of family, nurses, and others.

Emotion. (1990) Insight Media (30 minutes)
This video discusses both theoretical and applied issues in emotions. Theoretical highlights include a discussion by Paul Ekman of his theory concerning his hypothesis involving the possible connection between facial expressions and emotions. On the applied side, the program offers a brief discussion of the topic of sports psychology.

Emotions: Friend or Enemy. (1954) Indiana University, (30 minutes)
This film discusses the importance of emotions for adaptation and contrasts this with their capacity to disrupt behavior.

Emotional Styles in Human Behavior. (1962) University of California, (24 minutes)
Relates emotional response to personality functioning.

Face Value. Filmmakers Library, Inc., (38 minutes)
The video features Paul Ekman's cross-cultural research on emotional expression. This film presents faces as the key to individuality and as an important medium of communication. Research reveals how important faces are to us as a species.

Grief. (1976) Carousel Films, (18 minutes)
This film discusses the nature of grief and grief therapy.

Judging Emotional Behavior. (1953) Indiana University/WEXL, (24 minutes)
This classic black and white film shows two subjects responding to ten emotion-eliciting stories, first without sound, then with sound. This format allows students to learn about several interesting elements of emotions. First, they can determine how accurate they are at identifying emotions based on facial expression and body cues. Second, they can learn how environmental context can play a role in emotion identification.

The Mystery of Happiness. ABC, (55 minutes)
This ABC Special narrated by John Stossel details the research on happiness by Dr. David Meyers. Stossel reviews the various research strategies psychologists use to assess people's feelings of well being as well as the results of their work.

What Happens in Emotion. (1957) Indiana University, (30 minutes)
This is a brief overview of physiological and behavioral changes in emotion.

Feature Films

Meet the Parents (**Ben Stiller, Robert DeNiro**) Comedy
1.   What physiological responses does a polygraph test measure?
2.   How accurate was the test in the movie? How accurate are the tests in general?

3. Do you believe that Ben Stiller's character's results were affected by being interviewed by his girlfriend's father? Explain your answer.

11. Human Development Across the Lifespan	Videos	Films
Developmental (Overall / General)	20	
Prenatal & Newborn	9	
Child Development	39	6
Adolescent Development	17	12
Adult Development	17	6

Please note the subtopics in this section are organized *chronologically* by lifespan rather than alphabetically by subtopic.

* Development (Overall)

CNN ® Today Video Vol. III: Section 7: Human Development Across the Lifespan

The Age Wave (9:04)

Body Doubles: The Twin Experience. (1997) Films for the Humanities and Sciences, (50 minutes)
Recommended by MC Journal. The study of twins is vital to research in psychology. Twins separated at birth and later reunited are often quite similar. This similarity begs the notion that personality is formed by experience, and suggests that personality is genetically predetermined. This excellent HBO documentary contains powerful interviews with numerous twins, including those conjoined, and a history of twin research from Josef Mengele of the University of Minnesota Twin Research Center.

Citizen 2000: A Series on Child Development. (1993) Filmmakers Library, (various times)
This new and unique documentary series is following the lives and development of a group of children over a period of 18 years, from their birth in 1982 until they become adults in the year 2000. The series is being produced in consultation with experts in the fields of developmental psychology, sociology, linguistics, and pediatrics. The children, all British but from a wide variety of social, economic, and ethnic backgrounds, are filmed at home, in school, at play, and at major events in their lives. Because of the close relationship between the filmmakers and the children, the portraits are completely spontaneous. The series provides a compelling picture of childhood at the end of the twentieth century. Titles available now include: *Matthew: Portrait of a One-Year-Old,* 25 min.; *Turning 2: Out of Babyhood,* 51 min.; *Turning 4: New Skills,* 51 min.; *Rachel—A Difficult Year, The Death of a Sibling,* 25 min.; and *Fathers,* 52 min. Parts of this series have already won some film awards. Videocassettes may be purchased or rented as a series or individually.

Cognitive Development. (1990) Insight Media, (30 minutes)
This video offers an excellent review of the basics of Piaget's theory including the areas of: language, reasoning, and remembering.

Corporal Punishment: "Loving Smacks". (2000) Films for the Humanities and Sciences, (52 minutes)
In this program, noted psychologists discuss the myths, justifications, and effects of corporal punishment and present alternatives to the use of violence to maintain discipline.

81

The Developing Child, Discovering Psychology Series. (1990) Annenberg/CPB, (30 minutes)

This video from the *Discovering Psychology* series offers an excellent review of the nature (genetics) versus nurture (environment) controversy. Points out how early psychologists such as William James portrayed the infant as confused and totally helpless in confronting the world. Recent findings involving modern technology refute that view. Newborns are good at three tasks: gaining sustenance, defending against harm, and making social contact. They also have definite interests and abilities: they prefer human voices to artificial sounds; they can distinguish their mothers' face from other faces; and they can imitate certain expressions and sounds. From studying how children solve problems, Jean Piaget concluded that they pass through four stages in their understanding of the world. This program illustrates how today's researchers continue to study many of Piaget's concepts, including object permanence and conservation. As the chapter suggests, recent findings indicate that Piaget underestimated the onset of many of the abilities young children have and overestimated the rate of their development. This program uses personality development to illustrate the interaction of nature and nurture. Activity level and shyness, for example, are personality traits that show considerable hereditary influence. However, even these tendencies can be modified by training and experience. Contemporary psychologists realize that nature and nurture interact in the course of development.

The Developing Child Series. (1991-93) Magna Systems, Inc. (times vary between 20-30 minutes)

The Developing Child series videos present information on most of the key areas of child and adolescent development. Some of the best of the videos include: Module #10 (Infancy: Beginnings in cognition and language); Module #14 (Child in the family); Module #20 (Early childhood: Behavior and relationships); Module #22 (Language development); Module #23 (Self identity and sex role development); Module #28 (Preadolescence); Module #30 (Adolescence: Search for identity); and Module #31 (Adolescence: Relationships with others).

Development. (1971) CRM/McGraw-Hill, (33 minutes)

This film presents a sampling of research methods in the study of human psychological development. Featured are a number of different areas of study and the psychologists who work in these areas. Included is Jerome Kagan demonstrating inborn motor reflexes and some of the more complex perceptual responses in experiments with infants. Also shown is Mary Ainsworth's "strange situations" experiment in which a mother and child are placed in a room alone with toys for the child.

Erik Erikson (Volumes 1 & 2). (1966) Insight Media, (50 minutes each)

This video presents an in depth discussion with Erik Erikson in which he describes his eight stage model of psychosocial crisis.

Everybody Rides the Carousel. (1980) Pyramid Film & Video, (72 minutes)

This video presents psychologist Erik Erikson's theory of personality development, using delightful animation. The eight stages of life are presented in three main parts: infancy to childhood, school age to young adulthood, and maturity to old age.

Gender and Relationships. (1990) Insight Media, (30 minutes)

This program emphasizes that even the most respected authorities are not in agreement about what factors influence peoples' feelings of love, affection, and sexual attraction toward others. The film addresses such questions as "what is love? What makes sexual behavior "normal" or "abnormal"? Why and in what ways do men and women differ in their sexual attitudes, behaviors, and motives?

Inside Stories: Journey into Self-Esteem Series. (1992) Filmmakers Library, (30 minutes)

This award-winning four-part series shows how building self-esteem improves the quality of life and helps people deal more effectively with their problems. The programs are (1) *Self-Esteem Begins in the Family*—deals with parenting issues; (2) *Self-Esteem and How We Learn*—shows the important role of the teacher in developing a healthy self-image, especially during adolescence; (3) *A Family in Recovery*—follows a seemingly perfect family on the road back from alcoholism; and (4) *Seniors' Esteem Issues*—focuses on later life. In all four programs we learn that people who have healthy self-esteem become capable of dealing with life's challenges. Examples from life are intercut with commentary by authority H. Stephen Glenn.

Physical and Cognitive Development, Discovering Psychology Teaching Module 10. (1990) Annenberg/CPB, (various times)

The Discovering Psychology Teaching Modules contain excerpts from the *Discovering Psychology Series*. The most important programs in this module include: footage of Piaget performing conservation experiments; a demonstration of object permanence in infants; the acquisition of symbolic understanding in children; a discussion of memory loss and aging; and educational training of the elderly.

Seasons of Life. (1990) WQED Pittsburgh / University of Michigan, (60 minutes each)

This unique series consists of 5 hour-long videos and a supplementary series of 26 half-hour audiotapes (either may be purchased separately). The videos cover infancy and early childhood, childhood and adolescence, early adulthood, middle adulthood, and late adulthood. Each program is hosted by David Hartman, who interviews experts from a variety of sciences to examine how biological, social, and psychological forces affect our lives.

Sex Roles: Charting the Complexity of Development. (1991) Insight Media, (60 minutes)

This film looks at the cultural ramifications of sex roles and the myths associated with them. Three theories of socialization (Freudian, social-learning, cognitive-development) are analyzed regarding how each theory views the nature-nurture controversy. The negative impact of sex-role stereotyping is examined.

Socialization—Moral Development. (1980) Harper Collins, (22 minutes)

This video explores theories of morality and moral development through the demonstration of classic experimental work in social and developmental psychology.

Time to Grow, 2--Contexts of Development. (1992) Pennsylvania State University, (28 minutes)

This video shows how the interplay of social, economic, and cultural contexts influences the development process and considers the major contexts in which a child grows: interaction between genetic potential and environment, child-parent relationship, peer groups, social class, and culture.

Touchpoints: Pregnancy. (1992) Piper Films Inc., (50 minutes each)

A series based on the Brazelton Study. By watching twelve families, all in unique situations, we are shown how and why children develop the way they do. In part 1, *Birth and First Four Weeks of Life*, questions explored include: What kind of parent will I be? What will my baby be like? What will delivery be like? This part also covers birth to first few weeks, newborn assessment, the work of attachment, and issues in the first three months (crying and calming, the work of becoming a family). Part 2, *First Month Through First Year*, covers issues concerning communication and adjusting to being a parent, cognitive and motor development, feeding, sleep, negativism, tantrums, and teasing. Part 3, *One Year Through Toddlerhood,* covers sibling rivalry, discipline, and toilet training.

Toys. (1994) Filmmakers Library, (47 minutes)
This video airs divergent views of educators, from those who feel that natural materials such as wood, stones, and acorns are the only proper toys to those who believe that a child's world should be full of complicated objects, as this reflects the real world. It features psychologists Howard Gardner, Jerome Kagan, and others. The program highlights the dramatic changes that have occurred in the kinds of toys available, from blocks and stuffed toys to battery operated toys that simulate reality (some violently) to computer games.

Twinsburg, Ohio: Some Kind of Weird Twin Thing. (1992) Filmmakers Library, (23 minutes)
This award-winning film is about two very different identical twins living 3,000 mile apart who agree to meet at Twins Days in Twinsburg, Ohio. This documentary chronicles the continuing struggle of balancing the intimacy of a shared childhood against the adult need for individuality. Color.

* Prenatal Development and the Newborn

Babymakers. (1980) CRM/McGraw-Hill, (43 minutes)
This film explores the many controversies surrounding artificial insemination, egg-embryo manipulation (babies created outside the body—"test-tube babies"), and the use of surrogate mothers. It also offers unusual footage of the actual freezing of embryos.

Capabilities of the Newborn, from *The Mind Series Teaching Modules*, 2nd Edition #13
This video demonstrates the startling abilities that newborns have, as determined by modern technology.

Cells: Baby and Child. (1998) Films for the Humanities and Sciences, (20 minutes)
Section one of this program makes extensive use of microscopic imaging to create an overview of cells in their role as the building blocks of life. Section two describes the newborn experience, from birth to breastfeeding. Also covered are the mechanics behind a baby's improvement of vision and rapid language acquisition. Childhood play, social interaction, and schooling are touched upon as well. A BBC Production. Color.

The Effect of Hormones and the Environment on Brain Development, from *The Brain Teaching Modules*, 2nd Edition #17 (1998) Annenberg/CPB, (6:50)
This video presents some rather startling and significant findings that address the important topic of gender differences. The *in utero* photography is stunning.

Miracle of Life. (1983) Swedish Television and WGBH, Boston, (60 minutes)
This excellent film uses microphotography to show the complex sequence of events that lead to conception and to the birth of a human baby.

Newborn. (1978) Filmmakers Library, (28 minutes)
This film documents the amazing capabilities of the newborn. It demonstrates the infant's readiness to face challenges, perceive its environment, and establish its individuality. Neonatal researchers Barry Brazelton, Lewis Lipsitt, and Louis Sanders demonstrate the components of normal infant development and how these are measured.

Rock-A-Bye-Baby. (1972) Time-Life, (30 minutes)

The film explores some of the techniques used by psychologists to measure mothering practices around the world. Children raised in orphanages, who have not been cuddled and carried, become listless and withdrawn. The film shows that even monkeys raised in isolation from their mothers develop human-like schizophrenia. The film suggests that from birth to about three years, the mother-child relationship is critical in human development.

Simple Beginnings? Child Development from Birth to Age Five. (1994) Films for the Humanities and Sciences, (24 minutes)

This program explores the period of child development from birth to 4 to 5 years of age, providing an overview of several key topics in developmental psychology. The program features three experiments, which display early abilities of infants to recognize rules, faces, and biological motion. The experiments test short-term memory capacities of young babies, register a baby's reaction to the mother and to a stranger, and demonstrates how babies appear to discriminate at a young age between biodynamic and non-biodynamic motion. The program goes on to explore the parents' role in structuring infants' learning experiences in the early development of language.

Teratogens and Their Effects on the Developing Brain and Mind, from *The Mind Series Teaching Modules*, 2nd Edition #12

Teratogens are substances that can cause malformations of the fetus in the first and second trimesters of pregnancy. The embryonic stage when the major organ systems are developing, is an especially sensitive time for the developing prenatal child. This video looks at some of the more common hazards and effects of exposure to these harmful substances.

* Child Development (infancy and toddler)

CNN® Today Video Series:
Developmental Psychology Vol. I: Nutrition: Kids and Taste (3:04)
Developmental Psychology Vol. II: Toilet Training (4:00)
Developmental Psychology Vol. II: Terrible Twos (4:39)
Developmental Psychology Vol. I: Learning a Second Language (2:25)
Developmental Psychology Vol. II: Baby Language (3:56)
Developmental Psychology Vol. II: Dyslexia (2:02)
Developmental Psychology Vol. II: Brain Physiology and Bilingualism (4:32)

Basic Parenting Skills. (2000) Films for the Humanities & Sciences, (50 minutes)

This program presents an overview of basic parenting skills in a dramatic format. Practical techniques for dealing with tantrums and other undesirable behavior are included. Specific ideas for building a healthy parent-child relationship are examined.

Better Babies--Raising Intellectual "Superstars." (1991) Filmmakers Library, (28 minutes)

Does prenatal and early childhood learning produce geniuses? This video documents several early-learning programs. We see parents talking to their unborn children in the belief that they will accelerate verbal skills, and other parents in courses on how to raise geniuses. We are shown the hectic schedule of a toddler whose mother teaches him art, music, computers, geography, and Japanese. One couple displays pride in having raised four genius daughters, yet the eldest daughter does not plan to repeat her parents' experiments on her own children. This could be a good discussion-starter for your class.

Child Development. (1993) Films for the Humanities and Sciences, (60 minutes)

This program examines a range of the major subjects categorized under the rubric of child development. Topics covered include Genetic Counseling and Prenatal Testing, Fetal Alcohol Syndrome, Prepared Childbirth, Reflexes of Newborns, Learning in Infants, Temperament, Physical Abuse of Children, Learning Disabilities, Sexual Abuse of Children, and Teen Suicide. In addition to these, the videodisc contains still images.

Child Development. (1992) Insight Media, (30 minutes)

This program presents a historical overview of the contributions of Locke, Rousseau, Freud, Erikson, Bowlby, Watson, Gessel, and Piaget. The methods, challenges, and problems of studying development are considered.

Child Development. (2000) Films for the Humanities & Sciences, (60 minutes)

This program examines a range of the major subjects categorized under the rubric of child development. Includes a videodisc with still images.

Childhood. (1991) Ambrose Video, (57 minutes each)

This seven-cassette video series is one of the most complete documentary series currently available. It presents an insightful and richly textured examination of the various influences that shape us as individuals and as members of the families and societies in which we are raised. Through the observation of 12 families on five continents, the series looks at childhood from a number of perspectives: personal, scientific, historical, and cultural. Included are documentary sequences, provocative historic films, and vivid clinical illustrations with on-screen commentary by experts (Urie Bronfenbrenner was a program adviser). Since the following titles may not be explanatory of all content, you should check with your media specialist for a listing of specific content. The programs are (1) *Great Expectations,* (2) *Louder Than Words,* (3) *Love's Labors,* (4) *In the Land of the Giants,* (5) *Life's Lessons,* (6) *Among Equals,* and (7) *The House of Tomorrow.*

Child Sex Abusers. (1995) Films for the Humanities and Sciences, (28 minutes)

This is a specially adapted Phil Donahue show featuring mothers and their daughters who have been molested by brothers, half-brothers, and neighborhood kids. An expert who deals with abusive children counsels what to look for and what to do with abusive kids, and counsels kids who are being abused.

Cognitive Development. (1990) Coast Community College District Telecourses, (30 minutes)

This film explores cognitive development and Piaget's theories.

A Cross-Cultural Approach to Cognition. (1976) Harper and Row, (27 minutes)

This film illustrates Piaget's cognitive stages using children from Japan, Guatemala, and Kenya.

The Developing Child. (1990) Annenberg/CPB) (30 minutes)

Part of the *Discovering Psychology* series hosted by Philip Zimbardo, this film examines the impact of heredity and environment on the development of the child. The arguments of nature and nurture are discussed and supported with results from human and animal research. Ultimately the film concludes that, even though newborns are equipped to respond to their environment, biology alone is not destiny. Experience can alter the development of the child. This excellent examination of the nature versus nurture debate promotes active discussion among students.

Development. (1998) PBS Video, (55 minutes)

Part of *The Mind* series, this film discusses the development of the CNS in humans. The film presents graphic representations of neuronal changes from the single germ cell to the brain of a six-year-old. The effects of drugs, alcohol, and radiation on the developing brain are also examined in both human and animal models. The film contains excellent graphics depicting differentiation within the human brain.

Emotional Intelligence: The Key to Social Skills. (1997) Films for the Humanities and Sciences, (28 minutes)

There was a time when parents were expected to teach their children social skills, such as how to listen, share, and be kind. Today that job and the nurturing of emotional intelligence necessary to learn those skills, has been turned over to schools. This program from *The Doctor Is In* looks at innovative teaching techniques that are helping students to develop emotional intelligence and the social skills that will help them lead happier lives. Psychologist Daniel Goleman discusses the nature of emotional intelligence and how it develops; child psychologist Maurice Elias explains the concept of emotional literacy. A Dartmouth-Hitchcock Medical Center production.

Erik H. Erikson. (1992) Davidson Films, (38 minutes)

Using archival materials, interviews, and new footage, this video discusses Erikson's theory that the interplay of genetics, cultural influences, and unique experiences produces unique individual variability. The program also contains commentary by Erikson's colleague Margaret Brenman-Gibson, offering a sense of relationship between the life experience of a theorist and the work that is produced.

Gender Development: Social Influences, from *The Brain Teaching Modules*, 2nd Edition #3 (1998) Annenberg/CPB (4:02)

This is an excellent video that clearly demonstrates how we treat children as a function of their sex. The examples are clear and vivid. The point made here is cleverly presented and very convincing for what we already know to be the case. This module will elicit laughter from viewers when they observe the male child being disguised as a girl. It provides a good starting point for discussion of gender identity, gender role, gender typing, and the nature vs. nurture controversy.

Gender: The Enduring Paradox. (1991) University Film and Video, (56 minutes)

Part of the *Smithsonian World* series. This video explores the ever-changing role of gender in American society, from the formation of gender roles in early childhood to the socially constructed roles of masculinity and femininity experienced throughout life. Segments look at the women's movement, fathers who nurture their children, and cross-cultural differences between the sexes.

Incest: The Family Secret. (1984) Filmmakers Library, (57 minutes)

Another multi-award winning video (including APA) about childhood sexual abuse. In this video, women tell their childhood stories either in a self-help group or with their identity hidden. The program explores the role of the mother in an incestuous family. Additionally, a formerly abusive father who underwent treatment in a psychiatric hospital is presented.

Infant Cognitive Development, from *The Mind Series Teaching Modules*, 2nd Edition #14, Worth (7:34)

This video looks at recent research into the subject and demonstrates some of the recently developed research techniques for exploring the intellectual development of young children. It also points out where current findings differ from those of Piaget.

The Infant Mind. (1992) Insight Media, (30 minutes)

This fascinating video presents traditional Piagetian perspectives of objective permanence during the sensorimotor period. Then it challenges some of Piaget's assumptions to demonstrate that infants have a perception of cause and effect, number and object permanence much earlier than formerly believed.

Jean Piaget. (1969) Insight Media, (40 minutes each part)

This is a two-part interview that illuminates key concepts of Piaget's theories. Party I surveys each of the important stages of cognitive development. In Part 2, Piaget discusses Freud and Freudian concepts. He also discusses his reaction to Jensen's report on intelligence.

Language Processing in the Brain, from *The Mind Series Teaching Modules*, 2nd Edition #8, (1999) Worth (6:19)

This video discusses Neil Bohannon's work on children's development of receptive language, the precursor to productive language, and has insight into how kernel language structures are initiated.

Louder Than Words. (1991) University Film and Video, (57 minutes)

Part of the *Childhood Series*. Jerome Kagan, a professor of developmental psychology at Harvard, discusses the connection between shyness, sociability, and biology. Benjamin Spock is also featured offering advice for parents and teachers.

Music and Early Childhood. (1994) Filmmakers Library, (28 minutes)

This video makes a strong case for beginning music education at an early age because of its importance as a precursor to language skills. It shows groups of very young children engaged in musical activity, as well as psychologist Howard Gardner discussing musical intelligence.

Piaget's Developmental Theory: An Overview. (1989) University Film & Video, (28 minutes)

Using both archival footage of Piaget and newly shot footage of David Elkind conducting interviews with children of varying ages, this video offers an overview of the scope and content of Piaget's theory.

Piaget on Piaget. (1977) Yale University, (42 minutes)

Piaget's ideas and writings have been influential throughout the world in the study of child development and in education. In this film, he clarifies certain concepts and corrects some misunderstandings about his ideas. For example, Piaget sets forth his ideas on the nature and grounds of knowledge, as seen in some of the classic experiments in his research with children.

The Psychological Development of the Child. (2000) Films for the Humanities & Sciences, (21-26 minutes each segment)

This eight-part series covers the development of the child from the womb to the end of the first year, covering such topics as the birth process, prenatal development, attachment, breast-feeding across cultures, the family, psychological development and the discovery of the outside world.

Self-Esteem and the Child. (1990) Cox Entertainment, (45 minutes)

This video-based skill-building workshop includes dramatic vignettes and interviews with children and two self-esteem professionals. The program emphasizes five elements that lead to self-esteem: a sense of security, and sense of identity or self-concept, a sense of belonging, a sense of purpose, and a sense of competence. This video may be of special assistance for those teaching parents or for students who want to be teachers and counselors.

Self-Esteem Begins in the Family. (1992) Filmmakers Library, (30 minutes)
This video discusses the importance that self-esteem has throughout our lives. We meet three families: those of a divorced mother, a married couple, and a single father. They describe their difficulty with their own parents and their determination not to repeat the same mistakes. We see the nurturing environments they have created in their homes.

Social Development in Infancy, from *The Mind Series Teaching Modules*, 2nd Edition #15, Worth (6:44)
This video clip emphasizes the importance of social interaction in infancy in contributing to attachment and personality development.

Using What We Know: Applying Piaget's Developmental Theory in Primary Classrooms. (1991) University Film & Video, (35 minutes)
Using Piaget's work, David Elkind proposes educational practices that reflect thoughtful consideration of the application of Piaget's theories to today's primary classroom. Filmed in model classrooms, topics include classroom leadership, cooperation and competition, classroom learning, and assessment. This video stresses child-centered practices that enhance the quality of primary education. In an introductory psychology classroom, this is a good example of theory put into practice.

Walk Before You Run. (1989) Access Network, (29 minutes)
This video demonstrates through a dramatization how students differ in their development and thinking skills at different ages.

Where Angels Dare. (1993) National Film Board of Canada, (26 minutes)
This WPA award-winning film is an intensely personal exploration of healing from childhood sexual abuse. Six men and women share their journeys and the "angels" who helped along the way.

Why God, Why Me? (1988) Filmmakers Library, (27 minutes)
This multi-award-winning video about childhood sexual abuse dramatizes the life of those children who grew up never feeling safe in their own homes. It is compelling, but no graphic sexual or violent scenes are presented. The program ends on a positive note, showing that survivors can establish new, loving relationships.

Feature Films

A.I.: Artificial Intelligence (**Haley Joel Osment, Jude Law, Frances O'Connor**) Drama / Science Fiction
David (Osment) is a robot of the future who replaces Henry and Monica's comatose son. When the couple's natural child recovers, David is abandoned and sets out to become "a real boy." A science fiction film that can be used to illustrate a variety of developmental and technological issues.

Jack (**Robin Williams, Diane Lane, Jennifer Lopez**) Comedy / Drama
Jack (Williams) is introduced as a ten year old who looks like a 40 year old man. In a flash back it is discovered that Jack was born only ten weeks after his mother became pregnant, and has a disorder causing rapid aging. Home schooled until now Jack decides to go to public school where fellow fourth graders tease him. His classmates soon see an advantage to having him around and grow to love Jack. A good film to discuss various differences between child and adult development stages.

Look Who's Talking (**John Travolta, Kirstie Alley, Olympia Dukakis**) Comedy
Infant Mikey is a "talking baby" protagonist who is a sarcastic observer of his new world. Mikey's mother (Alley) is searching for a father for Mikey. The perfect daddy is right under her nose, cab driver (Travolta), who was on the scene when she went into labor on the sidewalk. While a preposterous premise, it nevertheless provides an illumination of adult life from a baby's perspective.

Trading Places (**Dan Akroyd, Eddie Murphy**) Comedy
1.   Is Eddie Murphy's character a product of his environment or of his heredity?
2.   What personality changes, if any, did the switch in roles dictate?
3.   Of the two men, who made the bet concerning "nature or nurture," who would you say won? Explain your answer.

Specific Scene Analysis:
Unforgiven (1992) (**Gene Hackman, and Frances Fisher**) Drama

- Central Concept: Moral development
- Approximate Scene Location: 3 minutes, 38 seconds into the 131-minute film
- Approximate Scene Length: 5 minutes, 38 seconds
- Opening Line: "You know how Skinny is, he says he is going to shoot them."
- Closing Line: "Not yet maybe.

Key Concepts: moral judgments, Kohlberg's theory of moral development, Gillian's criticisms of Kohlberg's theory
Characters/Actors: Little Bill (Gene Hackman), Clyde Ledbetter (Ron White), Women at the Brother: Strawberry Alice (Frances Fisher), Delilah (Anna Thomson), Silky (Beverly Elliott), Faith (Lisa Repo-Martell), Crow Creek Kate (Josie Smith), Little Sue (Tara Dawn Frederick), Cowboys: Quick Mike (David Mucci), David Bunting (Rob Campbell), Skinny (Anthony Jones)
Scene Description: Two cowboys were visiting the Billiard Club, a local brothel, and one of them got upset and cut a young woman several times on the face. The young woman, Delilah, had laughed when she saw his naked body. The owner of the establishment, Skinny, had threatened to shoot the cowboys. The local sheriff, Little Bill, is sent for, and he arrives to dispense justice. Little Bill's response to the scenario is to have the cowboys pay Skinny six ponies for the damage to the young woman. The women in the brothel, led by Strawberry Alice, are upset at little Bill's decision and bond together to pay a reward to anyone who will kill the cowboys for what they did to Delilah's face. They were offended by Little Bill's solution to the crime.

Questions/Discussion:
1.   What is the issue in the scenario? How did Strawberry Alice's approach to the issue differ from Little Bill's?
The issue is how to dispense justice for the behavior of the cowboys in cutting the face of Delilah. Little Bill views the incident as an issue of damaged property; the young woman was the property of Skinny, the owner of the brothel. Therefore, justice is compensating Skinny adequately for the future losses he would encounter because males would not desire a damaged woman. On the other hand, Strawberry Alice sees the issue as a grievous personal harm to Delilah. The women care about Delilah and think the cowboys should pay for the dangerous assault they committed toward her. The issue for Strawberry Alice is one of punishment for personal harm committed against a woman.
2.   What concepts from, and criticisms about, Kohlberg's theoretical approach to moral growth can partially explain these gender differences?

The cognitive-developmental approach to moral development developed by Kohlberg assumes that the core of morality is a sense of justice. Individuals are motivated to move to higher levels of morality by growth of the cognitive structures and social interactions. Carol Gilligan has criticized Kohlberg's theory for its focus on morality from a masculine perspective of abstract reasoning about justice and rules of society. Competitiveness, aggression, and the rights of the individual are stressed in the socialization of males. On the other hand, females are socialized to be more caring and nurturing; therefore, their approach to moral issues is from the premise of relationships that should have equal value with the male perspective. Because of different socialization practices and societal expectations for males and females, gender differences in moral perspectives exist. Thus Sheriff Little Bill and Strawberry Alice would differ in how they viewed the issues in the scenario.

3.   Is there empirical support for gender differences in moral development?

Empirical evidence indicates that males and females do not differ in their approach to reasoning about moral dilemmas; both use caring and justice in their moral judgments. In everyday living, however, observers have noted that females are more likely than males to extend a caring approach to others.

Suggested Children's Television Shows:
- Barney, Teletubbies, Blues Clues, Sesame Street

Analyze these shows to determine what methods they use (or don't use) to facilitate toddler cognitive development.

* Adolescent Development (young adulthood)

CNN® Today Video Series.
Developmental Psychology Vol. I: Teen Violence (2:25)
Developmental Psychology Vol. II: Resiliency in the Face of Physical Disability (2:39)
Developmental Psychology Vol. I: Teen Substance Abuse: Smoking (1:47)
Developmental Psychology Vol. II: Binge Drinking (2:06)
Developmental Psychology Vol. II: Teenage Sexuality (3:27)
Developmental Psychology Vol. II: Divorce Effects (4:44)
Developmental Psychology Vol. II: Impact of Bullying (2:17)

Adolescent Anxiety. (1985) PBS Video, (28 minutes)
Norman Kaplan hosts this *Here's to Your Health* series video, which focuses on the importance of communication between parents and their adolescent children. Maintenance and enhancement of self-esteem, identity acquisition, sexuality, and independence are the main topics. Behavioral management through reinforcement and modeling is stressed, along with open communication and active listening as methods of healthful parent-child interaction. This film discusses several problems that adolescents encounter during their transition into adulthood and thus is a good vehicle for stimulating introspection among your students.

Adolescent Development. (1990) Insight Media, (30 minutes)
Physical, psychological and social development during adolescence are explored by this video. Specific topics addressed include puberty, peer influence and moral development.

Adolescent Development. (1991) Pennsylvania State University, (30 minutes)
From the *Study of Human Behavior* series. Adolescents, mothers, and psychologists are interviewed about the physical changes, search for identity, and struggles for independence that accompany the transition from childhood to adulthood. The program also covers the stresses that

accompany the range of differences among teen peers and touches on cognitive and moral development during adolescence.

Adolescence: The Winds of Change. (1976) Harper & Row, (40 minutes)

The biological, sexual, and cognitive transitions of adolescence are discussed by teenagers in this frank, open film. Added commentary on this period of great change is provided by David Alkind, Janeway Conger, and Jerome Kagan. In addition, the parent-child relationship as it relates to the transition into adulthood is addressed in several candid scenes. This film's topics are of major importance to many students, so it usually promotes active classroom discussion.

Self-Esteem and How We Learn. (1992) Filmmakers Library, (30 minutes)

This program could also be used in the Learning topic unit. It focuses on the critical school-age years, especially adolescence, when self image is tested in an environment outside the home. The teacher may play a pivotal role in helping the adolescent feel accepted and productive. We are shown a model school where students and teachers work and learn with mutual respect.

Teenage Mind and Body. (1990) Insight Media, (30 minutes)

This video explores the areas of adolescent cognitive and physical development. Two highlights include David Elkind's discussion of formal operations and adolescent egocentrism, and a review of Kohlberg's theory of moral development and moral reasoning.

Teenage Suicide. Films for the Humanities and Sciences, (19 minutes)

This documentary explores some of the reasons teens commit suicide and the recent increase in the number of suicides. It describes some of the behavior patterns to which family and friends should be alerted. A young man who has attempted suicide tells his story.

Teenagers and Sex Roles. (1985) PBS Video, (30 minutes)

A production of WGBY-TV, this film depicts several male and female teenagers discussing sex roles in our society. The debate in the film is fairly constructive given the high level of emotion displayed by the participants. In general, the males are traditional in their beliefs and the females are more contemporary, stressing androgyny. This debate often produces active classroom discussion, because college students are often trying to establish their own sex-role identity and integrate it into their personality. Color.

Teenage Suicide: The Ultimate Dropout. (1978) PBS Video, (30 minutes)

Through a series of interviews, this film introduces viewers to three teenagers who have attempted suicide. Two females and one male explain why they wanted to end their lives. The film points out that many teenagers are candidates for suicide, because they frequently experience despair, hopelessness, estrangement, and isolation. The three subjects of this documentary cited depression and a lack of attention as the reasons for attempting to end their lives. The film strongly advises the use of support programs for potential victims and thus is highly recommended.

Teens: What Makes Them Tick. (1999) ABC, (43 minutes)

This ABC News special includes John Stossel talking to a variety of teens and their parents. He visits the Harvard Medical School's Brain Imaging Center to reveal some surprising physiological reasons for teen behavior. The adolescent years are not only a time of huge growth spurts, but also an age of irrepressible passion and enthusiasm. This program concludes that despite their rebellion, most teens want to please their parents.

The Unknown Generation X. (1995) Films for the Humanities and Sciences, (28 minutes)
(Recommended by Booklist). "Generation X " is called a myth by some, a reality by others. Whatever the case may be, the generation of young adults born between 1965 and 1980 faces challenges that no other generation has had to deal with. Unemployment, underemployment, a huge national debt, a depleting Social Security system, negative stereotyping, and endless bombardment from advertisers are just a few of the issues confronting this generation. This program examines some of the stereotypes and issues that society has created for "Generation X." Featured in this program are Wendy Kopp, founder of Teach for America; Neil Howe, author of *13th Gen;* and Richard Thau, president of Third Millennium. Color.

Feature Films

American Pie I (**Jason Biggs, Shannon Elizabeth, Alyson Hannigan**) Comedy
Jim (Biggs), a high school senior and his three friends Kevin, Finch and Oz make a pledge to go to bed with a woman the three weeks before the senior prom. Jim attempts to seduce a beautiful Czech exchange student but fails miserably and ends up going to the prom with an annoyingly chatty girl. Each of the other boys have prospects but none of them look too promising. While some scenes may push the envelope a bit, so also sometimes does adolescent behavior.

American Pie II (**Jason Biggs, Shannon Elizabeth, Alyson Hannigan**) Comedy
The teens from American Pie (1999) return home following their freshman year of college. They rent a summerhouse on Lake Michigan where they hope to score romantically. However complications arise and their well laid plans are laden with many flaws. A comical look at some late adolescent activities and fantasies.

Girl, Interrupted (**Winona Ryder, Angelina Jolie**) Drama
Winona Ryder gets diagnosed with borderline personality disorder and loses herself in an Oz-like netherworld, but more insane and dangerous.
1.   What disorder does the girl who commits suicide suffer from?
2.   Many of the girls in the institution suffer from low self-esteem. Choose one of the girls and explain how her esteem level has affected her life.
3.   Choose one character and explain how you would work with this client if you were her therapist.

Nell (with Jodie Foster)

The Piano (with Holly Hunter)

House of Cards (with Kathleen Turner)

Lean on Me (with Morgan Freeman)

Dangerous Minds (with Michelle Pfeiffer)

Sixteen Candles (Comedy)

The Breakfast Club (**Emilio Estevez, Judd Nelson, Molly Ringwald**) Comedy Drama
Nine hours of school detention bond five students who until this day were strangers and on different levels of the high school caste system. Faced with a villainous principal, who makes their lives miserable, the

group decides they have one thing in common – they do not like adult society. A sensitive look at adolescent development and issues during a cross section of a day in their lives.

Flowers for Algernon

Skulls

* Adult Development

The Adult Years—Continuity and Change Series. (1985) Pennsylvania State University Audio-Visual Services, (196 minutes)
>   This is a seven-part series which explores the aging process as a complex mixture of continuity and change rather than a series of predictable steps or stages.

Aging. (1988) PBS (55 minutes)
>   Part of *The Mind* series originally shown on PBS, this video reviews numerous key aging concepts including neural changes common in aging, and atypical aging problems (e.g., Alzheimer's, Parkinson's, cerebral vascular accidents).

Aging. (2000) Films for the Humanities and Sciences, (26 minutes)
>   This film covers the physical processes of aging and the various body systems to see how and why they change as they age. It is shown that not all of the changes in older people are inevitable and that some, in fact, can be slowed down or reversed.

Aging and Memory, from *The Mind Teaching Modules*, 2nd Edition #17, Worth (11:16)
>   This video illustrates how a common form of forgetting involving future intentions can be studied in the laboratory. This video presents a new study of age differences in a form of memory that is commonplace and that is now beginning to receive the attention of memory researchers.

Aging Well. (2000) Films for the Humanities and Sciences, (16 minutes)
>   This film discusses how people are living longer than their parents did and why they are staying healthier. The program covers medical advances that continue to boost our life expectancy rate, and the role that lifestyle changes play.

Brain Transplants in Parkinson's Patients, from *The Brain Teaching Modules*, 2nd Edition, #31 (1998) Annenberg/CPB, (11:09)
>   This video begins with a brief description of Parkinson's disease. One of the most promising new approaches to treating the disease involves the implantation of fetal tissue into the basal ganglia of Parkinson's patients. Note that it takes about one and a half years for the transplanted tissue to produce its full complement of dopamine. Even then, it does not produce all the dopamine needed by the patients, and so they continue to take L-dopa after surgery.

Death: An Overview. (2000) Films for the Humanities and Sciences, (50 minutes)
>   This step-by-step program takes the myth and mystery out of the process of dying and death itself, and presents both as biological and clinical realities.

Death and Dying. (1975) PBS Video, (30 minutes)

Through a personal interview with Elisabeth Kubler-Ross, this film introduces us to the Swiss psychologist and her work with dying people and their families. In this film, part of the *Death and Dying* series, Kubler-Ross discusses the importance of communication and of understanding the emotions of the dying individual, to help him or her achieve a peaceful death. This film concludes with Kubler-Ross discussing her view on mercy killings and life after death. Although somewhat dated, this film presents material that is of interest to all students, especially those who have cared for or are caring for a terminally ill person.

The Effect of Aging on Cognitive Function: Nature/Nurture, from *The Mind Teaching Modules*, 2nd Edition #16, Worth (10:09)

This video opens with still pictures of identical twins of many ages and races. The narrator tells us how the study of identical twins can help us to determine how factors such as lifestyle, diet, and stress may contribute to individual differences in the aging process.

Effect of Mental and Physical Activity on Brain/Mind, from *The Mind Teaching Modules*, 2nd Edition #18, Worth (9:27)

This video shows the effect of aging on both mental and physical decline.

Facing Death: Conversations with Caregivers. (1993) University Film & Video, (26 minutes)

This video offers advice and guidance for professional hospice workers to help them become more comfortable with death. Five hospice workers share their personal experiences as caregivers and relate perspectives acquired from years of working with dying patients. Although aimed at hospice workers, this video is also useful for members of a psychology class studying the other end of the life cycle.

Growing Old in a New Age. (1993) Annenberg/CPB (58 minutes each)

This thirteen-part series explores numerous facets of adult development through interviews with researchers, health care professionals, and older individuals. Some of the individual tape topics include: How the Body Changes; Learning, Memory and Speed of Processing; Intellect, Personality and Mental Health; Social Roles and Relationships in Old Age; Work, Retirement and Economic Status; and Dying, Death, and Bereavement.

Healing Your Spirit. (1992) Thinking Allowed Productions, (30 minutes)

This series of four interviews conducted by Jeffrey Mishlove concerns spiritual peace. In the first program, Wayne Muller suggests we can learn to let go of blaming others for our pain or even trying to understand why we were victims of misfortune. In the second program, Gay Gaer Luce proposes that the aging process need not occur in the manner prescribed by cultural stereotypes. In the third program, Rachel N. Remen discusses the loneliness and pain of illness as well as the opportunity for spiritual deepening that it affords. In the fourth program, Dale Borglum suggests that healing is facilitated when one does not deny the possibility of death. This series may be of special interest to those teaching a class of older students and adults.

Like Two Peas in a Pod. (1991) Filmmakers Library, (55 minutes)

This award-winning film from Quebec focuses on three sets of identical adult twins of various ages. It explores each set of twins and their combined and individual struggles for identity. Color.

To Live Until You Die. (1984) Time-Life Video, (57 minutes)

In this video, Elizabeth Kubler-Ross presents an interesting discussion of her stage theory of dying. She also offers her opinions on issues like hospice care, working with the terminally ill, and the need for spiritual assistance as death approaches.

Maturing and Aging, Discovering Psychology. Annenberg/CPB Project, (30 minutes)

This program is particularly effective in challenging society's myths about the aging process. For example, it shows that development is lifelong, as indicated by Erikson's theory. Similarly, it explains research demonstrating that when no physical illness is present, psychological deterioration is the exception rather than the rule. Problems such as depression, anxiety, and stress are no more common among the elderly than among other age groups. Training methods have been developed to enable the elderly to recover loss in inductive reasoning, spatial orientation, or attention. Differences in lifestyle, diet, and exercise, as well as in locus of control and level of optimism, influence response to the aging process. As noted, development of an education program that changes our cultural stereotypes about aging is only the first step in meeting the pressing needs of older adults. In addition, we need early intervention programs that provide therapy for those with problems, and a redesigned environment that makes our health care delivery system more accessible and accommodating to those with limitations.

Relationships in Old Age. (1993) Annenberg/CPB, (60 minutes each)

(8) *Family and Intergenerational Relationships,* (9) *Work, Retirement and Economic Status,* (10) *Illness and Disability,* (11) *Dying, Death, and Bereavement,* (12) *Societal and Political Aspects of Aging,* and (13) *The Future of Aging.* While in an introductory class, even a short series of these programs may be difficult to schedule, they are presented here because of special emphases an instructor may wish to cover.

Feature Films

Citizen Kane **(Orson Welles, Joseph Cotton, Buddy Swan)** Drama

Charles Foster Kane (Welles), a very wealthy and powerful man, dies after uttering his last word "Rosebud." Thompson, a reporter working on an obituary film, is told to find out what "Rosebud" means. Thompson's search leads him to five people in Kane's private life.

Magnolia **(Jason Robards, Jr., Julianne Moore, Tom Cruise)** Drama

Earl Partidge (Robards), a successful producer of television game shows, leaves his wife who is sick with cancer to marry a younger woman, Linda (Moore). After their marriage Earl discovers that he has cancer and his wife Linda takes care of him. Earl would like to reunite with his son but his son wants nothing to do with his father.

The Mirror Has Two Faces **(Barbra Streisand, Jeff Bridges)**

Two cerebral Columbia professors commit to a perfectly sensible but passionless paper marriage based on their intellectual common ground. The earth moves, however, when the wife redesigns her look in order to invoke the hots in her spouse and bolster her sagging self-esteem.

1. According to Sternberg's Triangular Theory of Love, which component was missing from their relationship?
2. Was the way they dealt with conflict predictive of success or failure in their relationship?
3. Why do you believe that Streisand's character was willing to enter into a relationship that would be void of passion? Explain your answer.

Pretty Woman (**Richard Gere, Julia Roberts, Ralph Bellamy**) Comedy
A self-involved corporate ladder climber Edward Lewis (Gere) makes the acquaintance of a hooker Vivian Ward (Roberts) and decides to put her on a $3000 retainer as his "date." Edward buys her a full wardrobe and cosmetic makeover. Some topics related to adult development are illuminated.

Specific Scene Analysis:
Steel Magnolias (**1989**) (**Julia Roberts and Sally Field**) Comedy-drama

- Central Concept: self-actualization
- Approximate Scene Location: 53 minutes, 30 seconds into the 118-minute film
- Approximate Scene Length: 7 minutes
- Opening Line: M'Lynn: "We have this new psychiatrist who comes in two days a week."
- Closing Line: Shelby: "I would rather have 30 minutes of wonderful than a lifetime of nothing special."

Key Concepts: self-actualization, peak experiences, Maslow's theory
Characters/Actors: M'Lynn (Sally Field), Shelby (Julia Roberts)
Scene Description: In a small town, M'Lynn is a member of a group of women who frequent the local beauty salon. The women have formed an active social support group for one another and enjoy, among other activities, gossiping about local people. They gather at the beauty salon, church, community activities, and one another's social gatherings. M'Lynn is very close to her daughter, Shelby, and she and her husband proudly give Shelby an elaborate wedding. M'Lynn is concerned about Shelby's health; she is diabetic and has been told by doctors that she should not have children. Shelby and her husband have decided to have a child. As the scene opens, Shelby is about to tell her mother she is pregnant.

Questions/Discussion:
1. Was Shelby's explanation to her mother an example of peak experience as described by Maslow in his theory of personality?
Maslow defines peak experiences as transient moments of self-actualization when the individual feels happiness and fulfillment. Shelby is trying to explain to her mother why she is willing to take the health risk against her doctor's advice so as to fulfill her deepest desire of creating a life. Shelby is satisfied with her decision and has reached a level of maturity that enables her to go beyond her mother's concerns to prioritize the importance of her personal goals.

2. Which behavior is Shelby exhibiting that leads to self-actualization as defined by Maslow?
Maslow notes that one of the behaviors that leads to self-actualization is listening to your own feelings in evaluating experiences rather than listening to the voice of tradition or authority or the majority. Shelby is listening to her feelings, not others', about the probable risks involved in pregnancy.

3. Which of the characteristics of self-actualizers is Shelby displaying?
The characteristic most exemplified by Shelby is a deep appreciation for the basic experiences of life.

The Truman Show (**Jim Carrey, Laura Linney, Ed Harris**) Comedy/Drama
Truman Burbank (Carrey) is not aware that his life is a popular 24-hour-a-day TV series. Every moment of his life is captured by concealed cameras. His friends and family are actors in reality. At age 30 he becomes suspicious and tries to leave but the show's producer devises ways to stop Truman's escape attempts. An impossible plot premise, however in the midst of this comes a variety of developmental issues.

12. Personality: Theory, Research & Assessment	Videos	Films
Humanistic Perspective	7	2
Psychoanalytic Perspective	15	2
Social Cognitive Perspective	3	1
Trait Perspective	6	2

* Humanistic Perspective

Being Abraham Maslow. (1972) Filmmakers Library, (30 minutes)
    This older film presents a sensitive interview with Maslow by Warren Bennis of the University of Cincinnati. Maslow discusses his humanistic theory and the factors that shaped his life and ideas. He also provides reasons for rejecting Freud's view of our need to repress instincts and rejects the behaviorists' position that our actions are simply responses to environmental stimuli. He describes his goal of trying to develop a more humanistic attitude in psychology.

Carl Rogers. (1969) Insight Media, (50 minutes)
    In this two-part series, Rogers compares his theory of personality with other theories. In Part I, he discusses motivation, perception, learning, and the self. In Part 2, he discusses his views on education.

Carl Rogers Interviews Phillip. (1981) Insight Media, (45 minutes)
    This video features a session in which Carl Rogers interviews a client,, Phillip, who wants to get in touch with his feelings and blames his lack of maturity for his anxieties.

The Humanistic Revolution: Pioneers in Perspective. Psychological Films, (32 minutes)
    This film begins with an interview with Maslow on self-actualization followed by interviews with other pioneers in this field: Gardner Murphy, Carl Rogers, Rollo May, Paul Tillich, Fritz Perls, Victor Frankl, and Alan Watts.

Maslow and Self-Actualization (Parts I and II). (1969) Psychological Films, (30 minutes each)
    Maslow discusses themes of honesty and awareness in Part I and of freedom and trust in Part II.

The Self. (1990) Annenberg/CPB, (28 minutes)
    Program 15 in the *Discovering Psychology* series. Host Philip Zimbardo leads viewers through an exploration of the inner mind. The film begins with William James's early concepts of the material, spiritual, and social mind. Other ideas examined include Freud's concepts of the id, ego, and superego and the ideas of Rogers, Bandura, and Maslow. Zimbardo then discusses perceived changes in communication, social status, and strategic self-presentation with Patricia Ryan of the Theatre Department of Stanford University. This program is helpful for reviewing the basic theories of some of the primary agents in personality theory and for demonstrating some practical applications of self and self-image as perceived through interpersonal communication.

The Self: Discovering Psychology Series. (1990) Annenberg/CPB, (28 minutes)
    This program is part of the *Discovering Psychology Series* hosted by Philip Zimbardo. The key premise of the video involves a discussion of the historical conception of the mind. Some of the theorists reviewed include: James (types of self); Freud (id, ego, superego); Rogers (humanistic perspective); and

Bandura (social-learning approach). The video also touches on the concept of cognitive factors in personality through an example demonstrating the possible role of self-image in thought.

Feature Films

Proof of Life (**Meg Ryan, Russell Crowe, David Morse**) Drama
Alice (Ryan), whose marriage is in trouble, finds herself falling for a new man as Peter's (Morse), her husband's, life is in danger. Terry (Crowe) is hired to rescue Peter from the radical Marxist faction gearing up for a revolution in Tecala. Alice and Terry work closely together to rescue her husband but at the same time Alice is having new feelings for Terry. A film that raises many issues related to personality and social relationships.

Schindler's List (**Liam Neeson, Ralph Fiennes**) Drama
Liam Neeson plays a shrewd German businessman who startles everyone--including himself--when he begins trying to save Jews during WWII.

1. How could internal and external locus of control affect the concentration camp prisoners?
2. Using Maslow's Hierarchy of Needs, what needs were met and lacking in the camp prisoners? Also, which needs were met if you were on Schindler's list? Which of your needs are satisfied and which are lacking?
3. What defense mechanisms did the Nazis use to justify their actions? Does Ralph Fiennes' character use any particular defense mechanism (support your view)?

* Psychoanalytic Perspective

Carl Jung. (1971) CRM/McGraw-Hill, (35 minutes)
This is an older film of historical significance. It presents an interview with Carl Jung about his ideas and theory of personality. The role of the conscious and unconscious are discussed, as well as his concepts of the opposites within our personality. The film also probes the influence of Freud on his ideas and theory and discusses the areas in which he differed from Freud.

Discussion with Dr. Carl Jung. (1968) Pennsylvania State University, (36 minutes)
In this film Jung talks about his theories of personality and discusses his differences with Freud and Freudian psychoanalysis.

Dr. Henry Murray (Part I). (1966) Pennsylvania State University, (50 minutes)
This is an introduction to the TAT in which Murray discusses Freud and Jung and their association techniques.

Freud: The Hidden Nature of Man. (1970) University of Illinois, (29 minutes)
This film depicts the life of Sigmund Freud from his youth to his later years. It shows his early work with patients in Vienna and presents his theories of the Oedipus complex, the role of the unconscious, and infantile sexuality.

Freud Under Analysis. (1987) WGBH/NOVA, (58 minutes)
This video, which was produced by WGHB for the *NOVA series*, provides a superior review of the psychodynamic theory of Sigmund Freud. In addition to describing the major tenants of Freud's

approach (e.g., the id, ego, super ego, psychosexual stages, and defense mechanisms), the video has actual footage of Freud in his famous office.

In Search of the Soul. (1982) University Film & Video, (30 minutes)

Part of the *Story of Carl Jung* series. This video provides a look at Jung's childhood and student years, his apprenticeship at Zurich's Burgholzli Mental Hospital, his relationship with Sigmund Freud, and the red book in which Jung recorded some of his most intimate and profound paintings and thoughts.

Personality: Early Childhood.   (1978) CRM/McGraw-Hill, (20 minutes)

From the *Developmental Psychology: Infancy to Adolescence* series. This interesting film could also be used when covering Chapter 11, which is about human development. This program describes four aspects of the preschool personality: dependency, identification, aggression, and anxiety. Dependency is discussed in terms of adult encouragement, identification is examined through psychoanalytic theory and social learning theory, and anxiety is studied through a segment showing a preschool girl who becomes lost.

Personality: Middle Childhood.   (1978) CRM/McGraw-Hill, (20 minutes)

From the *Developmental Psychology: Infancy to Adolescence* series. This program discusses peer-group interaction and the importance of social factors from ages 6 to 12. An upward spiral begins with group acceptance of the child, which enhances self-esteem, which promotes self-confidence and high achievement motivation. A downward spiral begins when children fail and come to believe the failure is due to lack of ability. They will begin to develop lower achievement motivation unless adult intervention allows them to see alternatives.

Personality: Adolescence.   (1978) CRM/McGraw-Hill, (21 minutes)

From the *Developmental Psychology: Infancy to Adolescence* series. Three teenagers are profiled as they face the challenges of finding their own identities. Issues of self-esteem, independence, and social and sexual identity are illustrated. Barbara Newman of Marymount Manhattan College discusses the roles of peer influence and conflict with authority in the development of concepts of independence and self-esteem, including Freud's concept of the superego.

The Psychology of Jung. (1991) Films for the Humanities and Sciences, (60 minutes each, #5 is 90 minutes)

This five-part series provides a thorough examination of the life and work of Carl Jung, including the sources and themes of Jungian psychology. Evocative dream recreations provide an additional avenue of access to Jung's work. Programs include (1) *Passions of the Soul,* (2) *Carl Gustav Jung: An Introduction,* (3) *Mind and Matter,* (4) *Symbols and Symbolism,* and (5) *Self-Knowledge.*

Reactions to Psychoanalytic Concepts. (1982) Karol Media, (30 minutes)

In this film Rollo May discusses his reactions to the ideas of Sigmund Freud, Otto Rank, Harry Stack Sullivan, Alfred Adler, Alan Watts.

Sigmund Freud. (1994) Insight Media, (50 minutes)

This video traces the life and work of Freud, from his childhood through medical school to the development of his psychoanalytic theory. It presents his early work on hypnosis with Jean Charcot and his collaboration with Joseph Breuer on the famous case of Anna O. The program explains how Freud discovered the value of dream analysis through self-analysis and how he eventually came to use free association in therapy. Other fundamental psychoanalytic concepts, including instinctual drives, the Oedipus complex, and transference, are covered.

The Story of Carl Gustav Jung. (2000) Films for the Humanities & Sciences, (93 minutes)
This three-part series from the BBC archives explores the life and work of Carl Jung. Part One is *In Search of the Soul* explores how Jung developed his pagan vision of reality, and how he attempted to reconcile science and religion. Part Two is *67,000 Dreams*, in which his search for the root of his conflict with Freud and his development of the concept of the collective unconscious are outlined. Part Three, *Mystery That Heals*, has a psychiatrist talking about how Jung's ideas are used in therapy.

The World Within. (1990) Insight Media, (60 minutes)
This video offers a tour-de-force of the philosophy and life of Carl Jung. Some of the more memorable moments include Jung's discussion of his ideas concerning dreams, archetypes, and memory.

Young Dr. Freud. (1980) Films for the Humanities and Sciences, (99 minutes)
This docudrama is an introduction to Freud's work and explores the influences that made Freud what he was: the effects of alienation, of medical studies which he neither enjoyed nor mastered, and of his discovery of a subject area in which he could make a unique contribution. Also discussed are the men who shaped his ideas: Breuer, Charcot, Janet, and Fliess as well as some of the famous cases, such as that of Anna O.

Feature Films

Freud (**Montgomery Clift**) Biographical Drama
Biography of the early days of Freud starring Montgomery Clift as Sigmund Freud. Some good background information here, and certainly much material for discussion and analysis.

Twins (**Danny DeVito, Arnold Schwarzenegger**) Comedy
Twin brothers, hardly identical, are separated at birth. One is raised on an island with the perfect environment, the other is left in New York to survive. When each discovers the other exists, they reunite and set off on a comic adventure in search of their mother.

1.   How much of an impact did the different environments play in the development of the "twins?" Explain your answer.
2.   Does the development of the "twins" follow Bandura's social learning theory? Why or why not?
3.   Do you think that twins reared in such different conditions would display some of the same traits, or would they be a product of their environment? Explain your answer.

* Social-Cognitive Perspective

Albert Bandura. (1988) Insight Media, (28 minutes)
In this interview with social learning theorist Albert Bandura, he compares his approach to the study of personality with other significant approaches. In Part I, he describes what influenced the development of his theories and research. He also discusses behavior modification, social learning, modeling, and aggression. In Part II, he discusses his classic Bobo doll experiment, as well as morality and moral disengagement and the effects of aggression and violence in the media.

Conscience of a Child. (1963) Indiana University, (30 minutes)
This film illustrates the development of personality, especially as it is affected by imitation and identification. A good portrayal of social learning theory.

Personality. (1971) CRM/McGraw-Hill, (29 minutes)
This case study from the *Psychology Today* series contrasts a college student's self-analysis with the opinions of his parents and friends. This film examines such personality evaluation methods as the self-report, multiple input, Holtzman inkblot, Thematic Apperception Test, and Allport's theory of maturity. It presents some good discussion topics.

* Trait Perspective

Discovering Who You Are: Theories of Personality. (1976) Insight Media, (34 minutes)
This video provides a nice general introduction to personality and the major personality theorists. The works of Freud, Adler, Erikson, Rogers, Pavlov, and Skinner are presented.

Outstanding Contributors to the Psychology of Personality Series. Pennsylvania State University, (50 minutes each)
Interviews with well-known personality theorists. Films appropriate for this chapter cover Gordon Allport and Raymond Cattell.

Personality. (1971) CRM/McGraw-Hill, (30 minutes)
An advertisement was run in a major newspaper asking for subjects for psychological testing. From the numerous replies, one individual was selected to be the subject of this film: the personality was described and psychologically assessed. The processes by which the description was derived include interviewing, outside descriptions, and self-description. The film also includes a discussion of standard psychological assessment tests—MMPI, Forer Sentence Completion, WAIS, TAT, and Holtzman Inkblot Test.

Personality. (1990) Insight Media, (30 minutes)
Psychoanalytic, humanistic, behavioral and social-learning approaches to personality are presented in this video. Also addressed are the "big five" factors of personality.

Reflections, Carl Rogers. (1976) American Association for Counseling and Development, (59 minutes)
This video shows Warren Bennis, President of the University of Cincinnati, interviewing Carl Rogers. Rogers' theories and how they were formed are discussed.

Theories of Personality. (1994) Insight Media, (20 minutes)
Interviewing clinical and research psychologists, this video examines five theories of personality, and is an excellent adjunct to any coverage of Personality. The subjects: psychoanalytic (Freud, Jung, Erikson, Adler), humanistic (Maslow, May, Rogers), social-learning (Pavlov, Thorndike, Bandura, Skinner), cognitive (Kelly), and trait (Allport, Cattell, Eysenck). It explores relative emphases and considers whether or not personality is stable over time.

Feature Films

The Wall Sci-Fi/Fantasy.
A rocker watching TV seeps into another world dominated by the sound of Pink Floyd. A fascinating portrayal of the traumas (sexual and otherwise) of childhood carried over into adulthood.

Specific Scene Analysis:
The Fisher King (1991) (**Robin Williams, Jeff Bridges, Mercedes Ruehl**) Drama

- Central Concept: personality
- Approximate Scene Location: 44 minutes into the 137-minute film
- Approximate Scene Length: 3 minutes
- Opening Line: Lydia: "My mother calls me once a week, like an ongoing nightmare."
- Closing Line: Lydia: "Really." (followed by laughter from Lydia and Anne)

Key Concepts: personality, social-learning theory, psychoanalytic theory, observational learning, modeling, rewards, punishments

Characters/Actors: Lydia (Amanda Plummer), Anne (Mercedes Ruehl)

Scene Description: Jack Lucas is a talk show host. During one of his broadcasts he makes an offhand remark to a caller named Edwin. In response to Jack's comments, Edwin goes on a shooting rampage at a popular bar, killing seven people. Three years later, Jack is still tortured by the incident. He has lost his radio show as a result of the incident and is employed in a video store. He lives with the owner, Anne, above the store. On a drunken spree, Jack wanders into a deserted part of the city, where he is set upon by two youths who soak him in gasoline and start to set him on fire. He is rescued by Perry and other homeless persons. Subsequently, Jack learns that Perry's wife was one of the patrons who was killed by Edwin in the bar. Jack wants to help Perry, who is now homeless and suffering from mental illness. Jack thinks he can turn his life around by helping Perry, to whom he feels indebted. Jack and Anne attempt to arrange a meeting between Perry and a young woman he fancies, Lydia. They arrange for Lydia to come to the video store, where she admires Anne's nails. Anne offers to do Lydia's nails for $40. Lydia comes to Anne's apartment to have her nails polished.

Questions/Discussion:

1.   How did Anne define personality? How is personality defined by social scientists?
Anne defines personality as a person becoming anything he or she wants to become. Personality is scientifically defined as a person's stable and enduring patterns of thoughts, emotions, attitudes, and behaviors.

2.   Can a person acquire any characteristic he or she wants, as suggested by Anne, to form his or her personality?
According to social-learning theory, individuals learn behavior patterns that form personality through rewards and punishments and through observational learning. This perspective also incorporates internal processes, referred to as person variables, in explaining personality. The current trend in this approach is to emphasize the active role of the individual in shaping his or her own personality. Thus, if a person wants to acquire a specific trait or any personality wanted, as suggested by Anne in the film, it is possible.

3.   How does social-learning theory's explanation for personality differ from the psychoanalytic theory's explanation?
Social-learning theory emphasizes environmental determinants of personality as contrasted with psychoanalytic theory's primary emphasis on internal constructs and conflicts.

13. **Stress, Coping, & Health**	Videos	Films
Alcoholism	6	3
Drugs & Substance Abuse	12	1
Stress	43	7

CNN® Today Video Vol. I: *Section 1: Mental Health and Stress*

Mental Health History (1:36)

Mental Health and Traumatic Events (2:24)

The Grieving Process (2:22)

CNN® Today Video Vol. I: *Section 5: Health*

Assisted Suicide (2:33)

Sleep Studies (2:17)

CNN® Today Video Vol. II: *Section 3: Health*

Miscarriage Depression (2:03)

Alzheimer's Boom (2:33)

Enjoying Anorexia (2:24)

CNN® Today Video Vol. II: *Section 4: Mental Health and Stress*

Honduras Mental Stress (1:54)

Prostitution (2:18)

Suicidal Tendencies (1:32)

CNN Today Video Vol. III: *Section 8: Stress, Coping and Health*

Elderly Depression (1:37)

* Alcoholism

The Addicted Brain. (1987) Films for the Humanities and Sciences, (26 minutes)
   This documentary takes viewers on a tour of the world's most prolific manufacturer and user of drugs– the human brain. The biochemistry of the brain is responsible for joggers' highs, for the compulsion of some people to seek thrills, for certain kinds of obsessive-compulsive behavior, even for the drive to achieve power and dominance. The program explores developments in the biochemistry of addiction and addictive behavior.

Addiction: The Family in Crisis. (1995) Films for the Humanities and Sciences, (28 minutes)
   This program tells the story of one man's addiction to alcohol. It explains the process of addiction in the brain and the role of the family in "enabling" the drinking behavior. The program follows the alcoholic through a treatment program as he learns the causes of his addiction and how to keep his alcoholism under control - abstinence.

Alcohol Addiction: Hereditary Factors, from *The Mind Teaching Modules*, 2nd Edition #29 (2000) Worth (11:40)

This video deals with alcoholism, addiction, biological evidence for hereditary traits and how science progresses through replication and the development of new technologies.

Alcohol and Human Psychology. (1985) Aims Media, (23 minutes)

Describes psychological aspects of alcohol consumption.

Alcoholism: Life Under the Influence. (1984) Ambrose Video, (57 minutes)

This Nova series film discusses the most common and least admitted disease. Alcoholism is related to 90 percent of all physical assaults, 50 percent of all homicides, and 25 percent of all suicides in America. In the film, an interdisciplinary panel of experts discuss the disease and its implications. In addition, therapists, researchers, and alcoholics are interviewed in order to gain a better understanding of the problem.

No More Shame: Addiction. (2000) Films for the Humanities & Sciences, (23 minutes)

This program explains current research into why people become addicted, what puts them at risk, and what the best treatments may be. The program profiles a recovering alcoholic.

Feature Films

28 Days (**Sandra Bullock**) Drama
1. Is Sandra Bullock's portrayal of an alcoholic believable? Why or why not? Give specific reasons for your answer.
2. What was the turning point that allowed Bullock's character to admit that she was an alcoholic and decide to remain sober?
3. Why do you believe that she was no longer able to stay with her boyfriend after completing her 28 days at the center? Do you believe that she would have been able to stay sober if she remained with the boyfriend? Why or why not?

Leaving Las Vegas (**Nicholas Cage, Elisabeth Shue**) Drama
Nicholas Cage goes to Las Vegas to drink himself to death in the pleasant company of a prostitute played by Elizabeth Shue.

When a Man Loves a Woman (**Andy Garcia, Meg Ryan**) Drama

* Drugs & Substance Abuse

The Addicted Brain. (1995) Films for the Humanities and Sciences, (26 minutes)

This documentary takes the viewer on a tour of the most prolific manufacturer and user of drugs—the human brain. This program explores the cutting edge of development in the biochemistry of addiction and addictive behaviors.

Addictions Caused by Mixing Medicine. FFS, (19 minutes)

An addictionologist and a clinical pharmacist explain how mixing medicines can lead to problems.

Addiction: The Mind Series. (1988) PBS, (60 minutes)

     This video provides an excellent introduction to the issue of drug addiction through a discussion of both physical and psychological dependency. Special attention is given to nicotine (tobacco), alcohol, and cocaine.

An Easy Pill to Swallow. (1980) CRM/McGraw-Hill, (28 minutes)

     As this film points out, anxiety has become a major medical problem and a very big business as indicated by the fact that well over one-quarter of the prescriptions filled in North America are for mood-altering drugs. This film explores this phenomenon in an examination of drug abuse issues illustrated by discussions with doctors and patients. It asks whether we have turned our common social and emotional problems into "diseases" and abandoned self-reliance or self-help in favor of drugs.

Animated Neuroscience and the Action of Nicotine, Cocaine, and Marijuana in the Brain. (2000) Films for the Humanities & Sciences, (24 minutes)

     Using 3-D animation, this program takes viewers on a journey deep into the brain to study the effects of the three substances. Actual neurons used in the animation create a realistic effect. Teacher's Guide is available.

Body Addicts. (1993) Filmmakers Library, (28 minutes)

     This award-winning video demonstrates that the stress of physical activity stimulates adrenalin, which causes the brain to release endorphins, the body's own morphinelike compound. Experiments are conducted to block the release of endorphins, causing athletes to become fatigued rather than euphoric. While the film does not ignore the positive aspects of exercise--increased concentration, feelings of well-being, and so on--it allows us to understand why some people are so driven that exercise becomes a harmful addiction.

Cigarettes: Who Profits? Who Dies? (2000) Films for the Humanities & Sciences, (49 minutes)

     This program features former cigarette models who are now dying of cigarette-related cancer. Looks at the tobacco companies and their new tactics for continuing addiction to nicotine.

Depressants and Their Addictive Effect on the Brain, from *The Mind Teaching Modules*, 2nd Edition #22, (2000) Worth (4:24)

     This video deals with states of consciousness, addiction, and alcohol-related abnormal behaviors.

Drugs: Uses and Abuses. (2000) Films for the Humanities & Sciences, 8-part series (20-35 minutes each)

     This eight-part series covers sedatives, narcotics, stimulants, hallucinogens, inhalants, THC, PCP, and steroids. The history, effects, and varieties of each drug are covered.

The Science of Addiction. (2000) Films for the Humanities & Sciences, (18 minutes)

     In this program, experts discuss the psychological, medical, and social aspects of chemical dependence in four teenagers. Includes computer animations and PET scan imaging as illustrations of the impact of drugs on brain chemistry.

Substance Misuse. (1995) Films for Humanities & Sciences, (30 minutes)

     This program discusses the most commonly misused substances including stimulants (amphetamines, caffeine, cocaine, nicotine, MDMA), depressants (alcohol, benzodiazapenes, barbiturates, solvents), hallucinogens (LSD, magic mushrooms), and opiates (heroin, morphine).

Treating Drug Addiction: A Behavioral Approach, from *The Mind Teaching Modules*, 2nd Edition #30 (2000) Worth, (4:24)

This video provides a salient example of how drug therapies incorporate the results of research on several levels of behavior.

Feature Films

Traffic **(Michael Douglas, Catherine Zeta-Jones, Benicio Del Torro)** Drama

* Stress

Biology, Brain, and Behavior: Seasonal Affective Disorder. (1992) Pennsylvania State University, (25 minutes)

This video concludes that for victims of seasonal affective disorder, an illness that grips them during the short days and long nights of winter, only half-hour doses of bright light during the darkness can alleviate their suffering. The program turns to the world of biology to gain insights into this strange illness, investigating such things as circadian rhythms and secretion of the hormone melatonin. You could also use this film in the Consciousness unit, if you cover circadian rhythms there.

Can't Slow Down. (1995) Films for the Humanities and Sciences, (28 minutes)

This program examines American's increasingly hurried lifestyle, working 160 hours a year more than they did in 1970. Because of the urge to acquire, the pressure to achieve or be fired, the need to achieve outside the home, and longer commutes to work, couples are too busy to talk to one another. The program asks how we are spending our time and how the constant rush is affecting our relationships and our health.

Coping with Stress. (2000) Films for the Humanities & Sciences, (23 minutes)

This program explains that stress is a biological response of an organism to its environment, and indispensable to survival. When stress becomes chronic it can lead to illness or even death.

Coping with Stress: Locus of Control and Predictability, from *The Brain Series Teaching Module*, 2nd Edition #22, Worth (2:49)

This video illustrates the importance of animal research as a means of promoting human well-being. This program can be used to lead into a lively discussion with students by having them identify stress-related factors in their lives and examines the elements they can control and predict which could reduce stress for them.

Emotions, Stress, and Health, from *The Brain Series Teaching Modules*, 2nd Edition, Worth (10:59)

This module goes into detail regarding the interaction of emotions, stress, and health. Students will be able to see and hear from patients dealing with life-threatening illness, and how they manage their emotions.

Getting a Handle on Stress. (1988) Films for the Humanities and Sciences, (26 minutes)

This film focuses on identifying stress factors, determining the effects of stress, and finding intervention strategies to handle stress. The film host, Jim Hartz, undergoes a battery of physical, psychological, and stress tests at Denver's Institute of Health Management and Stress Medicine to determine his susceptibility. The film explains what stress is and how it can be effectively managed by interviewing experts who demonstrate stress-reducing techniques to the viewer. This program is well produced and contains practical advice that all students will find interesting and useful.

Handling Stress: Today and Tomorrow. (2000) Films for the Humanities & Sciences, (30 minutes)
   This program helps students identify circumstances that can be stressful, and provides ways to mange the pressure. It also explains how to handle tension by channeling the energy to positive feelings and how individuals can accomplish goals rather than waste time worrying about failures.

Healing and the Mind, Volumes 1-5. (1993) Insight Media, (330 minutes total time)
   In this series, reporter Bill Moyer discusses numerous aspects of health psychology and behavioral medicine. Some of the highlights include: 1) a discussion and demonstration of biofeedback; 2) Eastern approaches to medicine (including meditation); and 3) changes in U.S. medical practices as a result of the incorporation of psychological issues in medicine.

Health, Mind, and Behavior: Discovering Psychology Series. (1990) Annenberg/CPB (30 minutes)
   This video from the *Discovering Psychology Series* presents an interesting review of how the new bio-psycho-social model (which emphasizes the role of psychological processes in medical problems) is replacing the traditional biomedical approach. Included among health psychology's concerns are the social and environmental factors that put us at risk for physical and psychological disorders. Hans Selye's general adaptation syndrome describes the body's typical reaction to stressful events. Richard Lazarus's concept of cognitive appraisal suggests that our perception and interpretation of an event are as crucial as the event itself in understanding the cause of stress. Health psychologists develop strategies for coping with stress and teaching behaviors that promote wellness. Their important contribution to the understanding and treatment of illness is reflected in Thomas Coates's recent work on the AIDS epidemic. Highlights also include a discussion of the utility of traditional Native American medical techniques in modern medicine and the use of biofeedback in stress management.

Health, Stress, and Coping. (1990) Insight Media (30 minutes)
   This video explores a variety of topics including stressors, physiological reactions to stress, and strategies for coping with stress.

Learning to Live with Stress: Program Minutes The Body for Health. (1979) Document Associates, (19 minutes)
   This film contains interviews with two authorities in the study of stress and its effects on the human brain and body: Dr. Hans Selye, who introduced stress into the medical vocabulary, and cardiologist Dr. Herman Benson of Harvard. Both describe stress as a force causing heart problems, hypertension, and a multitude of other known and unknown threats to health.

Male Stress Syndrome. (1987) Films for the Humanities and Sciences, (28 minutes)
   This film, presented by talk show host Phil Donahue, looks at the effects of stress on men. The etiology of the disease is discussed, along with the differences between male and female stress. Donahue is joined by Georgia Witkin-Laniol, who is an authority on stress in males, and sports figure Arthur Ashe. This presentation is an interesting examination of a gender-specific type of stress.

Managing Stress. (1989) CRM, (34 minutes)

This color film does an excellent job of describing the impact of stress in the work place. Students are introduced to numerous issues including: 1) sources of stress; 2) Type A and B personalities; and 3) stress reduction techniques (e.g., biofeedback, relaxation training).

Managing Stress. (2000) Films for the Humanities & Sciences, (19 minutes)

This brief program discusses the difference between negative and positive stress. The body can become stronger while under the influence of positive stress and weaker through the effects of negative stress. The film depicts the result of these two stresses on the individual and presents several ways to reduce their effects. Although an elementary introduction to the topic of stress, it should be considered when classroom time is limited.

The Mind-Body Connection. (1993) Ambrose Video, (58 minutes)

Bill Moyers talks with scientists and doctors who are on the frontier of mind-body research. Through careful studies to understand how our thoughts, emotions, and even our personalities can effect our physical health, they are gaining new insights into how the mind and body work together.

One Nation Under Stress. (1988) Films for the Humanities and Sciences, (52 minutes)

Stress is everywhere and it is being increasingly implicated in immune system dysfunction, cancer, hypertension, heart disease, ulcers, and a host of other illnesses. This program seeks to help viewers understand what causes stress, explain its consequences, and demonstrate ways in which stress can be turned into a positive force. Hosted by Merlin Olsen, the program emphasizes that stress is a different variable for everyone and shows different ways in which people are coping with it.

Post-traumatic Stress Disorder. Films for the Humanities and Sciences, (28 minutes)

Host Jamie Guth interviews a Vietnam vet and a woman who is an incest survivor, both of whom have PTSD. Treatment techniques are discussed.

Psychobiology of Stress. (1988) Insight Media, (10 minutes)

This video provides a nice, brief presentation of the body's stress response.

Relationships and Stress. (1980) Time-Life Video, (30 minutes)

This film from the *Coping with Serious Illness* series discusses ways of handling changing relationships between a terminally ill person and family, friends, and medical personnel. Several experts explain how a serious illness can change existing relationships and how a person can cope with the stress that inevitably follows a terminal diagnosis. This film is strongly recommended for its open portrayal of a serious topic.

Running Out of Time: Time Pressure, Overtime, and Overwork. (1994) Films for the Humanities and Sciences, (57 minutes)

This program explores the impact of time pressure and overwork on American society, how much activity people fit into their busy lives, how much responsibility they increasingly assume, and how little leisure time actually remains. The program contrasts expectations about saving time with the reality that there are more time-savers but less time to use them, and compares conditions in other countries and at other times.

Stress. (1995) Films for the Humanities and Sciences, (23 minutes)

This program explains that stress is a biological response of an organism to its environment and is necessary to survival. However, when stress becomes chronic it can lead to sickness and even death.

Stress: A Disease of Our Time. Time-Life, (35 minutes)

Different types of stress are demonstrated in experiments, and their implications are discussed.

Stress and Emotion. (1984) PBS Video, (58 minutes)

This film from *The Brain* series explains what is known about the chemical and physical changes that occur in the brain as a result of prolonged stress. The film focuses particularly on the stresses of pain and anxiety on the individual's behavior and contains a dramatization of the accidental frontal lobotomy of Phineas T. Gage in 1848. A segment on the stressful life of an air traffic controller is also included to further clarify the concept of stress and its effects on a person's well-being.

Stress and Hypertension. (1986) Encyclopedia Britannica Educational Corporation, (19 minutes)

This video's main focus is the effect of stress on blood pressure. Stress is defined as an unwanted by-product of an overly demanding lifestyle, the principal sources being one's family and work relationships. High stress can result in dangerously high blood pressure (hypertension), which can be life-threatening. The film discusses several methods of coping with stress that are beneficial to one's health, especially dieting, reducing salt intake, and meditating.

Stress, Health and You. (1980) Time-Life Video, (18 minutes)

From the *Stress, Health and You* series. The subject is the effect of stress on our physical and psychological health. Noted researcher Hans Selye explains how stress can be both beneficial and detrimental to our health. This film also has Richard Rahe, co-developer of the Life Change Scale, illustrating how changes in our life can affect our well-being. This is an important film that will allow your students to analyze the stress that affects their health.

Stress in the Later Years. (1983) Churchill Films, (24 minutes)

From the *Be Well* series. This film examines the special forms of stress that the elderly are likely to encounter, such as loss of a loved one, loneliness, retirement, failing health, and more. It explains the stress and health correlation and offers a variety of helpful suggestions for coping with life events and their consequences. Some examples are mental relaxation, physical exercise, hobbies, new relationships, and finding support groups. This should be of interest to viewers with elderly parents or grandparents.

Stress: Keeping Your Cool. (1994) Films for the Humanities and Sciences, (36 minutes)

This program looks at the impact that stress has on our society and describes positive and negative stress, stress control, and ways to simplify a hectic lifestyle. Experts identify what causes stress, why women are experiencing such high levels of stress in their lives, and how teenagers are particularly prone to stress. The program explores the relationship between stress levels and health and the growing recognition in medical circles that physical ailments are often linked to, if not caused by, mental and emotional stress and anxieties.

Stress Management: Coping With Stress. (1986) Insight Media, (30 minutes)

A variety of stress management techniques are presented in this video. They include cognitive reappraisal, imagery, deep breathing and other relaxation techniques.

Stress: The Body and the Mind. (1986) University of Illinois Film Center, (60 minutes)

Examines physiological manifestations of stress.

Women and Stress. (1987) Films for the Humanities and Sciences, (28 minutes)

Women are not shielded from stress and experience it just as men do, but they tend to conceal their stress reactions more than men. Host Phil Donahue is joined by Georgia Witkin-Laniol, author of the book *The Female Stress Syndrome*. Together with a panel of women, they discuss stress and offer suggestions for coping with overwhelming events. This film offers a variety of practical suggestions for handling stress and should be considered an adjunct to the *Male Stress Syndrome* film.

Wounded Healers. (1993) Ambrose Video, (58 minutes)

Bill Moyers visits Commonwealth, a retreat for people with cancer, and follows a group of people over the course of a week as they learn to navigate the life passage called cancer. The program addresses the afflictions that have wounded their minds and spirits.

Feature Films

Analyze This **(Robert DeNiro, Billy Crystal, Lisa Kudrow)** Comedy
Dr. Ben Sobel (Crystal) is a New York psychiatrist whose client is Mafia kingpin Paul Viti (DeNiro). Viti is having panic attacks brought on by stress and guilt over his father's assassination. Just as Sobel and Viti are having a breakthrough the FBI attempts to persuade Sobel that Viti is going to have him murdered. Comical situations, but still illustrates a variety of stress-related topics.

Specific Scene Analysis:
Bastard Out of Carolina **(1996) (Jennifer Jason Leigh)** Drama

- Central Concept: traumatic events/sexual abuse
- Approximate Scene Location: 63 minutes into the 101-minute film
- Approximate Scene Length: 4 minutes
- Opening Line: Glenn: "Come here, you" (as he pushes and pulls Bone up the steps)
- Closing Line: Glenn (to Anney): "Don't worry."

Key Concepts: child abuse, defense mechanisms, rationalization, repression
Characters/Actors: Anney, Bone's mother (Jennifer Jason Leigh), Bone, abused child (Jena Malone), Glenn, Bone's stepfather (Ron Eldard), Dee Dee, Bone's sister (Christina Ricci), Narrator (Laura Dern)
Scene Description: Anney is from a poor family in rural South Carolina and unmarried when she gives birth to Bone. A few years later, Anney marries and has another daughter by her husband, who is later killed in an automobile accident. She is a widow with two daughters when her brother introduces her to Glenn. Anney marries Glenn and becomes pregnant. On the night Anney gives birth to a stillborn infant, Glenn sexually assaults Bone. Anney's family is suspicious of Glenn and thinks something is wrong with him. Glenn moves Anney and the children away from her family. Glenn is unemployed and an embarrassment to his middle-class family. Anney works late at the café because Glenn's salary is not enough to support the family. Glenn increases his sexual and physical abuse of Bone. The Scene opens with Glenn pushing and pulling Bone up the stairs to the bathroom, where he beats her.

Questions/Discussion:

1. What possible impact will the sexual and physical abuse suffered by Bone have on her development?

The traumatic events portrayed in the film will more than likely have a lasting impact on Bone. People who have been assaulted in childhood are more likely to develop a diagnosable mental disorder.

2.   What characteristic of the abusive situation increases the likelihood that Bone will be traumatized by the events?
The instances of abuse by her stepfather are uncontrollable by Bone. The abuse is poignant not only for her lack of control, but also for the insensitivity of her mother to her predicament. Bone is in a situation in which she is helpless, vulnerable, and alone.

3.   According to Freud's conceptualization of defense mechanisms, which one does Bone appear to be using?
As persons often do, Bone appears to be using more than one defense mechanism. Bone rationalizes that the fault is hers, that she has done something wrong and thus deserves her treatment. Bone is repressing the painful feelings of her treatment by her stepfather and carrying the memories as her guilt and shame.

Falling Down (**Michael Douglas, Robert Duvall, Barbara Hershey**) Drama
William Foster (Douglas) after being laid off from his defense job, gets stuck in a major traffic jam. Abandoning his car, Foster begins walking and slowly unravels mentally. He finally snaps at a fast-food restaurant. It is up to Prendergas (Duvall), a cop on the eve of his retirement, to bring Foster and his arsenal of weapons to a halt.

Ferris Bueller's Day Off (**Matthew Broderick, Alan Ruck, Mia Sara**) Comedy
Teenaged Ferris Bueller (Broderick) is notorious for cutting classes and getting away with it. Just before graduation Ferris decides to make one last grand cut from classes with the principal on his trail. Ferris's sister joins in the fun and helps her sibling brother. Can be used to discuss stress, coping, and especially adolescent responses.

The Horse Whisperer (**Robert Redford, Kristin Scott Thomas**) Drama
The best-selling story features Robert Redford as the cowboy who knows just what to say to the unruly horse and its comely owner.
1.   Describe one stressful experience of this movie, relating your answer to the book and the movie.
2.   Describe Type A personality. Mention one character from the movie that had Type A personality. Support your view.
3.   How did the "horse whisperer" help the mother, daughter, and the horse cope with their stressful experience?

Men of Honor (**Cuba Gooding, Jr., Robert DeNiro**) Drama
Carl Brashear lets nothing stand in the way of his dreams. The son of a Kentucky sharecropper, Carl leaves home for what he expects would be a better life. He aspires to become a Navy Diver. "Never quit ... be the best," his father had told him, and Carl takes those words to heart.

1.   What was the symbolism of the radio? What letters were written on the radio, and what did they mean?
2.   How did "Cookie" cope with his obstacles in the movie? How did DeNiro's character cope with his obstacles throughout the movie?

3.   There are several styles of dealing with conflict. Which one (s) do you typically use and why?

Specific Scene Analysis:
Miss Evers' Boys **(1997) Alfre Woodard**

- Central Concept: health
- Approximate Scene Location: 88 minutes into the 118 minute film
- Approximate Scene Length: 4 minutes
- Opening Line: Miss Evers: "And the years went on and they had said that there would be treatment in six months but the six months became a year."
- Closing Line: Miss Evers: "Before you know it how time passes and ten years had passed and the men just had not had treatment, but we kept on studying them."

Key Concepts: health, ethics of psychological research
Characters/Actors: Nurse Eunice Evers (Alfre Woodard), Doctor Brodus (Joe Morton), Chairman of Senate Committee (E.G. Marshall)
Scene Description: In 1932, many people believed that the high mortality rate and incidence of disease among the Negro population, as African Americans were called in those years, was proof that they were "biologically inferior." The government, concerned that disease among rural Negro communities would spread to the white population, decided to implement special programs "for the Negro." The most notable is a study conducted in Macon County, Alabama, that became known as *The Tuskegee Study*. The study started in 1932 with private funding from a foundation in Chicago. The program treated the Negro population in Macon County as well as studied those with syphilis, known as "bad blood" among the participants. After the stock market crash in the 1930s, the foundation lost its assets and stopped funding the program. The program was renewed later by the Public Health Services of the U.S. government with only a research component. The empirical investigation was designed to compare previous findings from a study of white men with untreated syphilis in Norway, with data to be collected from untreated Negro men with syphilis in Macon County. The purpose was to see whether race was a factor in reactions to diseases. However, the earlier study financed by a private foundation had a treatment component, while the study designed by the Public Health Services did not. Negro professionals were promised that treatment was coming; the U.S. Department of Public Health wanted first to do a purely scientific study with blood samples containing no medication. To assure the validity of the study, it had to follow rigorous scientific guidelines. After the media exposed *The Tuskegee Study*, the U.S. Senate convened the Senate Subcommittee on Health in 1973 to obtain the truth about the study. The study had stated in 1932, and penicillin had become available for the treatment of syphilis in 1942, yet the participants had not received treatment. Miss Evers, a nurse connected with the program throughout its existence, is testifying before the committee.

Questions/Discussion:
1.   The American Psychological Association and the federal government have established ethical guidelines for conducting research studies with human participants. How did this study violate ethical guidelines?
The participants were not told the extent of their medical condition, only that they had "bad blood." The men were deceived and thought they were receiving medical treatment for their illness when in reality they were only being studied. The participants had not been told the risk involved in not receiving treatment in order for the study to have scientific validity as defined by the researchers.
2.   There is increasing value in empirical investigations of the interactions between biological responses of individuals to environmental factors and disease. These findings will be important for health issues as life expectancies increase. The researchers in this

study prioritized the needs of science over the needs of the individual for treatment. Discuss whether this is the appropriate position. What other instances of a similar scenario can the students recall?

The guidelines for psychological research should serve as the framework for the discussion.

3.   Currently there are investigations of the effectiveness of new drugs and medical techniques to improve the health of many infected persons and also to prevent health problems (e.g. AIDS) in developing countries, where the participants are often poor with limited health care and have little sophistication about research. Whose role is it to see that these participants are not exploited?

The guidelines for psychological research should serve as the framework for the discussion.

The Program **(James Caan, Halle Berry, Omar Epps)** Drama
Easter State University Coach Winters (Caan) is under considerable pressure to bring in a winning season since the college is not doing well. Coach Winters does just about anything to recruit some promising young players out of high school. He and the college overlook almost any obnoxious behavior of the boys.

Sleepers **(Kevin Bacon, Robert DeNiro, Dustin Hoffman)** Drama
Four childhood pals from Hell's Kitchen are sent to reform school after accidentally killing a man during a cruel prank. The boys are raped and beaten by several guards at the reform school. After the boys release, two of the boys, now grown men, kill one of the guards at a restaurant in cold blood. They stand trial and their other friends and Father Bobby (DeNiro) pledge to free their friends and get even with the guards.

Stepmom **(Julia Roberts, Susan Sarandon, Ed Harris)** Drama
Jackie (Sarandon) is a divorced, book editor, who is raising two children in Manhattan. Her ex-husband Luke (Harris) lives in the city with Isabel (Roberts), a woman half his age. Jackie learns that she has cancer and faces the horrors of chemotherapy. She realizes that Isabel must become a part of her life and her children's lives in order to prepare for what is to come.

Terms of Endearment **(Debra Winger, Shirley MacLaine, Jack Nicholson)** Drama
Widow Aurora Greenaway (MacLaine) and her daughter Emma (Winger) are at odds when Emma marries a wishy-washy college teacher Flap (Daniels). Emma and Flap have three children before Flap has an affair with a student. Aurora is pursued by next-door neighbor Garret Breedlove (Nicholson). The mood of the film changes when Emma discovers she has terminal cancer.

14. Psychological Disorders	Videos	Films
Abnormal Psychology – General	33	20
Anxiety & Relationships	13	11
Mood Disorders	8	1
Personality Disorders	2	3
Schizophrenia & Related Disorders	8	9

CNN® Today Video Vol. III: *Section 9: Psychological Disorders*

Schizophrenic Reality (4:33)

CNN® Today Video Vol. III: *Section 10: Treatment of Psychological Disorders*

Depression Treatment (1:55)

* Abnormal Behavior – General

Abnormal Behavior: A Mental Hospital. (1971) CRM-McGraw Hill, (28 minutes)

The purpose of this documentary is to describe the difference between popular myth and the reality of an actual mental hospital and its patients. Included are a series of patient-therapist sessions during which the therapists discuss symptoms, diagnosis, treatment, and general prognosis of their patients.

ADHD: What Can We Do? (1992) University Film & Video, (35 minutes)

This video focuses on ways to manage attention-deficit hyperactivity disorder (ADHD). It details parent training methods and demonstrates effective strategies for situations at home, at school, and in public places. It also provides examples of techniques teachers can use and describes medications for managing ADHD.

ADHD: What Do We Know? (1992) University Film & Video, (37 minutes)

This video outlines the history, etiology, and prevalence of attention-deficit hyperactivity disorder and discusses long-term outcomes for those affected. It documents the impact of this disorder on young people and their families, as well as the special problems presented at school.

Aggression, Violence, and the Brain, from *The Brain Teaching Modules*, 2nd Edition #24 (1998) Annenberg/CPB, (7:17)

The topic of aggression and violence is discussed.

Am I Being Unrealistic? (1978) Media Guild, (25 minutes)

Cerebral palsy is one of the most misunderstood disorders in our society. This film gives students excellent insight into a disorder that diminishes physical functions but in no way impairs intellectual abilities. It is a study of a young man with cerebral palsy and shows his struggle with and acceptance of the disorder. It also chronicles his academic experiences and progress through special education centers, mainstreamed schools, and university classes. This program was produced by the BBC for the British Open University.

tism: A Strange, Silent World. (1991) Filmmakers Library, (57 minutes)

This award-winning video takes a sensitive and comprehensive view of autism by focusing on three children of different ages, each with very different behavior patterns. It also introduces us to parents, teachers, and therapists who strive to maximize the potential of these children.

Behind Closed Doors. (1993) Filmmakers Library, (46 minutes)

This award-winning documentary portrays domestic violence from a very personal perspective. It focuses on two people, an abuser and, in a different case, a victim. Both discuss their difficult childhoods, their low self-esteem, their feelings of shame, and their determination to break the patterns of violence that have governed their lives.

Behind the Curtain: A Search for Solutions to Autism. (1993) Filmmakers Library, (28 minutes)

This brief but information-packed video explores the possible origins of autism and the therapies developed for treatment. It introduces us to a broad spectrum of professionals who have differing views on this disorder. The documentary shows four principal therapies for autistic children.

Borderline Syndrome: A Personality Disorder of Our Time. (1989) Filmmakers Library, (74 minutes)

Patients diagnosed with borderline personality disorder are a growing population in mental health facilities. Rare footage in this award-winning video shows in-depth conversations with patients and hospital staff members.

Bulimia.. (1987) Films for the Humanities and Sciences, (28 minutes)

If you cover the topic of eating disorders, which are becoming increasingly common in our society, you might want to use this video. It deals with the topic from the perspectives of both patients and therapists. Hosted by Phil Donahue, the program explores the pressure to be thin and how it may lead to the self-destructive eating disorder of bulimia. Low self-esteem, depression, and anger are both its causes and effects. This cycle is usually reversible through psychotherapy. Experts include Craig Johnson of the Psychosomatic-Psychiatric Center in Chicago and Susan Wooley of the Clinic for Eating Disorders in Cincinnati. Bulimic patients also discuss the illness from a first-person perspective.

Childhood's End. (1982) Filmmakers Library, (57 minutes)

This is a documentary portrait of three suicidal youngsters, one of whom succeeded in killing himself. The film does not try to simplify a complicated phenomenon and leaves a strong impression of the tragedy and waste of this irreversible action.

Dealing with Alzheimer's Disease. (1990) Terra Nova films, (21 minutes)

This video deals especially with communication techniques, both verbal and nonverbal, for Alzheimer's patients. It was produced with the Alzheimer's Treatment and Research Center, and Ramsey Foundation.

The Diagnosis and Treatment of Attention Deficit Disorder in Children. (1995) Films for the Humanities and Sciences, (27 minutes)

This program from *The Doctor Is In* shows how a diagnosis of Attention Deficit Disorder (ADD) is made and what treatments are working. The program follows children at home and school, both on and off medication. An innovative private school specializing in alternative education for children with ADD is profiled, and the program explains how best to structure school and home environments. Psychiatrists John Ratey and Ned Hallowell, experts in this field, provide background and perspective. A Dartmouth-Hitchcock Medical Center production.

Dyslexia: A Different Kind of Mind. (1997) Films for the Humanities and Sciences, (29 minutes)

(Finalist, AMA International Health & Medical Film Competition) Dyslexia, a learning disability that affects oral and written language, often masks the presence of a gifted mind. People with dyslexia learn differently. This program from *The Doctor Is In* explores that cognitive difference by examining how dyslexic students learn, and how new teaching techniques are helping them succeed in school. These teaching approaches are explored at the Washington Lab School – a pioneer in the implementation of innovative teaching methods. Thomas West, author of *In the Mind's Eye,* discusses our society's need for the visual talents possessed by many people with dyslexia. (May also be used with Ch. 6) A Dartmouth-Hitchcock Medical Center production.

Films for the Humanities & Sciences Catalog: Abnormal Psychology. (2000) Films for the Humanities & Sciences, (various times)

This reference is an entire 18-page catalog of films and videos in abnormal psychology. The catalog is available from the following address: P.O. Box 2053, Princeton, New Jersey, 08543-2053, or you may access their website at *http://www.films.com.*

John's Not Mad: Tourette Syndrome. (1993) Filmmakers Library, (28 minutes)

This powerful documentary portrays an adolescent who suffers from a severe case of Tourette's, which causes him to make involuntary sounds, including a constant stream of profanity. He feels that these words and sounds are forced out of him beyond his control. It should be noted to your classes that most people with Tourette's syndrome are not as severely affected as the patient in this video, who represents the extreme end of the spectrum.

Leonard's Travels. (1994) Filmmakers Library, (20 minutes)

Although brief, this video offers a human face to mental illness. Leonard is a seven-foot-tall bearded giant who has spent the first 20 years of his adult life in and out of mental institutions. We see a peer counseling session and hear the client's candid comments about an antiquated mental health system. It's worthwhile for any instructor wanting to present a brief case study of a sensitive person wanting to help others.

Living with Tourette's. (1992) Encyclopedia Britannica Educational Corporation, (25 minutes)

This program examines the personal, emotional, and communication difficulties involving a person with Tourette's syndrome. The short duration of this video may make it appropriate for classroom use, even though you may not emphasize Tourette's syndrome in classroom content.

Madness. (1992) Brook Productions, (58 minutes)

Produced for BBC television and KCET/ Los Angeles, this series has five parts: (1) *To Define True Madness*—explores past and present myths about mental illness and how our current-day perceptions and fears compare with earlier superstitions; (2) *Out of Sight*—looks at the history of institutionalized treatment for mental patients; (3) *Brain Waves*—discusses the history of medical discoveries about the structure and functioning of the brain; (4) *The Talking Cure*—looks at Sigmund Freud and some modern variations on his work; (5) *In Two Minds*—discusses schizophrenia, the most baffling of mental diseases.

The Mind of a Serial Killer. Films for the Humanities and Sciences, (60 minutes)

Originally produced for NOVA, this fascinating video goes behind the scenes to give the real story behind the special investigative unit of the FBI portrayed in the film *Silence of the Lambs.* Using a detailed psychological profile, this unit helps to catch a notorious serial killer who targeted prostitutes.

The Politics of Addiction. (1998) Films for the Humanities and Sciences, (57 minutes)

The story of how our society meets the challenge of translating what scientists, doctors, counselors, and recovering addicts have learned into rational public policy is complex and sometimes contradictory. This program looks at Arizona's recent struggle to find an alternative to current policies. Proposition 200 proposed a reassessment of the status of nonviolent drug addicts now serving time, and emphasized treatment over incarceration. The movement was supported by an alliance from across the political spectrum. On the Washington scene, members of Congress, doctors, and policy activists have joined in a movement with recovering people that is pushing for new public policy.

Psychopathology. (1990) Annenberg/CPB, (30 minutes)

This program from Zimbardo's *Discovering Psychology* series is excellent because it presents the text from a historical and a contemporary perspective. Symptoms and causes are the specific content areas covered. A cultural case study shows the impact of our society on the Native American population.

The Silent Epidemic: Alzheimer's Disease. (1982) Filmmakers Library, (25 minutes)

This film describes Alzheimer's disease and shows the problems raised by its ever-increasing incidence. The film notes that although the disease can be diagnosed, there is still no cure for its degenerative and ultimately fatal course. Also discussed is the issue of whether Alzheimer's patients should be cared for in their homes or in other facilities.

The Spiral Cage. (1991) University Film and Video, (28 minutes)

This video documents the life of Al Davison, a middle-aged English novelist born with spina bifida. Through interviews and illustrations, it captures the stigma and fear Al experienced as a taunted schoolboy. Al discusses the continuation of verbal and physical abuse into adulthood and his growing self-acceptance and determination to live a full life. This sensitive film should increase the acceptance level of your class.

Titticut Follies. (1971) Zipporah Films, (90 minutes)

This is a documentary about the lives of patients in a state mental hospital. It is a controversial film that presents a very stark portrayal of hospital conditions.

Twins: A Case Study. (1990) Filmmakers Library, (52 minutes)

This award-winning video provides a remarkable portrait of 45-year-old Yorkshire twins who dress alike, speak in unison, share everything, and are inseparable. Trusting no one but each other, they have fixated on one man as a love object. Among questions addressed is whether they are both psychotic or one is just imitating the other.

Understanding and Communicating with an Individual Who Is Experiencing Mania. (1990) (NurSeminars, Inc.) (61 minutes)

This video explains the effects of the manic portion of bipolar disorder. It describes the signs and symptoms of mania, alterations in brain function, medical management using lithium, and communication techniques to deal with the interpersonal dynamics that occur as a result of mania.

The Violent Mind. (1998) PBS Video, (60 minutes)

Program 9 in *The Mind* series. This research-oriented program deals with the anatomy and biochemistry of the brain and the changes that may cause violent behavior. Some conclusions suggest that even the violent acts of serial killers may have a biological or genetic origin. The program also discusses the ethical issues and legal complications of those conclusions. If you like to encourage spirited discussions with your class after media programs, this program provides much to discuss.

What is Normal? (1990) Insight Media, (30 minutes)
  This video discusses the distinctions between normal and abnormal behavior. Experts in the field explain at what point people need help, describe treatment strategies, and shows how professionals classify disorders using DSM—III-R. A discussion of the controversies surrounding classification is included.

The World of Abnormal Psychology, Volumes 1 – 13. (1992) Annenberg/CPB (60 minutes each)
  This highly acclaimed series from Annenberg covers a wide variety of topics including anxiety disorders, personality disorders, sexual disorders, mood disorders, schizophrenia, and disorders of childhood. Each of the disorders is vividly illustrated by the use of people actually diagnosed with the disorder. Causes, cures and prevention are all discussed.

The World of Abnormal Psychology #13-An Ounce of Prevention. Worth, (60 minutes)
  This program begins by noting that psychological disorders can emerge at any point in the lifespan and asks whether they can be prevented. The program explores several community-based projects that focus on specific life stages. Each project uses a unique combination of strategies that attempt to reduce the effects of known psychological, biological, and environmental risk factors that contribute to the development of psychological disorder.

Feature Films

Agnes of God **(1985)**
  Jane Fonda stars in a film depicting a confrontation between religion and psychiatry.

Alligator Shoes **(1982)**
  A family deals with the problems that arise when a mentally ill aunt moves in.

American Psycho **(Christian Bale, Willem Dafoe, Jared Leto)** Comedy
  Patrick Bateman (Bale), the son of a wealthy Wall Street financier, has a position with his father's firm. Although he presents himself as a successful and stylish person in reality he is a serial killer who murders without provocation. Donald Kimble (Dafoe) is a police detective who is on Bateman's trail.

A Bronx Tale **(Robert De Niro, Chazz Palminteri, Lillo Brancato)** Drama
  Calogero, (Capra) is witness to a murder committed by Sonny. Sonny befriends him and introduces the young man to the mob. Calogero idolizes Sonny but loves and respects his honest father Lorenzo Anello (DeNiro). It takes a major tragedy for the 17 year old boy to decide his true course in life.

Deep Red **(Michael Biehn, Joanna Pacula, Jack Andreozzi)** Drama / Science Fiction
  Gracie (Haun), a young person whose bloodstream is infected by a strange, extraterrestrial element known as "Deep Red," is possibly immortal. Thomas Newmeyer, a researcher, wants to drain all of the blood from her body but hero Joy Keys (Biehn) stops Newmeyer and in the process patches up his relationship with his wife.

The Deer Hunter **(1978)**
  Robert DeNiro stars in a powerful film which deals with the psychological consequences of war.

The Dream Team **(1989)**
  The character played by Michael Keaton leads three other psychiatric patients on an adventure through the streets of New York.

First Blood (Sylvester Stallone)
>   Post-traumatic stress disorder.

Frances (1982)
>   Jessica Lange portrays a woman who suffers as a result of her nonconformity.

Jackknife (1989)
>   A Robert DeNiro film which deals with post-traumatic stress disorder.

King of Hearts (1966)
>   Older than the rest, but a classic film starring Alan Bates in which mental patients take over a French town during World War I.

Misery (Kathy Bates)
>   1.   What DSM-IV diagnosis seems most appropriate for Annie?
>   2.   Annie is sexually attracted to Paul. How often is sexuality a feature of the diagnosis in Question 1?
>   3.   Is the portrayal of the disorder that Annie has believable? Why or why not?

Nuts (1987)
>   The concept of legal sanity is debated in a courtroom drama starring Barbara Streisand.

One Flew Over the Cuckoo's Nest (1975)
>   A classic film starring Jack Nicholson which raises the question of what is in the best interest of the institutionalized patient.

Rain Man (1988)
>   Dustin Hoffman plays an autistic adult. Also stars Tom Cruise.

Requiem for a Dream (Ellen Burstyn, Jared Leto, Jennifer Connelly) Drama
>   Four people are trapped by their addictions. Harry (Leto) and his best friend Tyron (Wayans) are heroin addicts living in Coney Island, NY. Harry's girlfriend Marion (Connelly) is also an addict who is trying to distance herself from her wealthy father. Harry's mother Sara becomes addicted to amphetamines when she goes to a doctor to loose weight for a game show she is appearing on.

Silence of the Lambs (Jodie Foster, Anthony Hopkins, Scott Glenn) Thriller
>   Clarice Starling (Foster) is a student with the FBI's training academy who is sent to interview Dr. Hannibal Lecter (Hopkins) who is behind bars for murder and cannibalism. Through the interview Clarice hopes to gain insight into a vicious murderer named Buffalo Bill. Lecter is willing to give her advice but it has a price. In exchange he wants to speak with Clarice about her past.

Seven
>   Narcissistic and/or Antisocial personality.

Silence of the Lambs (1991)
>   Frightening film starring Anthony Hopkins and Jodie Foster which focuses on various antisocial personalities and psychological profiles.

The Snake Pit **(1948)**
    Historically interesting portrayal of institutionalization and slow recovery with Olivia DeHavilland.

* Anxiety and Related Disorders

The Addicted Brain. (1987) Films for the Humanities and Sciences, (26 minutes)
    This documentary takes viewers on a tour of the world's most prolific manufacturer and user of drugs–the human brain. The biochemistry of the brain is responsible for joggers' highs, for the compulsion of some people to seek thrills, for certain kinds of obsessive-compulsive behavior, even for the drive to achieve power and dominance. The program explores developments in the biochemistry of addiction and addictive behavior.

Anxiety: The Endless Crisis. (1975) Indiana University, (59 minutes)
    This film explores a wide range of anxiety-producing situations—from the momentary flashes of anxiety that everyone experiences to extreme anxiety that can lead to death. Two mental health authorities discuss the difference between state anxiety and trait anxiety. The physiological as well as the mental reactions to anxiety are explained.

Case Study of Multiple Personality. (1973) CRM/McGraw-Hill, (30 minutes)
    This assemblage of scenes from the film *Three Faces of Eve*; it depicts multiple personality and includes actual interviews.

The Compulsive Mind. (1995) Films for the Humanities and Sciences, (28 minutes)
    This program focuses on a woman with obsessive-compulsive disorder (OCD) who has a fear of contamination. This woman describes her cleaning routine, which includes 200 hand washings a day. This video illustrates the role of medication and behavior modification in the treatment of OCD. This program observes the client as she works with her therapist.

Getting Anxious. (1984) Insight Media, (30 minutes)
    This video presents the common symptoms found in a variety of anxiety disorders including phobias, obsessive-compulsive disorders, and panic attacks. It also reviews the effectiveness of various therapies employed to treat anxiety disorders.

The Many Faces of Marsha. (1991) Insight Media (48 minutes)
    The fascinating case of Marsha is presented in this video from CBS's *48 Hours*. The video does a good job of presenting the mysteries of dissociative identity disorder as it explores many of Marsha's 200 personalities.

Mental Illness. (1990) Films for the Humanities and Sciences, (23 minutes)
    Everyone is exposed to some form of mental illness, observing, if not undergoing, what can range from a minor annoyance to a serious affliction. This program describes the most common mental illnesses: phobias, anxiety attacks, and nervous breakdowns, as well as schizophrenia, the most insidious and complex of mental afflictions. Although there is much we have yet to learn about them, mental illnesses are increasingly being deciphered by scientific and medical research.

Multiple Personalities. (1994) Insight Media, (30 minutes)
    This video does a good job of presenting dissociative identity disorder by depicting three individuals diagnosed with the disorder. It explores the roots of the disorder to be found in childhood abuse.

Multiple Personality, from *The Brain Teaching Modules*, 2nd Edition #23 (1998) Annenberg/CPB, (9:09)
    The program begins by defining dissociative identity disorders. DID starts in childhood, triggered by the need to flee psychologically from real physical or sexual abuse. DID elicits great interest among students due to the number of movies and TV epics that dramatize the disorder.

The Obsessive-Compulsive Neurosis: The Disordered Mind Series. (1963) PCR, (30 minutes)
    This is an excellent, older black and white film produced in 1963 and offers a superior introduction to obsessive-compulsive behavior. The information is presented along with a profile of an individual who has been severely impacted (e.g., lost his job) due to the effects the disorder.

Panic Attack: Causes and Treatments. (1991) Films for the Humanities and Sciences, (29 minutes)
    You are in a cold, clammy sweat, and pervaded by fear. These are two symptoms of a panic attack, a debilitating mental disorder that affects thousands of people worldwide. This program explores the possible causes of the condition and examines treatments, particularly cognitive therapy. Three patients talk about their lives lived under the pall of panic attacks. One patient, whose first occurrence was on a train trip, takes a short train journey as part of her liberating therapy. A BBC Production. Color.

Sybil. (1976) A made-for-TV-movie
A classic film in which Sally Field portrays a young woman with 17 personalities.

The Touching Tree. (1993) Awareness Films, (38 minutes)
    This short but sensitive drama portrays a young boy with obsessive-compulsive disorder: how he faces his fears and begins the slow process of recovery with professional help and the attention of an understanding teacher. You may want to show this if you have future teachers or counselors in your class.

Feature Films

As Good As It Gets **(Jack Nicholson, Helen Hunt)**
    1.   Is Nicholson's portrayal of a person with OCD accurate? Why or why not?
    2.   How much of an impact on his everyday life does the OCD have? Explain your answer.
    3.   If he were your client, how would you attempt to treat his problem?

Beaches (Bette Midler)
Histrionic personality

Copycat **(Sigourney Weaver)**
    Agoraphobia.

French Kiss **(Meg Ryan)**
    Aerophobia

High Anxiety **(Mel Brooks)**
    Fear of heights.

Me, Myself, and Irene **(Jim Carrey, Renee Zellwegger)** Comedy
    1.   What DSM-IV diagnosis does Jim Carrey's character have?
    2.   What events led up to Carrey's disorder?
    3.   Is this an accurate portrayal of the given disorder? Explain your answer.

Primal Fear (**Edward Norton**)
> Dissociative identity disorder.

Shattered Mind (**Heather Locklear**)
> Dissociative identity disorder.

The Three Faces of Eve (**Joanne Woodward, David Wayne, Lee Cobb**) Drama
A young Georgia housewife, Eve (Woodward), suffers from multiple personalities. Eve's husband (Wayne), seeks help from a psychiatrist (Cobb). With the use of hypnosis the doctor is able to find out that each of Eve's personalities are aware of the other's existence. After months of therapy, Eve is cured. Joanne Woodward stars as "Eve"—classic case study of Chris Sizemore which first brought dissociative identity (multiple personality) disorder to the public's attention.

Unstrung Heroes
> Obsessive-Compulsive

What About Bob? (**Richard Dreyfuss, Bill Murray**) Comedy
Bob (Murray) suffers from obsessive-compulsive disorder.

* Mood Disorders

Depression: A Study in Abnormal Behavior. (1973) CRM/McGraw-Hill, (26 minutes)
> In this film on abnormal behavior, the viewer follows a young housewife/teacher through the course of a depressive episode. The pattern of abnormal behavior becomes clear through watching her inability to function normally; her husband's attempts to ignore her erratic behavior; his growing awareness that she is disturbed; her suicide threat; his decision to get help; and the process of diagnosis, hospitalization, and treatment.

Depression: Beating the Blues. (1985) Filmmakers Library, (28 minutes)
> As this film indicates, unlike normal feelings of being blue which may last for hours or days, true clinical depression can last for weeks and months. The film investigates the latest research on the causes of depression and explores the variety of treatments available. Among the treatments highlighted are chemotherapy, electroconvulsive therapy, and psychotherapy.

Depression: Beyond the Darkness. (1991) Insight Media, (58 minutes)
> This video presents a nice discussion of the various psychological theories concerning the origins of depression (e.g., cognitive, biological). It also explores the nature of treatment through a review of intervention techniques including: cognitive therapy, drug treatments, and electroconvulsive therapy.

Mood Disorders: Hereditary Factors, from *The Mind Teaching Modules*, 2nd Edition, #32 (2000) Worth (6:11)
> This video discusses bipolar disorders. A ten year study involving 12,000 volunteers from an Amish community is discussed.

Mood Disorders: Mania and Depression, from *The Mind Teaching Modules*, 2nd Edition #31 (2000) Worth (7:34)
> This video presents vivid examples of the mood fluctuations of patients who suffer from periodic affective episodes.

Mysteries of the Mind. (1988) Films for the Humanities and Sciences, (58 minutes)

This program explores manic-depression, obsessive-compulsive disorder, alcoholism, and other mood disorders whose victims show a lack of control over their behavior and their life. It examines the neurochemical and genetic components of these disorders, as well as physiological, neurological, and biomedical research into the mysteries of the brain; the program also shows the nature of these mood disorders and the pain they cause patients and their families.

One Man's Madness. (1976) PCR, (31 minutes)

This is a remarkable documentary of a young writer experiencing bipolar disorder. Mood swings from ecstasy to severe depression (each lasting some months), feelings of elation, and psychological withdrawal are seen at home and in the hospital. Memorable footage of the hospital and treatment is included. The film also shows how people can detect early warning signs and begin to understand this cyclic disorder.

Suicide—It Doesn't Have to Happen. (1976) Phoenix/BFA Films And Video, Inc., (20 minutes)

This film presents a dramatization, based on case histories, about a high school teacher who helps a suicidal student.

Feature Films

Mr. Jones **(Richard Gere)**

Bi-polar disorder (mania then depression).

* Personality Disorders

Personality Disorders. (1981) Insight Media, (45 minutes)

This still-image video dramatizes antisocial, paranoid, schizoid, avoidant, narcissistic, passive-aggressive, histrionic, and compulsive personality disorders. The differences between personality disorders, neurosis, and psychoses are explained.

What Sex Am I? HBO

Takes a fascinating look at the minds and lives of transsexuals. It helps students to see the distinctions between transsexualism, transvestism, and homosexuality.

Feature Films

At Close Range **(1986)**

Sean Penn stars in a film which depicts the effects that a psychopathic father has on his sons.

Cape Fear **(Robert DeNiro)**

Antisocial personality.

Girl, Interrupted **(Winona Ryder, Angelina Jolie)** Drama

Winona Ryder gets diagnosed with borderline personality disorder and loses herself in an Oz-like netherworld, but more insane and dangerous.

1. What disorder does the girl who commits suicide suffer from?
2. Many of the girls in the institution suffer from low self-esteem. Choose one of the girls and explain how her esteem level has affected her life.
3. Choose one character and explain how you would work with this client if you were her therapist.

* Schizophrenia and Related Disorders

Abnormal Psychology: The Psychoses. (1980) Harper and Row, (23 minutes)
 This is an excellent film if you cover schizophrenia and treatment in your course, as it was shot on a schizophrenia ward in a mental institution. Interviews with schizophrenic and depressive patients are included. The film provides an excellent introduction to etiology, behavior, treatment, and prognoses.

Full of Sound and Fury: A Film About Schizophrenia. (1985) Filmmakers Library, (54 minutes)
 What is it like to suffer from schizophrenia? This film explores the lives of three individuals who have been profoundly affected by this elusive mental disorder. For the families of those suffering from schizophrenia, the experience is tragic, and the film presents an interview with the mother of a young man whose torment ultimately drove him to suicide.

I'm Still Here: The Truth About Schizophrenia. (1996) Insight Media, (67 minutes)
 This video debunks a number of myths about schizophrenia. Illustrates how patients afflicted with the illness are still able to live extraordinarily productive lives.

Leslie: A Portrait of Schizophrenia. (1990) Filmmakers Library, (57 minutes)
 This award-winning video is about a young black man suffering from paranoid schizophrenia. Hearing voices and hallucinating as a child, abandoned by his parents in his teens, 21-year-old Leslie obeyed voices telling him to jump from a fifth-floor apartment window. This is an especially interesting video in that Leslie himself conceived and developed the outline for the program, including drawing the artwork and graphics and composing the original music. This allows your students to see a contributing side to schizophrenia.

Psychotic Disorders. (1990) Coast Community College District Telecourses, (30 minutes)
 Part of the *Psychology - The Study of Human Behavior Series*, this video discusses schizophrenia, its treatment and possible causes.

Schizophrenia: Etiology, from *The Brain Teaching Modules*, 2nd Edition #27 (1998) Annenberg/CPB, (14:45)
 This video shows the impact of both organic and environmental factors on schizophrenia.

Schizophrenia: Symptoms, from *The Brain Teaching Modules*, 2nd Edition #26 (1998) Annenberg/CPB, (5:39)
 This video focuses on schizophrenia as a disease. This is a realistic view of what the disease involves and how disabling it can be.

Through Madness. (1993) Filmmakers Library, (30 minutes)
 Winner of numerous awards, this powerful documentary demystifies mental illnesses and humanizes those who suffer from them. We hear about psychological disorders from three people who describe them from the inside out: a schizophrenic, a paranoid schizophrenic, and a manic-depressive. Each of these individuals presents an engrossing tale of despair and hope and teaches us about the fragile boundary between sanity and insanity. Color.

Feature Films

A Beautiful Mind **(Russell Crowe, Jennifer Connelly, Ed Harris)** Drama
The film is based on the true story of prominent mathematician John Forbes Nash, Jr. who is played by Crowe. Nash is a brilliant professor with a bright future and a beautiful wife, Alicia (Connelly). Everything begins to fall apart as his paranoid schizophrenic activities are revealed. Nash learns to live with his illness and wins the Nobel Prize for his work. An award-winning film.

Benny and Joon **(1993)**
Johnny Depp and Mary Stuart Masterson (schizophrenic) star in a film in which two troubled young adults find love.

Beyond Reason **(1985)**
The tables turn as a psychologist begins to lose touch with reality. This film stars Telly Savalas.

Crumb **(1970s)** (119 minutes)
This movie documents a recent period in the life of 1970s counterculture cartoonist Robert Crumb. A legitimate case can be made for Robert Crumb having a schizoid personality disorder. There is also footage of Robert's two brothers, one of whom appears to have schizoptypal personality disorder; the other has been diagnosed and treated for schizophrenia. This documentary allows a direct comparison of these three related disorders in real lives. (Check video stores under "special interest" to find the video.)

Specific Scene Analysis:
The Fisher King **(1991) (Robin Williams and Jeff Bridges)** Drama

- Central Concept: schizophrenia
- Secondary Concept: hallucinations
- Approximate Scene Location: 92 minutes into the 137-minute film
- Approximate Scene Length: 5 minutes
- Opening Line: Jack: "I don't believe in little floating people. There is no magic."
- Closing Line: Perry: "The Red Knight."

Key Concept: hallucinations
Characters/Actors: Jack Lucas (Jeff Bridges), Perry (Robin Williams)
Scene Description: Jack Lucas is a talk show host. During one of his broadcasts he makes an offhand remark to a caller named Edwin. In response to Jack's comments, Edwin goes on a shooting rampage at a popular bar, killing seven people. Three years later, Jack is still tortured by the incident. He has lost his radio show as a result of the incident and is employed in a video store. He lives with the owner, Anne, above the store. On a drunken spree, Jack wanders into a deserted part of the city, where he is set upon by two youths who soak him in gasoline and start to set him on fire. He is rescued by Perry and other homeless persons. Subsequently, Jack learns that Perry's wife was one of the patrons who was killed by Edwin in the bar. Jack wants to help Perry, who is now homeless and suffering from mental illness. Jack thinks he can turn his life around by helping Perry, to whom he feels indebted. He finds Perry in the street and tries to convince him that some of his thoughts are not true.
Questions/Discussion:
      1.   Why does Perry think Jack should have seen the Red Knight?

Perry is unaware that he has been hallucinating. Persons experiencing hallucinations are suffering from thought disturbances and think their perceptions are as real to others as they are to them.

2.   What are hallucinations?
Hallucinations are defined as sensory experiences in the absence of relevant or adequate external stimulation.

3.   Why is Perry running and screaming from the Red Knight?
Hallucinations are often frightening and terrifying to the person experiencing them.

I Never Promised You a Rose Garden **(1977)**
    Story of a schizophrenic teenager starring Kathleen Quinlan.

K-PAX **(Kevin Spacey, Jeff Bridges, Mary McCormack)** Drama, Science Fiction
Prot (Spacey) claims that he is an alien from the Planet K-PAX. After an incident at New York's Grand Central Station, Prot is placed in a mental hospital under the care of Dr. Mark Powell (Bridges). Powell becomes involved with his patient and wonders if his patient's story of being from another planet is true. Prot claims that he must leave Earth and the pressure is on for a psychiatric breakthrough before the departure date.

12 Monkeys **(Brad Pitt)**
    Schizophrenia-disorganized.

Prince of Tides **(Nick Nolte, Barbra Streisand, Blythe Danner)** Drama
Tom Wingo (Nolte) is stuck in a hopeless marriage and feels trapped in his life and is suddenly awakened when his sister tries to kill herself. He goes to his sister's side in New York where he meets Susan Lowenstein (Streisand), his sister's psychiatrist. Susan and Tom begin a relationship as Tom learns to deal with the feelings he has for his mother and his wife.

15. **Psychotherapy**	Videos	Films
Biomedical Therapies	14	2
Behavior Therapies	14	4
Insight Therapies	7	1
Therapy Options	13	2

CNN® Today Video Vol. I: *Section 3: The Mind and Therapy*

>   Aversive Therapy (2:12)

>   Thought Control (3:46)

CNN® Today Video Vol. II: *Section 2: The Mind and Therapy*

>   Road Rage (2:02)

* Biomedical Therapies

Actualization Through Assertion. (1976) Research Press, (25 minutes)
>   This film illustrates the development of a more assertive style through the use of group
techniques.

Autistic Child: A Behavioral Approach. (1983) CRM, (26 minutes)
>   This film portrays what is known about autism, as well as what is unknown, and includes its
cause(s). It focuses on the use of behavior modification in teaching autistic children social and verbal
skills.

Back From Madness: The Struggle for Sanity. (2000) Films for the Humanities & Sciences, (53
minutes)
>   This program provides a view of the world of insanity that few ever see, following four
psychiatric patients for one to two years, from the time they arrive at Harvard's Massachusetts General
Hospital. Includes rare archival footage demonstrating how their conditions were treated in the past. An
HBO production.

Back Wards to the Back Streets: The Deinstitutionalization of Mental Patients. (1987) Insight Media,
(55 minutes)
>   This video follows the lives of some of the mental patients released from mental institutions as a
result of the Supreme Court ruling in 1975. Many of the patients who were supposed to receive
supportive care ended up on back streets around the country. Profiles of successful programs through
which patients are led back to normal lives are also presented.

The Biochemical Revolution: Modes of the Future. (1976) Document Associates, (19 minutes)
>   Mind control and manipulation are possible misuses of drugs discussed in this program. Statistics
indicate that 75 million prescriptions are filled yearly, a conservative estimate that does not count illegal
drug use. Our society is drug indulgent, if not drug dependent, and the use of drugs to control human
behavior is a distinct possibility that needs to be addressed. Although not strictly a therapy film, this
presentation does raise the issue of ethics and moral judgment in the area of psychopharmacology.

Health, Mind, and Behavior. (1990) Annenberg/CPB, (30 minutes)

Program 23 in the *Discovering Psychology* series. This presentation discusses the new biopsychosocial model of treating the mentally ill. Host Philip Zimbardo discusses the history of treatments for mental illness and presents a recent model that integrates the traditional biomedical and psychological approaches with a new social awareness that relationships with others can affect our health. This film clearly indicates that the field of psychotherapy is changing and adapting to meet the needs of people in the 21st century.

Madness and Medicine. (1977) CRM/McGraw-Hill. (49 minutes)

Parts 1 and 2. This film from the *ABC News Closeup* series examines the use of drugs, electroconvulsive shock, and psychosurgery to treat the mentally ill. It discusses the moral and ethical use of such treatments, in which the side effects are often more troublesome than the disorder itself. The therapeutic effectiveness of these treatments is discussed with patients, families, and medical experts. Mental institutions, which often admit patients more readily than they discharge them, are also examined. This is an excellent film because of its presentation of various biomedical therapies.

Mood Disorders: Medication and Talk Therapy, from *The Mind Series Teaching Modules*, 2nd Edition, #33, Worth, (6:08)

As this module opens, a female patient suffering from mania discusses her reaction to medication taken for her disorder. The narrator indicates that the medication is beginning to mute her long-term manic reaction. Paul Wender, University of Utah, then distinguishes between the physical and psychological factors responsible for depression. As he talks, we see a bipolar disorder patient named Doug Barton tracing his family genealogy. We learn that Doug's medication has relieved most of his pain. With the aid of an action graphic, the narrator describes where the chemical action of the medication has its effect—at the synapse. Antidepressant drugs seem to alleviate a deficiency of serotonin and norepinephrine in the synapses of depressed patients. Conversely, manic patients seem to have an excess of certain neurotransmitters. For them, lithium dampens or eliminates mania in 80% of the cases.

The Placebo Effect: Mind-Body Relation, from *The Mind Series Teaching Modules*, 2nd Edition #3 Worth, (6:14)

The opening shows an old, black and white movie of someone selling Vita-zone, a so-called cure-all. The narrator indicates that the imagination can work miracles through its faith in anything from voodoo to Vita-Zone. The power of belief, called the placebo effect, has made it more difficult for modern medical researchers to gauge the effectiveness of new drugs. At the same time, it offers the promise that in some cases, the Mind can heal the body. Jon Levine, University of California, San Francisco, is shown conducting an experiment designed to study the placebo effect. His male patients have had their wisdom teeth extracted and are administered saline solution in place of a real analgesic. A patient in the recovery area is approached by Levine, who is dressed in a white coat, stethoscope in pocket. Levine injects the contents of a syringe into the patient's I.V. hookup. As he does this, he says he is giving him a shot for the pain and that it will take about 20 minutes for it to take effect. Next we see another patient whose saline solution is administered by a computer. The two patients' reactions are dramatically different. The patient who thinks his analgesic was administered by a doctor reports feeling much less pain. The second patient reports that his pain has only gotten worse. The patients' responses indicate that mere belief in the healer and the healing agent can alleviate pain.

Schizophrenia: Pharmacological Treatment, from *The Brain Series Teaching Modules*, 2nd Edition #28 Worth, (6:06)

Two researchers are interviewed, and they talk about how drugs have changed their outlook for actually being able to help people with schizophrenia. Then, a patient named Augustine is interviewed about his reaction to drug treatment for his schizophrenia. Augustine has been on medication for approximately 4 weeks. He describes how he now looks to the future and the prospect of returning to work. He is much more realistic after 4 weeks of drug treatment.

Too Much Medicine? The Need for Clinical Evidence. (2000) Films for the Humanities & Sciences, (50 minutes)

This controversial program presents the need for well-designed trials and promotes a spirit of inquiry into the benefits, risks, and ultimate value of medical interventions.

Treating Depression: Electroconvulsive Therapy (ECT), from *The Mind Series Teaching Modules*, 2nd Edition #34 Worth, (5:41)

The module opens with a very depressed patient, Mary, being interviewed about her suicide attempts. She says she feels worthless, that she is the devil, that she smells and is generally disgusting. She describes how she tried to take her own life. Mark Fink, State University of New York, describes the desperation that led to Mary's suicide attempt. She was discovered by her husband after taking an overdose of aspirin. After recovering physically, she became a continuous risk, requiring around-the-clock surveillance. All she could think about was trying to kill herself. Fink indicates that it became necessary to treat her as rapidly and effectively as possible. Mary is then shown being wheeled into a treatment room under sedation. She is being prepared for ECT. Fink describes the preparation and treatment procedures in detail. Mary is seen as the treatment is administered. She displays a grand mal convulsion. When the treatment is over, Mary is seen rubbing her face. In the next scene, Mary looks dramatically different from her initial appearance. She is being interviewed by an offscreen therapist. She answers questions readily, smiling on occasion. She says she doesn't remember much about her depression but does remember some of the events leading up to her suicide attempt. Fink ends the module saying: "ECT has a very important place in the treatment of certain depressions. It's not a panacea. It doesn't help everyone. By and large, it is still probably the single most effective treatment we have for severe depression."

When Panic Strikes. (1992) Films for the Humanities and Sciences, (19 minutes)

This program begins with a description of how it feels to have a panic attack. The victim found no physician who correctly diagnosed the condition. When she was finally diagnosed as agoraphobic, treatment included medication and exposure therapy. Panic attack patients can lead nearly normal lives with the proper combination of medication and behavioral therapy. Color.

Feature Films

Girl, Interrupted (**Winona Ryder, Angelina Jolie, Clea Duvall**) Drama
19 year old Susanna (Ryder) commits herself to a mental hospital and spends 18 months exploring her troubled psyche and learning the ways of a mental hospital. She meets several other patients with troubled minds and decides that she must work harder with her psychiatrist in order to get well. Getting out of the hospital is not as easy as getting in as Susanna quickly discovers.

* Behavioral Therapies

Approaches to Therapy. (1990) Insight Media, (30 minutes)

This video contrasts psychodynamic, humanistic and cognitive-behavioral approaches to therapy by showing how the same client would be treated by each of the therapies.

Behavior Modification: Teaching Language to Psychotic Children (1969) Prentice-Hall, (42 minutes)

This film, based on the work of Ivor Lavaas at UCLA, demonstrates reinforcement and stimulus fading techniques used in teaching language skills to psychotic children. Frequent use of graphs and charts illustrates the effects of the treatment program and rates of improvement.

Behavior Therapy: An Introduction. (1978) Harper and Row, (23 minutes)

This video depicts how therapists use three models of learning theory to treat disturbed individuals. Principles of operant conditioning, classical conditioning, and observational learning are demonstrated in the form of contingency management, counterconditioning, and role playing to change problem behavior. The film contains interviews with and demonstrations by several behavioral therapists, such as Joseph Wolpe, Harry Kalish, and Virginia Roswell. The area of behavioral therapy is very well represented in this film, and the demonstrations are appropriate and clear.

Biofeedback: Medical Applications of Psycho-Physiologic Self-Regulation. (1987) Insight Media, (54 minutes)

This video introduces students to the use of biofeedback as a treatment for problems like: hypertension, anxiety, and post-traumatic stress. One interesting aspect of this video is that it reviews the treatment technique from the view of the therapist and patient.

Don't Panic: The Promise of Intensive Exposure Therapy. (2000) Films for the Humanities & Sciences, (17 minutes)

ABC News anchors Diane Sawyer and Sam Donaldson and correspondent Jay Schadler document a young woman's struggle to overcome the feelings of fear that have reduced her world to the narrow confines of her own home. Through intensive exposure therapy, an alternative to medication and psychotherapy for treating panic attacks with agoraphobia, many patients return to normal living within mere days.

Harry: Behavioral Treatment for Self-Abuse. (1980) Research Press, (38 minutes)

The patient shown in this film, Harry, has spent most of his life in institutions, wearing various types of physical restraints. Although he is only mildly retarded, the severity of his self-abuse defeated all attempts to educate him, and past treatment programs had failed to eliminate his unusual behavior and need for physical restraints. The film shows the inauguration of a behavioral treatment program and the use of fading, extinction, time-out, and positive reinforcement in the treatment of Harry.

Locking Up Women. (1993) Films for the Humanities and Sciences, (48 minutes)

This video provides a look inside Britain's Holloway prison, at the institution itself, and at questions about criminality in women.

Madness and Medicine. (1977) CRM/McGraw-Hill, (45 minutes)

This film explores the mental institution and its patients, the quality of life in the institution, and the patients' feelings about the treatment they receive. The use of chemotherapy, psychoactive drugs, electroshock therapy, and psychosurgery are discussed by both doctors and patients.

Peer-Conducted Behavior Modification. (1978) Research Press, (24 minutes)

Jeff assaults and provokes his classmates. A program is developed to change Jeff's behavior and that of his peers. The role of peers in shaping and reinforcing deviant behavior and the value of peers as positive behavior modifiers are demonstrated.

The Power of Positive Reinforcement. (1978) CRM, (28 minutes)

Behavior modification, with its emphasis on positive reinforcement, is recognized as a powerful tool for managing human performance. This film documents the systematic on-site application of this principle at a 3M plant in California where the result was five million dollars saved through increased worker efficiency. Additionally, the film examines its use in the less traditional settings of Valley Fair Amusement Park in Minnesota, on the defensive line of the Minnesota Vikings, and in the streets of Detroit with the City Sanitation Department.

Stroke Seeking Behavior: Therapeutic Traps and Pitfalls. (1976) APGA, (30 minutes)

Excerpts from group therapy sessions are used to illustrate common stroke-seeking behavior by clients which serves to divert efforts from therapeutic progress. Ways in which counselors are manipulated are illustrated as well as suggestions for ways in which to get clients to change.

Token Economy: Behaviorism Applied. (1972) CRM, (23 minutes)

The film begins as B. F. Skinner cites the five classic victims of behavioral mistreatment: old people, orphaned children, prisoners, psychotics, and retardates. He goes on to explain the use of tokens in a program of reinforcement therapy. Finally, to demonstrate Skinner's theories, the film takes the viewer to a facility of the Illinois Department of Mental Health where the program director explains how token economies are practiced.

Treating Drug Addiction: A Behavioral Approach, from *The Mind Series Teaching Modules*, 2nd Edition # 30 Worth, (5:55)

This module opens with a street scene in a run-down section of Philadelphia. Jim Sloan, who was a drug addict for 17 years, describes how plentiful the drugs are. For a former addict, he says the triggers for drug use are numerous: money in you pocket, the smell or sight of cigarettes, people who stop and ask you if you want drugs. Jim discusses his progress with Anna Rose Childress, VA Medical Center, Philadelphia. She asks him questions about the triggers he encounters and how he is able to deal with them. The narrator notes that for 8 months, Jim has been involved in a program designed to desensitize him to the triggers of drug use. Jim is being shown a movie of two individuals smoking illegal drugs. He is asked to rate how tempted he feels by what he sees, on a scale from 1 to 10. His response is good: He is unlearning some of his own triggers. Jim is then asked to prepare cocaine for smoking. He goes through all the preparations up to the point of lighting the match. He repeats this procedure while his physiological reactions are measured. His temperature remains normal. It has taken him 20 sessions to achieve this level of desensitization. Jim says, "You eventually can handle these things without the craving because you know you are not going to complete the act."

Understanding the Brain Through Epilepsy, from *The Brain Teaching Modules*, 2nd Edition #30 (1998) Annenberg/CPB

This video illustrates that drug therapy may be amelioration, and surgery as possible complete cure.

Feature Films

A Clockwork Orange (**Malcolm McDowell, Patrick Magee, Michael Bates**) Science Fiction
Alex (McDowell) and his "Droogs" terrorize writer, Mr. Alexander (Magee) and rape and kill his wife. Alex is later jailed for bludgeoning the Cat Lady to death and submits to Ludovico behavior modification

technique to gain his freedom. He is conditioned to abhor violence and even Beethoven. Returned to the world defenseless, Alex is victim to his prior victims. This was a controversial film when produced, but illustrates some extremes to which behavioral conditioning may be taken.

Fight Club (**Brad Pitt, Edward Norton, Helena Bonham Carter**) Drama
Jack (Norton) is a depressed young man who is caught up in the world of big business. He doesn't like his work and receives no sense of reward from it. Attempting to drown his sorrows he tries crashing support groups for patients with terminal diseases. On a business flight he meets Tyler Durden (Pitt) who introduces him to fighting. More men join the Fight Club which quickly becomes an underground sensation but a closely guarded secret. Some could develop the idea of sublimation as a form of therapy.

Good Will Hunting (**Matt Damon, Robin Williams**) Drama
1.   Identify the different kinds of therapies and techniques used to try to treat Will.
2.   What do you believe caused Robin Williams' character to continue working with Will?
3.   If you had a client that presented himself like Will, what approach would you use to try to treat him? Explain your answer.

Specific Scene Analysis:
One Flew Over the Cuckoo's Nest (**1975**) **Jack Nicholson** Drama

- Central Concept: electroshock therapy
- Approximate Scene Location: 57 minutes, 18 seconds into the 129-minute film
- Approximate Scene Length: 2 minutes
- Opening Line: Nurse Pilbar: "Mr. McMurphy, please follow me."
- Closing Line: McMurphy: "Um-m."

Key Concepts: electroshock therapy, depression, antidepressant drugs, neurotransmitters, norepinephrine, serotonin
Characters/Actors: R.P. McMurphy (Jack Nicholson), Chief Bromden (Will Sampson), Nurse Pilbar (Mimi Sarkisian)
Scene Description: The film is about daily life in a mental institution. R. P. McMurphy was arrested for statutory rape and sent to a work farm. While at the work farm he has frequent fights and is sent to the mental institution for evaluation. The authorities at the work farm think McMurphy is faking his behavior to get out of work detail. At the hospital, he is assigned to a ward administered by Nurse Ratched. The patients on the ward are heavily medicated and following a strict daily routine organized by Nurse Ratched. Some of the inmates participate in group therapy sessions. Nurse Ratched is in charge of the group therapy sessions and is a very controlling therapist. McMurphy begins to needle her and disturb her routine for the ward by getting the patients involved in physical activities, e.g., basketball. He also engages the inmates in forbidden activities (e.g., gambling) and into demanding changes in the routine (e.g., watching the World Series baseball game instead of listening to light classical music). In one of the group sessions he gets some of the inmates so aroused that they are demanding their cigarettes and other privileges denied or controlled by Nurse Ratched. After one of the group sessions, a fight breaks out and McMurphy is sent along with Chief Bromden to receive electroshock therapy.

Questions/Discussion:
1.   What is the history of the use of electroshock therapy?

In the period between 1940 and 1960, electroshock therapy was frequently administered to patients because of the limitations in treatment alternatives and the prevailing belief that the major cause of mental illness was biological. The use of the procedure decreased with the coming of psychoanalytic therapy and anti-psychotic and antidepressant drugs.

2.   When do therapists recommend electroshock?

Therapists sometimes recommend electroshock therapy when drug therapy has not been effective for patients with depression. Contemporary therapists are recommending electroshock therapy as a treatment alternative.

3.   How has electroshock therapy changed, and how does it work for the benefit of the patient?

Electroshock therapy has changed since the time period in the film. The procedure is gentler, with only a mild electrical current being administered. A muscle relaxant is also injected to prevent the convulsive muscle spasms seen in the film. It is not clear why electroshock therapy is effective with some patients. It is postulated that insufficient levels of the neurotransmitters norepinephrine and serotonin are a factor in depression. Electrical current in the nondominant side of the brain evokes seizures that cause massive release of these neurotransmitters. Generally, antidepressant drugs work by blocking the reuptake of these neurotransmitters, thus enhancing their effects. There are three classes of medications available for the treatment of depression: (a) tricyclates, e.g., Elavil; (b) selective serotonin reuptake inhibitors, e.g., Prozac; and (c) monoamine oxidase inhibitors, e.g., Nardil.

* Insight Therapies

Anxiety: Cognitive Therapy with Dr. Aaron T. Beck. (1989) Psychological and Educational Films, (43 minutes)

In this program, Beck discusses his theory of cognitive therapy and presents an assessment outline for the treatment of anxiety. He demonstrates his theory and techniques in a session with a young man whose problems of procrastination are seated in his fears of how other people view him. Beck is a professor of psychiatry, director of the Center for Cognitive Therapy at the Pennsylvania School of Medicine, and the author of several books. This film is an excellent presentation of cognitive therapy and is well produced.

Carl Rogers Conducts an Encounter Group. (1975) Extension Media Center, (70 minutes)

Carl Rogers discusses factors that he believes are important in successful facilitation of a group. Highlights include Rogers in a group setting interacting with individual members.

Existential-Humanistic Therapy. (1998) Insight Media, (100 minutes)

Although a bit long for the typical class, this video presents the basic philosophy behind existential-humanistic therapy. It illustrates the approach through the use of a counseling session.

The Human Potential Movement: Journey to the Center of the Self. (1975) Pennsylvania State University, (18 minutes)

This film focuses on the human potential movement and Dr. William Shutz, founder of the Esalen Institute. There are scenes of encounter group sessions emphasizing techniques for releasing aggression.

Rational Emotive Therapy. (1982) Institute for Rational Emotive Therapy, (29 minutes)
This film overviews "rational emotive therapy" originated by Dr. Albert Ellis in 1955. Interviews Ellis who explains why he rejected traditional therapies and discusses the evolution of RET.

The Talking Cure: A Portrait of Psychoanalysis. (1988) Insight Media, (56 minutes)
A rare recording of Freud opens this program. Experienced therapists explain and describe what happens in traditional psychoanalysis and how patients commonly respond to the process.

What is Gestalt? (1969) Pennsylvania State University, (24 minutes)
This film features a discussion by Fritz Perls and includes an illustration of awareness training.

* Therapy Options, When to Seek Therapy, and General Topics on Psychotherapy

Can You Stop People from Drinking? (1992) Nova Videos, (57 minutes)
This video looks at how Russia and the United States are attacking the problem of alcohol abuse. It covers prohibition, hypnotism, imprisonment, surveillance, deception, aversion therapy, and group therapy such as Alcoholics Anonymous.

Coping with Phobias. (1993) Films for the Humanities and Sciences, (28 minutes)
This program explains why people have phobias and how phobias can usually be overcome. It focuses on fear of flying. The program also visits a speech class to explain the dynamics of this phobia and provide specific suggestions on overcoming the fears involved.

Depression and Manic Depression. (1996) Films for the Humanities and Sciences, (28 minutes)
Winner of many awards. Depression affects over 17 million Americans each year, and it's been estimated that only one-third of this group gets any treatment, largely because of stigma and fear. The lack of treatment results in a high number of suicides, making this illness as fatal as any other illness and public epidemic. This program from *The Doctor Is In* explains the disease through the experiences of several people, including *60 Minutes* host Mike Wallace; Kay Redfield Jamison, psychiatrist and author of a book on her life with manic-depressive illness; artist Lama Dejani; and State Dept. official Robert Boorstin. The program also provides an overview of the medications and therapy currently in use. A Dartmouth-Hitchock Medical Center production.

Escape from Madness. (1978) Films Incorporated, (52 minutes)
This film examines progress in treatment of the psychotic individual. It discusses new drugs that eliminate problem behaviors and tendencies toward developing psychoses. The film also presents a brief history of treatment and introduces some experimental programs, such as group communities and home care. This approach is especially interesting because of its blend of social and medical treatments.

Having Your Cake: Goodbye to Bulimia. (1997) Films for the Humanities and Sciences, (23 minutes)
"How do you stay so thin?" In this powerful documentary, four women openly share the details of their personal journeys of self discovery as they battled bulimia. Through intimate interviews, each describes how she first became aware of her self-destructive behavior and how she disarmed it, freeing herself to move forward towards physical and emotional health. The program is currently being used by teachers, therapists, and health professionals as both an early-warning device and an inspirational guide to recovery. Color.

Obsessive-Compulsive Disorder: An Alternative Treatment. (1996) Films for the Humanities and Sciences, (15 minutes)

The startling fact is that 1 in every 40 Americans is affected by OCD to varying degrees. A recently developed program, however, is bringing hope to millions of sufferers. Dr. Jeffrey Schwartz believes that many patients, by gaining self-awareness, can cure themselves. Two patients in this program believe it too, and testify that Schwartz's three-step treatment has helped them to successfully control their obsessive-compulsive behaviors. The patients include a man who compulsively saves newspapers, and a women who counts and recounts the items in her refrigerator. An ABC News 20/20 production.

Psychotherapy: Discovering Psychology Series. (1990) Annenberg/CPB, (30 minutes)

In this video from the *Discovering Psychology* series, Dr. Philip Zimbardo discusses the relationship between theory, research, and practice in the treatment of mental disorders. Perhaps the most outstanding feature of this video is its review of the numerous forces (e.g., history and culture) which influence our attitude and treatment of individuals with mental disorders. This program is an excellent preview to the major forms of psychotherapy. It divides psychotherapy into the psychological and the biomedical. Psychosurgery is perhaps the most radical biomedical treatment, with many considering the cure to be worse than the illness. The prefrontal lobotomy can impair memory, emotional expression, and the ability to plan ahead. ECT is also controversial but continues to be used in the treatment of depression. Drug therapy became popular back in the 1950s, with the use of tranquilizers and antipsychotic drugs. Not only do drugs alleviate suffering, they make psychotherapy possible. The program divides the psychotherapies into four categories: psychoanalysis, behavior therapy, cognitive therapy, and humanistic therapy. It provides useful descriptions of the specific treatments, their history, and the kinds of problems that they are most useful for.

Psychotherapy. (1979) CRM/McGraw-Hill, (26 minutes)

This video provides an opportunity for the viewer to consider reasons for psychotherapy and to learn about successful elements in the therapy experience. Three common elements of successful treatment are discussed: providing a safe relationship, working through feelings, and developing new cognitive and behavioral patterns. The film focuses on these themes and, through a series of three vignettes, describes how they are dealt with in therapeutic sessions. Color.

Reality Therapy. (1998) Insight Media, (100 minutes)

Although a bit long for the typical class, this video does a good job of presenting Glasser's reality.

The Scandal of Psychiatric Hospitals: When the Goal Is Insurance Reimbursement. (1988) Films for the Humanities and Sciences, (52 minutes)

This video presents the idea that while mentally ill patients are being discharged into the streets, healthy Americans are being locked up in mental hospitals so that hospitals can draw on their health insurance.

Therapy: What Do You Want Me To Say? (1974) CRM/McGraw-Hill, (15 minutes)

This film presents a young woman who has been pressured into seeing a psychologist, and her immediate reactions are hostility and fear. As the film shows, for most young people the stigmas attached to therapy are many. The film attempts to create a climate in which viewers can achieve insights about therapy and the role it can play in troubled lives.

Thinking Allowed: Putting Psychotherapy on the Couch. (1988) Thinking Allowed Productions, (30 minutes)

Bernie Zilbergeld expresses his feelings that to achieve personal transformation through psychotherapy one must be motivated to work hard and make difficult and disturbing changes in one's life. He believes that temporary emotional relief does not generally lead to lasting changes.

The World of Abnormal Psychology, #12—Psychotherapies. PBS, (60 minutes)

This program describes the wide range of approaches that therapists use in treating psychological disorders. Therapists demonstrate psychodynamic, cognitive-behavioral, and humanistic strategies in both individual and group therapy sessions.

Feature Films

***Don't Say a Word* (Michael Douglas, Sean Bean, Brittany Murphy)** Thriller

Therapist Dr. Nathan Conrad (Douglas) learns that his daughter has been kidnapped by Koster (Bean). Koster is in need of a critical piece of information known only to Elisabeth Burrows, one of his patients. Conrad must unlock the secret stored in Elisabeth's mind, while a detective is close to discovering Conrad's problem. Useful illustrations of personality, disorders, and treatment.

Specific Scene Analysis:
Patton (1970) George C. Scott War drama

Central Concept: Criteria for therapy
Approximate Scene Location: 134 minutes, 3 seconds into the 171-minute film
Approximate Scene Length: 2 minutes, 30 seconds
Opening Line: Patton: "Oh God, thou are my God. Early I seek thee."
Closing Line: Patton: "Dismissed."

Key Concepts: psychodynamic therapy, biological therapeutic approach, therapy
Character/Actor: General Patton (George C. Scott)
Scene Description: The setting for the film is World War II in Europe. Patton has been assigned commander of an American army unit attached to the Allied Forces as the push is made across Europe, fighting the Nazi army. He is known as a tough general with the nickname of "Blood and Guts." He has an idealistic and somewhat romantic view of war, yet he is realistic enough to recognize and admire the tough, self-sacrificing fighting soldier. He is also a person of deep religious faith. He did not permit battle fatigue to be recognized as a legitimate ailment; rather, he sees it as an act of cowardliness. While visiting the army hospital to issue medals to soldiers who exhibited bravery on the battlefield and to lift the morale of others, he sees a soldier crying. He asks the soldier what the problem is, and the soldier replies that his nerves cannot take it anymore and he cannot stand the shelling anymore. Patton calls him yellow-bellied and a coward, among other terms. Patton slaps him twice on the head with his gloves and orders him sent to the front line of battle. The incident is reported in the U.S. papers, and uproar is made in the United States against Patton. General Eisenhower orders Patton to apologize to the soldier that he slapped, doctors and nurses in the hospital at the time, and all the soldiers under his command. The scene opens with General Patton praying in church before going outside to address the assembled persons to apologize.

Questions/Discussion:

1. Is Patton's response to the soldier's suffering from possible depression and anxiety unusual? Patton's response is not unusual. Most people fail to recognize when an individual, friend, or loved one is in need of professional care. Family and friends use different remedies to try to get the person to stop

displaying the symptoms rather than treat the underlying causes. People often dismiss symptoms of mental illness displayed by an individual because there is a tendency to view them as controllable. Patton's behavior was an attempt to change the attitude and behavior of the soldier to make it consistent with the environment in which he finds himself, the partial goal of most therapy. Patton's intent may have been positive, however, his technique was questionable.

2. Why do people and therapists vary in their selection of therapeutic techniques?
The techniques of therapy vary with the theoretical explanations of mental illness. The concepts accepted by the therapists to explain normal behavior and within that framework, what is subsequently considered abnormal, will influence their selection of therapeutic techniques. For example, if the therapists' position is that normal behavior develops from early interactions within the family in the formation of internal constructs, then abnormal behaviors reflect a breakdown in the constructions or internal conflicts among the mental constructs. Thus, the therapeutic technique selected will more likely involve attempts to resolve internal conflict, or psychoanalysis.

3. What are the two major approaches to therapy?
Two major approaches to therapy are the psychodynamic and the biological. The basic assumption of the psychodynamic approach is that the basis of mental illness is psychological. There are various techniques that fall within this rubric; however, they all have this basic assumption in common. On the other hand, the common factor that unites the various biological techniques is the assumption that mental illnesses are caused by biochemical problems in the brain and failures in other parts of the physiological system.

16. Social Behavior	Videos	Films
Prejudice & Discrimination	10	2
Social Influence	12	2
Social Relationships	33	8

* Prejudice and Discrimination

Avoiding Conflict: Dispute Resolution Without Violence. (1995) Films for the Humanities and Sciences, (47 minutes)

This program details ways of stemming the rising tide of aggression in our schools and playgrounds, our streets and homes. It shows ordinary problems that can ignite into violence, and how the problems can be resolved peacefully. The program focuses not on the problems but on solutions as it highlights anti-violence programs that have made a difference by teaching dispute resolution, avoiding conflict, solving problems nonviolently, and averting domestic and street violence.

Brother of Mine: Youth Violence and Society. (1993) Films for the Humanities and Sciences, (50 minutes)

By the time most children reach the age of 18, they have seen 28,000 murders on TV. This compelling documentary takes a penetrating look at why children are becoming more violent at home, at school, and on the streets. Interviews with educators, police personnel, psychologists, and the youths themselves – both perpetrators and victims – reveal that violence, accepted as an everyday occurrence, has become a reflection of culture, not a contradiction of it. Proactive school-based programs such as group feedback sessions, student mentoring, and parenting classes demonstrate peaceful conflict resolution.

A Class Divided. (1985) PBS Video, for the *Frontline* series, (54 minutes)

This is an update of the famous experiment on discrimination based on eye color, constructed in 1968 by Jane Elliott, a third-grade teacher in Riceville, Iowa. The original footage is featured in *The Eye of the Storm* (described later in this listing). This program features interviews with the original students and reviews their reactions to the experiment, as well as the positive changes in attitudes that resulted. It explores these long-term effects through interviews with Elliott and her students.

Crimes of Hate. (1990) ADL – Anti Defamation League Film Library, (25 minutes)

This video reveals the twisted thinking of perpetrators of hate crimes, the anguish of the victims, and the strategies used by law enforcement officials, community organizations, and individuals to address these crimes.

Eye of the Storm. (1970) ABC/XEROX, (25 minutes)

This film documents the original experiment by Jane Elliott, a third-grade teacher in Riceville, Iowa, in which she demonstrated to her students the strong impact of prejudice and discrimination. The class was separated into two groups based on eye color, blue and brown. Each group was given superior status over the other group for one day. The results taught the students in a largely homogeneous school population about prejudice, discrimination, and the ease of changing attitudes. The experiment, conducted during National Brotherhood Week, was developed by Elliott following the assassination of Martin Luther King. This film is updated in the program *A Class Divided,* described earlier in this listing.

Fear and Present Danger. (1981) Indiana University, (55 minutes)

This film examines the growing fear of crime among Americans. Private citizens, believing self-protection is the answer, are taking up weapons and barring doors as never before. The program also explores the sources of the fear and the variety of responses to it—from learning to use small arms for self-defense to organizing protection groups like the Guardian Angels.

Street Life: Inside America's Gangs. (1999) Films for the Humanities and Sciences, (46 minutes)

In this program, ABC News correspondent Cynthia McFadden interviews female members of two Los Angeles gangs—the Drifters and Tepa 13—while correspondent John Quinones talks with King Tone, the radical leader of New York City's notorious Latin Kings. In addition, extensive unscripted video footage shot by members of these three gangs provides a glimpse as raw as it is rare of life inside the net that is snaring young people all across the country. Some content may be objectionable.

Understanding Prejudice. (2000) Films for the Humanities & Sciences,(50 minutes)

Gold Medal, New York Festivals. Highly recommended by *The Book Report*. This program discusses the nature of prejudice and its effects on individuals and society. The focus is on the following questions: Where does prejudice come from? Why does it exist? Where are we headed as a society? Included are a historical overview of prejudice and definitions of key terms, such as discrimination and bigotry. Interviews illuminate different kinds of prejudices and stereotypes. The timely topics of multiculturalism, homosexuality, "politically correct" language, the role of the media, and religion are discussed. This is an excellent classroom tool for promoting tolerance. A Cambridge Educational Production.

Understanding Prejudice. (1992) Thinking Allowed Productions, (86 minutes)

The demographics of society are forcing us to come to terms with cultural diversity. In this two-part video, Jeffrey Mishlove interviews Price Cobbs, who describes the principles of ethnotherapy designed to facilitate a deep examination of the ways we think about other groups.

Understanding Race: Race. (1996) Films for the Humanities and Sciences, (52 minutes)

No gene has quantified it, yet it continues to polarize the world's populations like no other concept. This compelling program examines the history and power of the artificial distinction called "race," viewing it within historical, scientific, and cultural contexts. Topics include the anthropological unity of Homo sapiens; sanctioned discrimination, such as segregation cultural biases based on racial stereotypes; and the underlying humanity that inextricably links us all.

Feature Films

***American History X* (Edward Norton, Edward Furlong, Fairuza Balk)** Drama
Upon hearing from his younger brother Danny Vinyard (Furlong) that blacks are breaking into his car, Derek (Norton) gets his gun and shoots the youths dead. Derek is convicted of murder and sent away where his racist attitude changes. Meanwhile his brother Danny is following in his brother's footsteps. Derek tries to detour Danny away from the group led by a white supremacist.

***The Outsiders* (Thomas Howell, Matt Dillon, Ralph Macchio)** Drama
The movie tells the story of the ongoing conflict between the Greasers and the Socs in rural Oklahoma. Ponyboy (Howell) is the youngest of three orphaned boys and hangs with the Greasers. When Ponyboy and his friend (Macchio) get into a deadly confrontation the two go on the run from the cops, and are faced with growing up very quickly.

* Social Influence (persuasion, advertising, etc.)

Conformity and Independence. (1975) Harper & Row, (23 minutes)

From the *Social Psychology* series. At some point, each person has conformed to group pressure or to an authority's expectations, despite the inclination to behave independently. This program presents classic social psychological research in both field and laboratory settings. Featured are Asch's research on group pressure and Crutchfield's variation, Sherif's experiments on the formation of group norms, Milgram's experiment on conformity, Kelman's three processes of compliance, and some theoretical constructs from Moscovici.

Dream Deceivers: The Story Behind James Vance vs. Judas Priest. (1991) University Film & Video, (60 minutes)

On December 23, 1985 two young men in Reno, Nevada put shotguns to their own heads after drinking alcohol and smoking marijuana as they listened to a record by the rock group Judas Priest. One died, the other was grossly disfigured. Their parents filed suit against CBS Records claiming that subliminal messages mesmerized the young men into their suicide pact. The program examines this tragedy through interviews with the young man who survived, the parents of both men, and members of Judas Priest. This video is meaningful to students who may recall this incident from news stories.

For All Practical Purposes: The Prisoner's Dilemma. (1986) Penn State University, (30 minutes)

(program 5 in the *Social Choice* series). If you conduct one of the Prisoner's Dilemma exercises in class, this is an excellent video to show the day after the experiment. It illustrates decision-making strategies in games of partial conflict. Prisoner's Dilemma and games of "chicken" are used as primary examples. The program then enlarges its scope to include business-oriented examples, such as negotiations, corporate takeovers, labor relations, and other industrial/organizational examples. This program allows students to see the Prisoner's Dilemma in a broader context.

The Famine Within. (1990) Direct Canada Limited, (90 minutes)

This video documents our society's obsession with an unrealistic body size and shape for women and the eating disorders that accompany that obsession. This excellent documentary was produced with the Ontario Film Development Corporation.

Frosh. (1993) Insight Video, (98 minutes)

This documentary follows a year in the life of freshman students at Stanford University. It traces the social experimentation and intellectual curiosity, cultural clashes, spiritual cries, academic pressure, and adjustment problems and illuminates the individual self-discovery within a diverse community.

Group Dynamics: Groupthink. (1973) CRM/McGraw-Hill, (23 minutes)

(from the *Behavior in Business* series). This is an excellent film that provides historic examples of groupthink and its eight symptoms, as proposed by Irving Janis. The causes of groupthink include multiple agendas and motives and conflicting communication. Means of preventing groupthink includes effective leadership, open communication, and positive group dynamics. The program also demonstrates historic examples of group decision-making processes that influenced events, such as Pearl Harbor, the Korean War, and the Bay of Pigs invasion.

Media Impact. (1997) Films for the Humanities and Sciences, (28 minutes)

This program emphasizes the seductive nature of films and television. The pervasiveness and sheer volume of electronic images in daily life make it extremely difficult for viewers to discern fact from fiction, as with Oliver Stone's controversial *JFK*. The manufactured reality of films and TV also plays a role in popularizing certain behaviors – some of which are unhealthy or antisocial, like smoking and violence. Studies show that as audiences become saturated with violent images, they can all-too-easily become desensitized to real-life situations. In addition, some suffer from media narcosis, a form of addiction which, when TV is removed from the environment, causes symptoms of withdrawal. This program is an essential component of any course that addresses the importance of critical viewing skills and an awareness of the media's impact on perceptions.

Negotiation and Persuasion. (1989) Insight Media, (30 minutes)

This program demonstrates techniques used to influence attitudes and behaviors, focusing on such elements of nonverbal communication as body language, facial expression, and touch. It discusses persuasive techniques, including ingratiation, supplication, intimidate, foot-in-the-door techniques, door-in-the-face techniques, and the that's-not-all technique.

Obedience. (1969) Pennsylvania State University, (B&W, 45 minutes)

This documentary of the original experiment by Stanley Milgram at Yale University is an excellent resource, especially if you emphasize the classic research in social psychology. Subjects in an alleged experiment on learning were asked to administer electric shocks of increasing voltage to another person. A variety of obedient and defiant reactions are illustrated. Debriefing sessions discuss the subjects' reasons for their responses. This program is the only authentic film footage of the Milgram experiment.

The People of People's Temple. (1979) Films Incorporated, (24 minutes)

This program is a documentary of the Jonestown, Guyana tragedy, where 900 people committed mass suicide under the orders of their leader, Jim Jones. Footage shot by the investigating team is combined with historic film records of the People's Temple, photographed over the years it operated. Interviews with survivors describe the social environment, and clinical experts describe the relationship between Jones and his followers. They discuss the atmosphere of the 1970s as encouraging the rejection of "establishment" ideas and acceptance of bizarre ideas and leaders. This topic elicits much controversy and emotion, and postviewing discussion is encouraged. The film was produced and directed by James Ruxin and David Gottlieb.

The Power of the Situation. (1990) Annenberg/CPB, (30 minutes)

Program 19 in the *Discovering Psychology* series. If your class time tends to be short at the end of the semester or quarter, and you plan to skim over the topics at the end of the book, please note: if you show no other program on social psychology, this video should be the one. It is a superior program that blends very well with the textbook material. It reviews all the major social psychology research, beginning in the 1930s with Kurt Lewin's experiment with three groups of boys under authoritarian, laissez-faire, and democratic leadership styles. It also includes Solomon Asch's famous experiment on conformity, Stanley Milgram's controversial experiment on obedience, and footage of the Stanford University prison-guard simulation that had to be stopped prior to its scheduled completion because of the severity of participants' responses. Program host Philip Zimbardo was one of the research principals in the Stanford experiment. The program also demonstrates the Harvard research on vision and flight simulators in improving vision for pilots.

When Will People Help? The Social Psychology of Bystander Intervention. (1976) Harcourt Brace Jovanich, (25 minutes)

Hosted by Daryl Bem, this film explores the public murder of Kitty Genovese and investigates bystander intervention. Why do people sometimes ignore emergency situations? What makes people help in a crisis? Social psychological experiments are used to attempt to answer the question. Results indicate that nonintervention stems from fear of physical danger, fear of legal problems, embarrassment, and need for a quick solution. For bystanders to help, they must feel the weight of responsibility, recognize the situation as an emergency, and not be deterred by the presence of others or the assumption that someone else will intervene.

* Social Relations

CNN® Today Video Vol. II: *Section 7: Diversity*

Brazil: New Beliefs (2:29)

CNN® Today Video Vol. III: *Section 11: Social Behavior*

Teen Culture (2:20)

About (Romantic) Love. (1995) Insight Media, (60 minutes)

This video investigates the connection between love and authentic self-creation. Hosted by Robert Solomon, it offers a rigorous and wide-ranging discussion of the role of love in the formation of human consciousness and individual personality.

Cognitive Social Psychology, Discovering Psychology Teaching Module 14. (1990) Holt, Reinhart and Winston (various times)

This module from the *Discovering Psychology Teaching Module* series contains several interesting programs addressing several critical aspects of social cognition: 1) a review of the Festinger and Carlsmith study of cognitive dissonance (3:48 minutes); 2) historical footage of Jane Elliot's famous "brown-eye" versus "blue-eye" study of discrimination and attitudes (2:00 minutes); and 3) a discussion of attitudes by John Mack (3:00 minutes).

Conformity and Independence. (1975) Harper & Row, (26 minutes)

Depicts reenactments of several classic social psychology studies, including the work of Sherif, Asch, and Milgram.

Conformity, Obedience, and Dissent. (1990) Insight Media, (30 minutes)

This program explores why people conform, obey, and dissent in social situations. It covers Milgram's obedience study, the Asch studies, research on styles of leadership, and the phenomenon of "groupthink."

Constructing Social Reality: **The** *Discovering Psychology Series.* (1990) Annenberg/CPB (30 minutes)

This videotape focuses on the power of cognitive control. Our perception and interpretation of reality shape all our social relationships and behavior. Three studies involving young students are used to illustrate the principle. The major focus of the video is on identifying processes that help us become more empathic and independent members of society. In 1968, Jane Elliot, a third-grade school teacher in Riceville, Iowa, used eye color as the basis for discriminating among her students and dramatically altered relationships among them. Robert Rosenthal demonstrated how teachers' expectations shape their students' academic performance. Rosenthal identifies four factors that seem to mediate the effect. Finally, Elliot Aronson and Alex Gonzalez describe how the jigsaw classroom can foster cooperation when students come to see themselves as independent.

The Dating Bill of Rights. (1998) Films for the Humanities and Sciences, (26 minutes)

Recommended by *The Book Report* and *Video Librarian*. Dating is an important part of becoming an adult, but it can also be confusing and frightening. This program presents basic guidelines that clarify common myths, such as that "no" really means "yes." Abuse and respect, sexual stereotypes, how to break up, and preventing violence are all discussed, along with what true love is and is not. Skits, dialogue, and quizzes engage the audience and present sensitive material in a very hip format.

Dealing with Conflict. (1992) University Film & Video, (20 minutes)

This short video describes the five basic positions people take in conflict and explains the choices people have for constructive or destructive outcomes. It also presents key skills for directing conflict toward positive results. Based on the Thomas-Kilmann conflict mode instrument.

Domestic Violence: Which Way Out? (1994) Filmmakers Library, (30 minutes)

This video deals with a successful treatment program in Bellevue, Washington that results in a low 4 percent repeat offense rate for those completing the intensive treatment. This video could also be used in a Psychotherapy unit, depending on your approach.

Encounters with Grief. (1992) University film & Video, (14 minutes)

This somewhat basic video explores the individuality and commonality of grief following a loss and offers perspectives on the process of recovery. It includes interviews with a mother who lost her teenaged son, a woman widowed in her 60s, and a man whose wife died at 52.

Face Value: Perceptions of Beauty. (1995) Films for the Humanities and Sciences, (26 minutes)

This video examines the belief that our perceptions of attractiveness may be universal and biologically programmed and that certain features of the face have an instinctive appeal—large eyes, high cheekbones, smooth skin texture, and a narrow jaw. This video is guaranteed to spark interesting discussion in the classroom.

The Gay Gene.   (1992) Films for the Humanities and Sciences, (29 minutes)

The science behind the controversial genetic research into the so-called "gay gene" is the focus of this program. A geneticist explains how the study was carried out, from initial interviews with gay men and their families, to the plotting of family trees, the extraction of DNA, and the analysis of samples in the lab. The program also considers the findings of the research: that homosexuality is, in part, genetically determined. It discusses whether these finds will advance the cause of gay rights and promote tolerance and understanding in society at large.

Group Dynamics: Groupthink. (1973) CRM, (22 minutes)

In this film, Janis and Kanouse discuss the symptoms of "groupthink" including self-censorship, shared stereotypes of the opposition, and the illusion of invulnerability, and viewers are shown how it influenced such historical events as the Korean War and the Bay of Pigs.

Groups and Group Dynamics. (1991) Insight Media, (30 minutes)

This video describes categories of groups and explains how they function, how they differ from other social entities, and how membership is determined.

Human Aggression. (1975) Insight Media, (24 minutes)

This program hosted by Stanley Milgram explores real-life incidents of aggression, the Bobo doll studies, the psychological training of police, and Milgram's studies of the influence of groups on aggression.

Interpersonal Processes, Discovering Psychology Teaching Module 15. (1990) Holt, Reinhart and Winston (various times)

This superior video from the *Discovering Psychology Teaching Module* series contains actual footage from several of the most important social psychological experiments ever conducted. Two of the highlights include: 1) Milgram's obedience experiment (4:29 minutes); 2) Zimbardo's prison simulation experiment (6:30); and 3) Aronson's jigsaw puzzle cooperation versus competition study. Additional modules cover topics like the groupthink behavior displayed during the Bay of Pigs incident and a discussion of tactics used by sales people.

Invitation to Social Psychology. (1975) Harper & Row, (25 minutes)

From the *Social Psychology* series. This program explores social psychology and illustrates the unique methods of research used in social settings. Three subtopics are explored: What is the subject matter of social psychology? What are its methods of investigation? What are some of the findings? Social psychological processes discussed include aggression, attribution, conformity, affiliation, and cognitive dissonance. These are illustrated by examining reactions of bystanders on a city street, Milgram's experiment in obedience, interpersonal reactions in a restaurant, and Zimbardo's prison simulation at Stanford.

Methodology: The Psychologist and the Experiment. (1975) McGraw-Hill, (31 minutes)

The film clarifies the essentials of experimental research as used in Schachter's social psychology experiment on fear and affiliation, and Austin Reiesing's physiological study of light deprivation and visually guided movement in kittens.

Obedience. (1969) New York Film Library, (45 minutes)

This classic black and white film contains actual footage from Stanley Milgram's original studies on obedience to authority. The film's images (especially the facial reactions of the subjects) create powerful impressions which can lead to intense student discussions concerning the nature and ethics of this project.

Pulling the Punches. (1994) Filmmakers Library, (30 minutes)

This video could be used in a Psychotherapy unit as well as in this social psychology chapter. It provides an intimate view of one man's therapy to control his abusive behavior toward his wife. The patient was treated at Everyman's Center in London. The video goes inside the Center to record his interactions with his counselor.

The Power of the Situation: Discovering Psychology. Annenberg/CPB Project, (30 minutes)

This program will bolster both students' knowledge of the history of social psychology and their understanding of person/situation interaction as a source of behavior and mental processes. It traces contemporary social psychology back to Kurt Lewin's thesis that behavior is a function of both the person and the environment. Beginning with Lewin's early work on autocratic, laissez-faire, and democratic leadership styles, the program covers research on conformity, the fundamental attribution error, and obedience. Original footage from Stanley Milgram's obedience studies is highlighted. The program also introduces students to the second most controversial experiment in social psychology, Philip Zimbardo's famous Stanford prison simulation. The prison study showed how the boundary between social role and personal identity can be erased. Both the obedience and prison studies raise questions about ethics in experimentation. In fact, they are the principle causes of a major revision of the APA's Code of Ethics in Psychological Research, which would preclude any such studies today. The program concludes with an example of positive social influence—Ellen Langer's study of visual acuity. ROTC cadets treated as pilots in an active training simulator demonstrated significantly improved vision over those in an inactive simulator.

Quiet Rage—The Stanford Prison Experiment. Insight Media, (50 minutes)
This is the full-length version of the second most controversial experiment in social psychology. It is narrated by Phil Zimbardo, who explains the real purpose of the experiment, shows examples of all the kinds of behavior changes that took place during the experiment, including his own, which he is brutally frank in revealing, and describes precautions taken to prevent harm to his participants, which failed to predict what actually took place. The experiment had been designed to continue for two weeks but had to be discontinued after only 6 days due to the deterioration of the personalities of the participants, especially those in the role of prisoners. A truly chilling example of just how pliable human behavior is under certain circumstances.

Responsible Assertion. (1978) Research Press, (28 minutes)
This film examines different styles of behavior through three dramatic scenes in which a graduate student confronts her advisor about the demanding requirements of her assistantship. These scenes demonstrate the different consequences of nonassertive, aggressive, and assertive behaviors. After each scene Dr. Pat Jakubowski comments on the cognitive and behavioral aspects of responsible assertiveness.

Save the Males: An Endangered Species. (1992) PBS Video, (57 minutes)
This video follows three men as they experience a "wildman weekend," gathering with others to perform healing rituals and search for answers to questions about their male identity and their place in a culture that has cast aside many of its traditional male rituals. It includes interviews with men from both city and country, and with psychologists and counselors.

Social Psychology. (1971) CRM, (33 minutes)
This classic color film incorporates documentary footage of the busing of African-American children into all-white school districts as a backdrop for a discussion of the issues of: attitude formation, racial prejudice, and social comparison theory.

Social Psychology. (1990) Insight Media, (30 minutes)
Social psychology attempts to explain the social forces that influence attitudes and actions. This video discusses studies on stereotyping and prejudice, attribution theory, and the power of social roles. It also analyzes Zimbardo's prison experiment and in-group/out-group experiments.

Social Psychology Series. (1989) Pennsylvania State University Audio-Visual Services, (30 minutes)
This eight-part series covers various topics in social psychology, including communication and persuasion, friendship, prejudice, conformity, group decision making and leadership, aggression, and helping and prosocial behavior.

The Unquiet Death of Eli Creekmore. (1988) Filmmakers Library, (55 minutes)
This powerful documentary on a brutal child abuse case has won many awards. Through moving accounts by family members, teachers, and doctors, we learn how the three-year-old was repeatedly mistreated by his father. A brutal beating when he couldn't stop crying was the cause of his death. This tragedy has caused some states to reexamine their child-protection laws.

Violence: An American Tradition. (2000) Films for the Humanities & Sciences, (55 minutes)

Using archival photos and footage, as well as the words of both historical figures and current experts in sociology, medicine, and history, this program explores the recurring patterns of violence that have emerged in our society as a result of insurrection, anger, prejudice, and ignorance. Hosted by civil rights leader Julian Bond, the program examines many of the most notorious acts of violence that have scarred the American psyche over the past 200 years.

Voices. (1991) Colorado State University, (35 minutes)

Participants from diverse cultural backgrounds discuss how their self-images developed, how they are perceived in our society, and how self-image and image of others combine to affect relationships. This video trains and teaches about intercultural relationships.

The Wave. (1984) Insight Media, (46 minutes)

This Emmy Award winning video recounts a classroom experiment in which a teacher was able to re-create his own "Reich." The information in the film can be used to demonstrate how social psychological techniques were used to get the people of Germany to embrace Nazism.

Women and Self-Esteem. (1990) Nicholas J. Kaufman Productions, (30 minutes)

This video presents a workshop that clarifies the difference between self-concept and self-esteem and explains how both real and ideal self-concepts are learned – the greater the gap between the two, the lower the self-esteem. The program also discusses parental and societal influences on self-esteem. Workshop attendees participate in four experiential learning exercises. This video may also work for a unit on Development, depending on your emphasis.

Feature Films

The Breakfast Club (**Emilio Estevez, Judd Nelson, Molly Ringwald**) Comedy/Drama
Nine hours of school detention bond five students who until this day were strangers and on different levels of the high school caste system. Faced with a villainous principal, who makes their lives miserable, the group decides they have one thing in common – they do not like adult society. A sensitive look at adolescent development and issues during a cross section of a day in their lives.

Dangerous Minds (**Michelle Pfeiffer, George Dzundza, Courtney Vance**) Drama
A school teacher discovers that it takes more than ordinary teaching skills and knowledge to get through to a class of "rejects from hell." With the use of bribery and intimidation, Lou Anne Johnson (Pfeiffer), a nine year veteran of the Marine Corps, reaches out to students who need her the most.

Girls Gone Wild (**Sue Carol, Nick Stuart, William Russell**) Drama
A young woman is angry when her boyfriend's father, a motorcycle cop, pulls her over for speeding and sends her to court. She dumps her boyfriend who later comes to her rescue when she gets herself in trouble with some gangsters. After a high speed chase the father and son team save the girl and she forgives both of them.

Girl, Interrupted (**Winona Ryder, Angelina Jolie, Clea Duvall**) Drama
19 year old Susanna (Ryder) commits herself to a mental hospital and spends 18 months exploring her troubled psyche and learning the ways of a mental hospital. She meets several other patients with

troubled minds and decides that she must work harder with her psychiatrist in order to get well. Getting out of the hospital is not as easy as getting in as Susanna quickly discovers.

Specific Scene Analysis:

Glory **(1989) (Morgan Freeman, Denzel Washington, and Matthew Broderick)** War Drama

- Central Concept: attribution theory
- Approximate Scene Location: 49 minutes, 15 seconds into the 122-minute film
- Approximate Scene Length: 5 minutes
- Opening Line: Major Forbes: "Excuse me, sir." Col. Shaw: "Yes, what is it?" Major Forbes: "We have caught a deserter."
- Closing Line: Mr. Rowlins: "The boy was off trying to find hisself some shoes, Colonel. He wants to fight same as rest us, more even."

Key Concepts: fundamental attribution error, internal dispositional attribution, external dispositional attribution

Characters/Actors: Col. Robert Gould Shaw (Matthew Broderick, Mr. Rowlins (Morgan Freeman), Trip (Denzel Washington), Major Forbes (Cary Lewis), Sergeant Mulcby (John Finn), Soldiers: Jihmi Kennedy, Andre Braugher, Donovan Leitch, and John David Cullum

Scene Description: The setting for the film is the Civil War. The narrative is from the letters of Colonel Robert Gould Shaw. Colonel Shaw was the son of wealthy abolitionists, and he enlisted in the army when he was 23 years old. He wrote home frequently, describing his experiences during the war. The letters are collected in the Houghton Library at Harvard University. When the film opens, the war is going badly for the North. With the urgings of Frederick Douglass, a noted "colored" leader, as African Americans were called during that time period, the governor of Massachusetts has decided to form a regiment of colored soldiers. He commissions Shaw to be the colonel of the regiment known as the 54th Massachusetts Infantry. Fugitive slaves and free colored men volunteered by the hundreds. Trip, an escaped slave, joins the regiment. Mr. Rowlins, a former slave who has worked in the battlefield in the Union Army burying the dead soldiers, joins also. The men are drilled in army routines and, according to Shaw, learn the routines very quickly. The men are issued rifles and taught shooting skills for the battlefield in contrast to their skills at shooting small game. Nonetheless, high-ranking officers in the Union Army do not plan to use the 54th regiment as fighting soldiers, but as men for manual labor to suit the war needs. Therefore, they do not issue the regiment shoes because they are needed for white soldiers whose units are engaged in battles. The men of the 54th regiment are drilled and trained until their feet are bloody in their shoddy shoes or from no shoes while training. Trips feet are bloody, and he decides to go to a nearby farm for a meal of biscuits and gravy and to try to find some shoes. Mr. Rowlins warns him not to go because he will be shot if he is caught. The scene opens with Trip being led into camp with his feet hobbled.

Questions/Discussion:

1. What concept in social psychology explains the events and personal interactions in the film clip?

The concept of fundamental attribution error is the best explanation. Fundamental attribution error refers to a tendency to overestimate the impact of internal characteristics of an individual and underestimate the impact of the environmental setting in making attributions about behaviors.

2.   How were the components of fundamental attribution error displayed in the film clip?
Major Forbes and Col. Shaw viewed Trip's running away as deserting the military. They attributed the behavior to personal cowardliness or fear of fighting. As Mr. Rowlins explains to Col. Shaw, Trip's leaving was not from a personal fear of fighting but rather from a desire to find some shoes. His feet were bloody, and Trip had difficulty walking and training because of his ill-made shoes. Trip wanted to fight as much, if not more, than other soldiers; he was not a deserter.

3.   Why do people make these types of errors in judgment?
There is a tendency for people to try to attribute cause and effect to events in the daily world because it assists in adjustments. People tend to prefer a quick internal, dispositional or personality explanation rather than an external or situational, environmental one. Personal behaviors in an event are considered more salient than environmental factors.

Powder Drama
An abused albino boy is cursed as different when he is integrated with teens his own age at school. His classmates, teachers, and others around him are both inspired and terrified by the strange-looking boy who apparently possesses certain inexplicable powers.

1.   What influence did Powder's appearance have on the way he was treated?
2.   In one scene, Powder revives one of the guys who has bullied him. What effect does this have on the social attitudes of the bullies?
3.   How does groupthink and conformity affect you? Explain.

The Shawshank Redemption (**Tim Robbins, Morgan Freeman**) Drama
A banker (Tim Robbins) gets life for murder and discovers that prison can provide personal growth despite foul degradation.

  1. How obedient was Tim Robbins' character? Explain.
  2. Did Robbins' character exhibit any prosocial behavior? Give examples.
  3. Did the social and group influences change Tim Robbins' character? Support your answer.

The Wild Ones (**Marlon Brando, Mary Murphy, Robert Keith**) Drama
Brando is part of a motorcycle gang who invades a small town where they raise hell all day. The Sheriff's daughter is fond of Brando. When Brando tries to escort her out of harms way the town's people assume that Brando wants to rape the girl and an angry mob attacks Brando who inadvertently strikes and kills a pedestrian. At his hearing the girl is quick to defend Brando.

17. Gender and Sexuality	Videos	Films
Gender Roles	17	6
Sex & Gender Research	3	

CNN® Today Video Vol. I: *Section 6: Gender and Sexuality*

> Depression Drugs (2:13)
> Brain Differences (2:12)

CNN® Today Video Vol. II*: Section 5: Gender and Sexuality*

> Developmental Psychology Vol. II: Teenage Sexuality (3:27)
> Gay by Nature (5:02)

* Gender Roles

The Brain: The Sexual Brain. (2000) Films for the Humanities & Sciences, (28 minutes)
> Part of the six-part series *The Brain*, this video shows some startling effects of hormone injections on brain structure and raises provocative questions about the sexual and reproductive roots of structural differences between males and females.

Childhood Sexual Abuse. (2000) Films for the Humanities & Sciences, (26 minutes)
> This program looks at the ways in which adult women learn to work out the problems caused by sexually abusive fathers. Includes input from psychiatrists, social workers, and law enforcement officials.

Child Sex Abusers. (1995) Films for the Humanities and Sciences, (28 minutes)
> This is a specially adapted Phil Donahue show featuring mothers and their daughters who have been molested by brothers, half-brothers, and neighborhood kids. An expert who deals with abusive children counsels what to look for and what to do with abusive kids, and counsels kids who are being abused.

Exploring Your Brain: Men, Women, and the Brain. (2000) Films for the Humanities & Sciences, (56 minutes)
> Part of the three-part series *Exploring Your Brain*, this video explores a number of the intriguing and sometimes puzzling differences between the brains of men and women.

Finding Out: Incest and Family Sexual Abuse. (1984) Kinetic Films, (25 minutes)
> This film concentrates on the role of the victim's mother in dealing with family sexual abuse. Viewers are shown Robin, a victim since age nine, who talks about the devastating emotional effects of sexual abuse. Her mother tells how she dealt with the disclosure and the subsequent breakup of her marriage.

Gender and Relationships. (1990) Coast Community College District Telecourses, (30 minutes)
> Part of the *Psychology - The Study of Human Behavior Series*, this video explores the complexities of emotional interactions and attachments.

Incest: The Family Secret. (1984) Filmmakers Library, (57 minutes)

As this film indicates, incest is a widespread problem that occurs in all kinds of families. Most commonly, it takes the form of sexual child abuse inflicted by the father on a non-consenting daughter while she is still a child. In this very frank program, adult women talk about the childhood experiences which so traumatized their later lives.

The Opposite Sex. (1993) Insight Media, (55 minutes)

Human beliefs about differences between the sexes inform social organization, law, religion, literature, and humor. This video considers men's and women's bodies, brains, emotions, and public and private behavior. Using a combination of science, observation, and opinion, it links biological and psychological studies to generate composite interpretations of gender difference.

The Sexes: Roles. (1978) Filmmakers Library, (28 minutes)

This film surveys the evolution of male-female roles from prehistory to our current industrial age. Judith Bardwick points out the stresses caused by the clash between traditional expectations and new realities while Matina Horner presents her classic studies on women's "fear of success," and sociologist Jean Lipman-Blumen relates how "girls are socialized to destroy their own dreams at an early age."

The Sexes: What's the Difference? (1978) Filmmakers Library, (28 minutes)

This film addresses the sensitive question, are "male" and "female" traits inborn or are they learned in childhood? Students can observe the research methods of such noted child development experts as Jerome Kagan and Elinor Maccoby as they attempt to isolate biological factors from cultural factors.

Sexuality: The Human Heritage. (1976) Indiana University, (59 minutes)

This film traces the development of human sexual identity--from the influence of prenatal sex hormones *in utero* to the external influences of family and society that help to shape our perceptions of what is feminine and what is masculine. In addition, Jerome Kagan discusses how children acquire gender and role identity.

Understanding Sex. (2000) Films for the Humanities & Sciences, (51 minutes)

Narrated by Candice Bergen, this program explores the biology, genetics, and psychological components of sex, including sexual orientation and assisted conception.

Why God, Why Me? (1988) Filmmakers Library, (27 minutes)

This multi-award-winning video about childhood sexual abuse dramatizes the life of those children who grew up never feeling safe in their own homes. It is compelling, but no graphic sexual or violent scenes are presented. The program ends on a positive note, showing that survivors can establish new, loving relationships.

Feature Films

The Age of Innocence (**Daniel Day-Lewis, Michelle Pfeiffer, Winona Ryder**) Drama
A romance between an upper-class gentleman and an ostracized lady is doomed by 19th century New York Society. Newland Archer (Day-Lewis) is engaged to May Welland (Ryder) when he happens to meet May's cousin Ellen. He falls in love with Ellen but cannot disregard the codes of New York

manners and marries May. When he happens to see Ellen again his yearning for her is even greater than before.

The Crying Game (**Stephen Rea, Jaye Davidson, Miranda Richardson**) Drama
Fergus (Rea) is an IRA member who takes part in the kidnapping of a black British soldier, Jody (Whitaker), stationed in Ireland. The IRA wants to use Jody to gain the release of an IRA operative. Fegus becomes friends with Jody and promises to look in on Jody's girlfriend if anything should happen to him. Jody escapes but is hit by a British police vehicle. Fergus escapes to London where he is wanted by the law for Jody's kidnapping and also by his former girlfriend, IRA operative Jud (Richardson). Fergus keeps his word to Jody and tracks down his girlfriend whom he enters into a love affair with.

A Disney Analysis
Try this exercise to allow students to examine changes in gender roles in children's videos over the past decades. How do these fantasy videos differ from reality?
 Early Disney videos—Peter Pan, Snow White, Sleeping Beauty, Cinderella
 Later Disney videos (1990s and beyond)—The Hunchback of Notre Dame, Hercules, Mulan, Pocahontas, The Little Mermaid

The Marriage of Maria Braun (**Hanna Schygulla, Klaus Lowitsch, Ivan Desny**) Drama
Maria Braun (Schygulla) marries a soldier during the allied siege of Germany. Her husband is killed Maria becomes a barmaid where she befriends a black soldier who sees to it that Maria's family receives food and supplies. Maria eventually takes a job with a wealthy importer (Desny). She sleeps with her employer but her heart still belongs to her dead husband.

Specific Scene Analysis:
The English Patient (1996) (**Ralph Fiennes and Kristin Scott Thomas**) Drama

- Central Concept: sexual orientation
- Approximate Scene Location: 91 minutes, 34 seconds into the 162-minute film
- Approximate Scene Length: 2 minutes
- Opening View: Count Almaay, an explorer who is mapping the terrain of northern Africa, is about to enter a cave in the desert in northern Africa when he observes Bermann, an English member of the expedition, embracing Kamal, a young Arabic male assistant. In the next scene, Count Almaay and Bermann are riding in a truck with Kamal on the roof. Bermann taps the roof of the truck, and Kamal leans over. Bermann puts food into Kamal's mouth and turns to Count Almaay and says, "How do you explain to someone who has never been here, feelings that seem quite normal?"
- Closing Line: "I do not know my friend."

Key Concepts: sexual orientation, genetic predisposition, heterosexual, homosexual, bisexual, lesbian, gay
Character/Actors: Count Almaay, an explorer (Ralph Fiennes), Bermann (Peter Ruhring), Kamal (Samy Azaiez)
Scene Description: Count Almaay leads an expedition for the royal Geographic Society to map the terrain of the desert located in northern Africa. The members of the expedition are European, and the people indigenous to the area are nomadic tribes of Arabic and African ancestry. The time period is before World War II, and the expedition has been underway for some time. Young males from the local tribes have been hired to perform the manual labor necessary for the project.

Questions/Discussion:

1.   How do you explain why Bermann feels that his same-sex sexual orientation seems normal? The display of sexual orientation is strongly influenced by cultural settings. In European cultures in the 1940s, the display of sexual orientations toward persons of the same sex was not encouraged, although there were probably lesbians and gays living in those countries during that time period. Bermann probably had experienced those feelings when he was living in Europe; however, now that he is living in a different culture, he feels comfortable with his feelings. He no longer feels constrained by the opinions of his European friends in the expression of his sexual orientation.

2.   Why do people desire to have an intimate relationship with persons of the same sex? There are different theoretical explanations for the development of sexual orientation. Psychoanalytic theory explains the development of homosexuality, a sexual orientation toward members of the same sex, as caused by family patterns in the early life of the person. Currently, the term *homosexuality* is not the preferred description of a person with same-sex orientation. The term *lesbian* is used for females who are sexually oriented toward other females, and *gays* for males who are sexually oriented toward other males. Heterosexuality refers to persons oriented toward members of the opposite sex, and bisexuality refers to persons oriented toward members of both the same and opposite sex. According to psychoanalytic theory, a child growing up in a household with an aggressive, intrusive mother and a passive, detached father will probably prefer establishing an intimate relationship with members of the same sex. Learning theorists use the basic concepts of reinforcement, modeling, and punishment to explain how persons become sexually oriented. Biological models for explaining sexual orientation have gained support in recent years. Genetic predisposition as a strong factor in persons' sexual orientation is suggested by identical twins usually having the same sexual orientation. In other words, if a person is a lesbian or gay, and a member of an identical twin pair, the other member is probably also gay or lesbian.

3.   Which theoretical explanation is supported by empirical findings? Empirical studies have not confirmed the psychoanalytic explanation based on early childhood experiences in the family. Current consensus for determinants of sexual orientation is an intertwining of the biological and social-learning positions.

Specific Scene Analysis:
Thelma and Louise **(1991) (Geena Davis and Susan Sarandon)** Drama

- Central Concept: gender identity
- Approximate Scene Location: 125 minutes, 19 seconds into t he 127-minute film
- Approximate Scene Length: 4 minutes
- Opening Line: Louise: "Oh my God." Thelma: "What the hell is this?"
- Closing Scene: No dialogue. The cast list.

Key Concepts: social learning theory, gender identity, rape
Characters/Actors: Thelma (Geena Davis), Louise (Susan Sarandon), Hal/Investigating Officer (Harvey Keitel), Max/FBI Agent in Charge (Stephen Torolowsky)
Scene Description: Louise, a waitress with repressed memories of a traumatic event, and her friend Thelma, a traditional housewife, start off on a vacation to a cabin in the mountains. Thelma has brought along a gun to ward off bears, snakes, and serial killers. She does not know how to use it, so she puts it in Louise's handbag. While driving toward their destination, Thelma and Louise decide to stop at a western bar and restaurant for food and drinks. During their time at the bar, they decide to have fun by drinking and dancing. Thelma, who has had a few drinks, is attracted to a local womanizer, who gets her dizzy by

twirling her around excessively while they are dancing. He takes her outside to the parking lot for air, where he starts to rape her. Louise comes upon the scene and uses the gun to get the man off Thelma. As they leave the scene, the man shouts obscenities at the two of them. Louise shoots him, and the two women leave the scene of the crime. Because they think no one will believe their version of the rape scenario, they attempt to resolve their predicament by driving to Mexico. During their efforts, there are encounters with males who are supportive and sympathetic toward their predicament and others who are devious, sexist, and a hindrance to their efforts. The scenes are scripted to illustrate the treatment of women and those accused of a crime. The women are changed in the process of fleeing. As they express their feelings and thoughts of what is occurring, they realize they cannot go back to the way they were. In the final scene, law enforcement personnel have found them after a chase across the western states. Thelma and Louise are in their car near the brink of the Grand Canyon.

Questions/Discussion:

1.   The women choose the option of driving off the cliff. Do you think their version of the attempted rape scene would have been believed?

It is highly unlikely that the women's version of what happened in the parking lot would be believed. Thelma was seen dancing and having fun with the male figure before he attempted to rape her. One of the enduring myths about rape in American society is that women are "asking for it" when they are overfriendly with men. Male sexuality is viewed as biologically overpowering, and if a female entices a male, he just has to have her, even if it means forcing her. Under those conditions, rape of a woman is justifiable and her fault.

2.   The women stated that they could not go back to the way they were. Consider social-learning theory's explanation for the development of gender identity as the conceptual framework for discussing the views of Thelma and Louise.

Social-learning theory considers the development of gender identity as following the same rules and psychological principles as all other instances of learning. An individual learns gender identity through the processes of observational learning, rewards, and punishment. Thelma was a traditional housewife who submitted to her husband and was passive and dependent. During the course of the events that were taking place in her life, she was forced to be aggressive, assertive, and independent. From her perspective, she could not go back to being a dependent, passive person. She had learned to function in a manner that was incompatible with her previous life. Louise had repressed an experience from early childhood that was very traumatic with possible sexual overtones. During the events in the film she had learned to speak up and defend herself. She thought she could not go back to being a person who reacted passively to detrimental environmental events.

3.   Do you think society's views of rape have changed such that a woman's perspective of the scenario would be believed?

Have students discuss their views of rape and society's reactions to the victim.

* Sex/Gender Research

The Differences Between Men and Women. (1995) Films for the Humanities and Sciences, (23 minutes)
        The old question "Are the differences between men and women conditioned by biology or by family and social environment?" is answered with recent research, which claims that the male and female brains are far from identical. The video also looks at cultural influences on gender-related behaviors.

Homosexuality: What Science Understands. (1987) Insight Media, (54 minutes)

This video traces research on homosexual behavior from the original Kinsey studies in 1954 through the late 1980s. Highlights of the video include a discussion of the decision to remove homosexuality from the DSR III and the issues of homophobia and AIDS.

Sex Hormones and Sexual Destiny. Insight Media, (26 minutes)

A Reuters laboratory is visited where research has demonstrated that hormones have a measurable effect on masculine and feminine behavior and the structure of male and female brains is different. The influence of the environment on female behavior is also discussed. The film features Dr. June Rainiest, director of the Chinese Institute for Research in Sex, Gender, and Reproduction.